The Official Guide to

Family Tree
Maker 2006

The Official Guide to

Family Tree Maker 2006

Tana Pedersen Lord

Ancestry®

Library of Congress Cataloging-in-Publication Data

Pedersen Lord, Tana
    The official guide to Family tree maker 2006 / Tana Pedersen Lord.
        p. cm.
    Includes bibliographical references and index.
    ISBN 1-59331-294-6 (soft cover : alk. paper)
    1. Family tree maker. 2. Genealogy—Computer programs. 3.
Genealogy—Data processing. I. Title.
    CS14.P43 2005
    929'.10285536—dc22

                                                                    2005024457

Published by MyFamily.com, Inc.

360 West 4800 North

Provo, UT 84064

All rights reserved.

Table of Contents

Installation
Errors During Install
General Info
Program Errors
Specific File Names

Select a Product
FTM 16
FTM 2006
FTM 2005

Answer

CAUSE

There are several different editions of Family Tree Maker. Some Family Tree Maker editions contain a Macromedia Flash presentation as an introduction to Family Tree Maker. On these CDs, setup.exe is usually located in a different folder.

RESOLUTIONS DISCUSSED IN THIS ARTICLE

- Look for ftm.exe
- Check the fscommand folder

STEPS FOR RESOLUTION

Look for ftm.exe

The ftm.exe file starts the Flash introduction on the CD. You can start ftm.exe, view the presentation, and then start the installation. To start the introduction:

1. Place the Family Tree Maker CD into your CD drive.
2. Cancel any installation error messages.
3. Click the **Start** menu, choose **Run**, and then click **Browse**.
4. In the **Look In** dropdown menu at the top of the "Browse" dialog box, choose the letter for your CD-ROM drive. It should have a picture of a CD to the left of it, and on many systems it is the D: drive.
5. When the CD-ROM drive letter appears in the **Look In** field, look in the large box for the file called ftm or ftm.exe.
6. Double-click this file to return to the **Run** dialog box, and click **OK** to start the installation.
7. Inside the introduction, when you are ready to install Family Tree Maker, click the **Install** button.

Check the fscommand folder

The fscommand folder contains the installation program for Family Tree Maker. If you would like to skip the introductory Flash presentation and go straight to the installation program for Family Tree

Print Answer

Email Answer

FamilyTree Maker 16

We've got answers
Get answers to the most frequently asked Family Tree Maker questions.

| Overview | Highlighted Features | Related Products | Help Center | FAQ |

Ask Family Tree Maker ▸ Email FTM Support ▸ My Profile

Select a Topic ⓘ
All ▸

Select a Product ⓘ
All ▸

Search for Answers
[   ] Search Tips

Search

Powered by RIGHT NOW

Answer ID
2559

Products & Services
Software Help

"Cannot find setup.exe" during installation

Question
When I try to install Family Tree Maker, I get the message Cannot find setup.exe or one

Acknowledgments

This book is a reflection of the hard work and dedication of many individuals. I would like to thank Rhonda R. McClure and Esther Yu Sumner whose previous versions of the guide provided a solid framework for me to build on. Thanks also to Jennifer Utley, Director of Publishing, for her confidence in me and the freedom to make this project my own. Thank you to Anastasia Tyler for her valuable and timely edits, and to David Van Valkenburgh and Thomas Caswell for contributing their technical expertise. And to Matt Wright and Rob Davis, thanks for their advice and encouragement. Also, thank you to the entire Editorial team, whose good humor and support made this project enjoyable. And finally, much appreciation and love to my son, Braden, and my family and friends who motivate and inspire me every day.

Introduction

This guidebook will help you learn Family Tree Maker 2006 quickly, leaving you more time to research your family history. You will learn many of the convenient features a casual Family Tree Maker user never discovers, resulting in more efficient data entry and navigation, and more ways to enhance your research visually to share with others. Even if you have never used a genealogy program before, you will find that Family Tree Maker's interface and options make it possible to keep track of even the most tangled of family trees. This book introduces you to many of the features available in Family Tree Maker so you can enjoy your research.

Who Should Read This Book?

This book is written with the novice computer user in mind. You are taken on a hands-on trip through the Family Tree Maker program. The many illustrations let you check your progress as you master each new feature or process. Even if you are familiar with computers, though, you may have only recently been introduced to Family Tree Maker, or simply want to know what great features you have not yet discovered in the program. This book offers you an easy-to-follow tour of the program and all that you can accomplish. As you compare your own screen to the screen images in the book you will be able to see if you are using the program correctly.

This book is organized by tasks. Some tasks may require many steps, and others may branch off into enhancements or additional features. A quick perusal of the Table of Contents should lead you right to the process you are trying to accomplish, or check the index in the back of the book.

Special Features of This Book

As you work with this book, you will accomplish many tasks. This is by design, so that you can master what you need in an easy-to-follow format. There are a couple of features, though, that will supply you with additional information as you work with the Family Tree Maker program.

Tips offer you useful hints about features in Family Tree Maker that can speed up the task at hand or enhance your report output.

Notes offer additional information about Family Tree Maker or about genealogy and sharing your family tree.

In the appendixes you will find help for installing the Family Tree Maker software and useful tables of keyboard shortcuts to make your data entry speedier.

Good luck, and have fun.

PART

I

Introduction to Family Tree Maker

1

Getting Started with Family Tree Maker

Before you can take advantage of the many features of Family Tree Maker 2006, you must know how to launch or open it. Be sure you have some of your family history information ready to enter so that you can begin to see how the program handles your family data. Family Tree Maker offers different methods for opening the program and beginning a new Family File. In this chapter, you will learn how to:

- Start Family Tree Maker from the Start menu or desktop
- Use the Welcome Screen
- Create, open, and find Family files
- Enter basic information in Family View
- Close Family Tree Maker

Get started with Family Tree Maker by learning how to launch the program and by creating a Family File. If you do not understand the meaning of a term used in Family Tree Maker, check the glossary in the back of the book, which addresses technical computer terms (click, dialog box, icon, etc.), Family Tree Maker terms (Edit Individual dialog box, Family View, etc.), and genealogy terms (GEDCOM, Ahnentafel, etc.)

Starting Family Tree Maker 2006

When you install Family Tree Maker (see Appendix A, "Installing Family Tree Maker") the installation creates two different ways to launch the program.

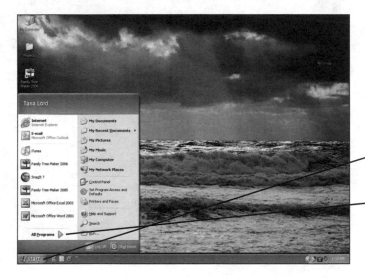

Launching Family Tree Maker from the Start Menu

For each program installed on your computer, there is a Start menu option that lets you launch the program. Family Tree Maker is no different.

1. Click **Start** on the Windows taskbar. The Start menu will appear.

2. Select **All Programs**. The Programs menu will appear.

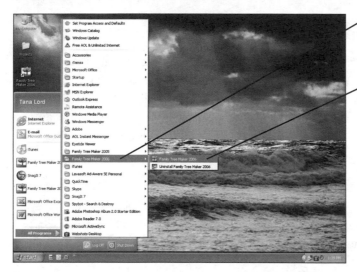

3. Select **Family Tree Maker 2006** from the Programs menu. The Family Tree Maker menu will appear.

4. Click **Family Tree Maker 2006**. Family Tree Maker will launch.

Launching Family Tree Maker from the Desktop

When you install Family Tree Maker on your computer, the program places an application icon on the Windows desktop. You can use this icon to launch the Family Tree Maker program instead of using the Start menu.

1. Double-click the **Family Tree Maker 2006 icon** on the desktop. Family Tree Maker will launch.

Using the Welcome Screen

If this is your first time using Family Tree Maker 2006 on this computer, Family Tree Maker will greet you with a one-time Welcome Screen. The Welcome Screen will allow you to view a Getting Started tutorial (if you have an Internet connection), as well as choose whether you want to create a new file or open an existing file from a previous version of FTM, an Ancestry Family Tree file, or a GEDCOM (GEnealogical Data COMmunications format).

WHAT IS A GEDCOM?

GEDCOM is a file format that lets you share genealogical data with others, even if they are using a different genealogy program. Family Tree Maker can import and export GEDCOMs. Learn more about sharing Family Files and GEDCOMs in Chapter 15.

The Welcome Screen has three options:

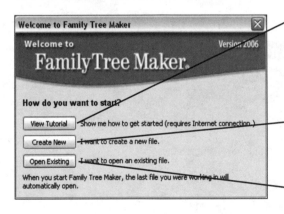

• Click **View Tutorial** to complete an online tutorial. You can also complete the tutorial at a later time by selecting **Getting Started Tutorial** from the **Help** menu.

• Click **Create New** if you are a new user and want to create your first Family File in Family Tree Maker.

• Click **Open Existing** if you already have a Family File or GEDCOM.

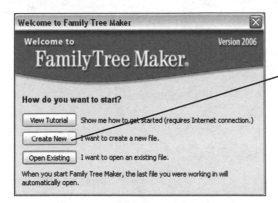

Creating a New Family File

1. Click **Create New** on the Welcome Screen. If Family Tree Maker opened but skipped the Welcome Screen (which indicates you have opened this program previously), click **New** from the **File** menu. The New File dialog box will open.

TIP

A typical Family File name for the Spencer family tree might be "SpencerFamily" or just "Spencers." Or, you can combine names and dates. For example, if you are a Spencer and your spouse is a Reed, you might call the file, "SpencerReed2006." You are free to choose any name, but you may find it easier to keep it short.

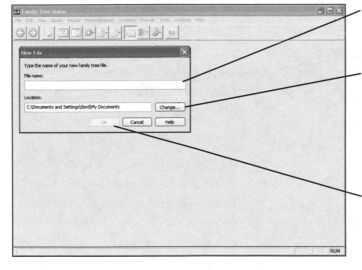

2. Type the name you want in the **File name** field. The Location field displays where the file will be saved.

3. If you want Family Tree Maker to save the file to the default location (which is in your My Documents folder, in a folder called FTM), skip to step 4. If you want to change the location, click **Change** and choose a new location.

4. Click **OK**. Family Tree Maker automatically defaults to the "Family Tree Maker (*.FTW)" file format. The New File dialog box will close and Family Tree Maker will open in Family View. You are ready to begin adding information to your Family File.

> ### NOTE
>
> Family Tree Maker will automatically open the last file you were working in when you launch the program, but it's a good idea to make a note of where you have saved your file in case you need to locate the file later.

Opening an Existing Family File

You may already have a Family File or GEDCOM you want to open in Family Tree Maker.

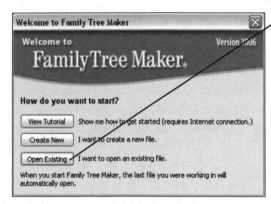

1. Click **Open Existing** on the Welcome Screen. If Family Tree Maker opened but skipped the Welcome Screen (which indicates you have opened this program previously), click **Open** from the **File** menu. The New File dialog box will open.

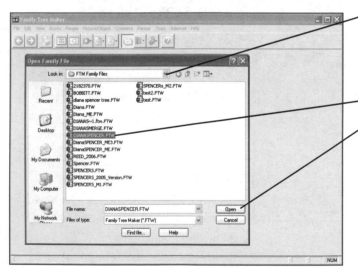

2. Click the **Look in** drop-down list to find the folder where the file is located, then click the folder when you find the file location.

3. Click the file you want.

4. Click **Open**. The Open Family File dialog box will close and Family Tree Maker will open to Family View with the details of the individual whose file you opened. You are ready to continue adding information to your Family File.

As you enter information in your Family File, Family Tree Maker will automatically save the details as you go.

Finding an Existing Family File

If you can't find the Family File that you want to open, you can use Family Tree Maker to help you find it.

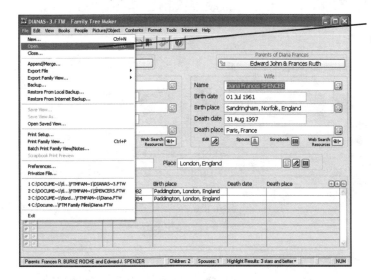

1. Click **Open** from the **File** menu. The Open Family File dialog box will open.

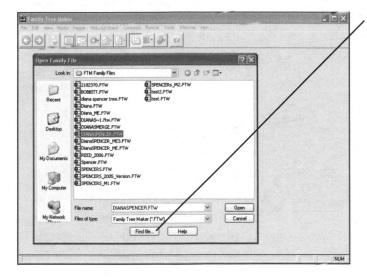

2. Click **Find file**. The Find File dialog box will open.

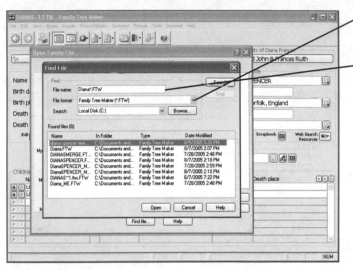

3. Choose a format from the **File format** drop-down list.

4. If you know the name of the file you are looking for, enter the name in the **File name** field. Make sure that you leave the file extension as it is. For example, enter "Spencer*.FTW".

TIP

Even if you do not know the name of the file, leave the default file extension in the File name field. That way, Family Tree Maker will filter the search results to those with the relevant file type.

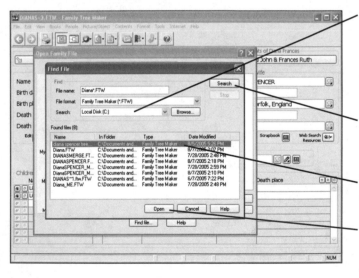

5. Choose a drive to search from the **Search** drop-down list. If you want to search in a specific folder on your hard drive, click **Browse** and choose a directory.

6. Click **Search**. The Found files section displays a list of the relevant search results.

7. Click the file you want in the **Found files** section.

8. Click **Open**. The Open Family File dialog box will close and Family Tree Maker will open the selected file. You are ready to continue adding information to your Family File.

Entering Names

Family Tree Maker automatically defaults to the Family View, where you will see a view representing three generations of a family. In this chapter, you will fill in very basic information for the two primary individuals in Family View—**Husband** and **Wife**. You will learn how to use Family View in greater detail in Chapter 3.

> **TIP**
>
> A common practice in family history record-keeping is to start with what you know best—basic details about yourself, your children, and your parents—and then to work backwards to ancestors.

Entering Information About a Husband or Wife

These instructions are for the Husband fields, but also apply to the Wife fields. Make sure you are still in Family View.

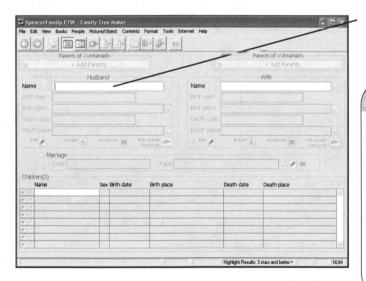

1. Click in the Husband's **Name** field, and type the person's name (first name, middle name, last name).

> **NOTE**
>
> You can change the label from "Husband" to a different title (e.g., Father, Spouse) in the Preferences dialog box (see Chapter 16). When recording names for women, use maiden names only. (You may choose to display their married names in reports and charts if you want.)

2. Press the **Tab** key to go to the next field. Type the birth date in the **Birth date** field.

TIP

In addition to using the Tab key, you can move from one field to the next by pressing the Enter key or by clicking in the field.

Understanding Names in Family Tree Maker

Generally, when entering the name of an ancestor in Family Tree Maker, you will simply type the name (as it appears in the record or resource you are viewing) directly into the **Name** field in Family Tree Maker's Family View. However, there are a few instances where the surname (last name) is not just a single word. In such instances, you will need to identify the surname for Family Tree Maker with backward slashes (\). There are many different reasons that a surname may be more than one word. This is especially true in the research of European names. Here are some examples, with the backward slash mark included:

George \de la Vergne\   Peter \Van Der Voort\

Pierre \Bourbeau dit Lacourse\   Teresa \Garcia Ramirez\

Another instance in which you might need to use backward slashes is when entering someone who does not have a last name, such as a person of Native American descent. For instance, your ancestor might have been known as Running Bear. This name would be entered in Family Tree Maker as Running Bear\\.

A common practice in genealogy is to write the entire last name for each individual in capital letters. This makes it easier to distinguish names in documents. For example, Arah Shumway would be written Arah SHUMWAY. If you use the capitalized last name, you will probably want to make sure the Family Tree Maker spell checker does not search for capitalized words. You can do this in the Preferences dialog box discussed in Chapter 16.

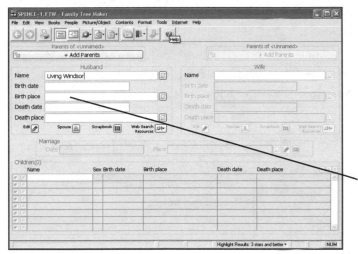

NOTE

NOTE

The date will be displayed in the standard format used by most genealogists: day month year. You may change how this is displayed in the Preferences dialog box (see Chapter 16).

3. Press the **Tab** key to go to the next field and type the individual's birth location in the **Birth place** field.

TIP

Family Tree Maker has a special feature called "Fastfields," through which the software remembers locations you have typed previously. You may notice the program automatically finishing the name of a location for you as you begin to type it, because it "remembers" the word. If the Fastfield offers an incorrect suggestion, you can continue typing over the location. You can also click the trash can icon, which appears when Fastfields is activated, to make Family Tree Maker forget that particular Fastfield term.

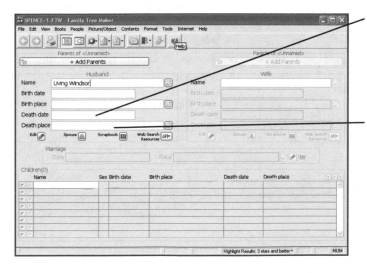

4. Press the **Tab** key to go to the next field and type a date in the **Death date** field. If the individual is living or you do not know the death date, simply skip over this field and the next.

5. Press the **Tab** key to go to the next field and type the place of death in the **Death place** field.

> ### NOTE
>
> You must first enter information in the Name field before Family Tree Maker will allow you to enter other information about an individual. However, you can enter a question mark and then replace the question mark with a name later.

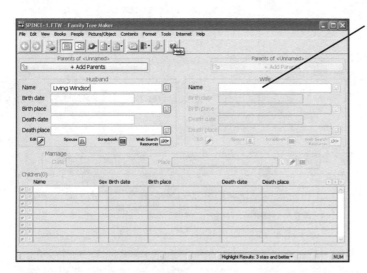

6. Click in the Wife's **Name** field and enter a name. Complete the Wife fields the same way you completed the Husband fields.

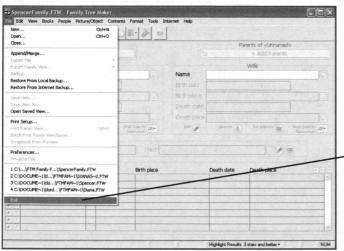

Closing Family Tree Maker

You have now seen the basics of entering information into Family Tree Maker. When you finish a session, you can close the program.

1. Click **Exit** from the **File** menu.

> ### NOTE
>
> You can also close the program by clicking the "X" in the upper-right corner of the Family Tree Maker window.

Learning General Family Tree Maker Features

Learning any software program requires an introduction to its interface. There are usually some new menu items, toolbar buttons, and choices that are specific to the program. This is certainly true of Family Tree Maker, and this chapter introduces you to those items. In this chapter, you will learn how to:

- Use menus and toolbars
- Understand dialog boxes and scroll bars
- Explore the Family View
- Explore the Pedigree View
- Explore Tree Charts
- Explore Reports

Using Menus and Toolbars

As you look at the top of the Family Tree Maker window, you will see some text and a number of small icons. These are the menu and toolbar buttons, which were referenced in Chapter 1. This section introduces you to these features.

By now you should have entered a Husband and Wife in Family View or filled in the information by opening an existing file or importing a GEDCOM. If you have not done so, please go back to Chapter 1 and follow those steps. Many of the menu and toolbar items discussed in this chapter will not be activated until you begin entering family information.

Using Menus

Menus are lists of the functions built into software programs. As in most software programs, the Family Tree Maker menus are activated by clicking the text that appears along the top bar of the Family Tree Maker window. Each menu contains a list of related commands that will appear in a drop-down list.

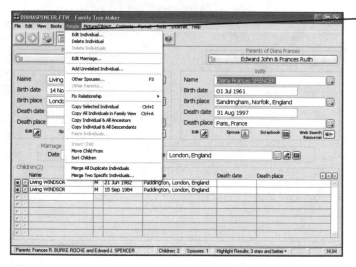

1. Click **People** in the top bar of the Family Tree Maker window. A drop-down menu will appear below the menu name.

NOTE

In Family Tree Maker, like in many software applications, options that are not available are grayed out.

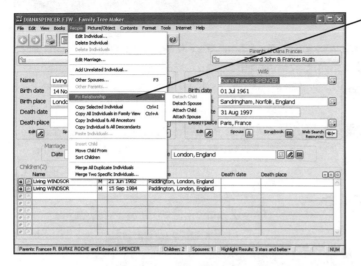

2. Select **Fix Relationship** from the **People** menu. A sub-menu will appear. Note that you only had to select Fix Relationship, not click on it, in order for the sub-menu to appear. If you planned to perform a function from this sub-menu, you would simply click on an item from the sub-menu.

Keyboard Shortcuts

Menu options have keyboard shortcuts. You can use these shortcuts to execute commands, rather than using the menus.

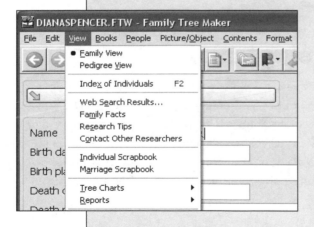

a. Press **ALT** to view the shortcuts. Each menu option now has one letter underlined. If all your menu options are grayed out, you may not have entered enough information yet, or you may need to click to select an item first. You may also need to close a dialog box.

b. Press **ALT** plus the underlined letter of the menu that you want to open. For example, after you press the **ALT** key, the V in "View" is underlined. Press **V**. This will open the View menu. Notice that each menu option in the View menu also has one underlined letter.

c. Press one of the underlined letters in the menu. For example, press **F**. The Family View will open. Now you know that **ALT, V, F** in succession will open Family View in Family Tree Maker.

Using Toolbars

There is one main toolbar in Family Tree Maker. (Family Tree Maker also has a vertical toolbar for charts and reports, which will be covered in Chapter 8.) The toolbar offers buttons to access some of the more popular windows, as well as a few shortcut buttons to some of the unique commands.

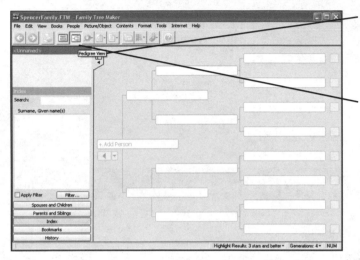

1. Place your mouse pointer over the toolbar buttons. The name of the function of that toolbar button will appear as a ToolTip (a small pop-up window).

2. Click the **Pedigree View** button on the toolbar. The Pedigree View will open.

Understanding Dialog Boxes

Dialog boxes are small windows that appear in front of your Family Tree Maker window and that require an action. Each dialog box has a different purpose, but generally, dialog boxes contain command buttons and various options to help you carry out a command or task. You had to view a dialog box before you could begin entering information in Family Tree Maker, either an Open Family File dialog box or a New File dialog box. Try the following example to view another of the many dialog boxes used in Family Tree Maker.

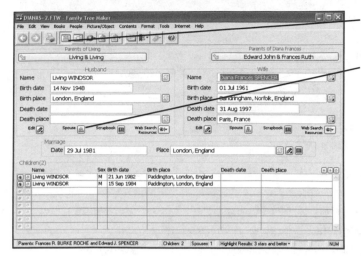

1. Click the **Family View** button to return to Family View.

2. Click the **Spouse** button below the Husband's Death place field. The Spouses dialog box will open. This is the dialog box that lets you add additional spouses (e.g., a widower re-marrying) to an individual or to view other spouses (e.g., an ex-wife).

3. Click **Cancel** to close the dialog box without making any changes.

Family Tree Maker offers a variety of views, charts, and reports to display your family data. Some displays focus on a single-family unit, while others are multi-generational, including ancestors and descendants. This section gives a quick overview of these Family Tree Maker features and explains how to access them. You will learn more details on how to use each view, chart, and report in following chapters.

Exploring the Family View

The Family View is the window in which you entered information about a husband and wife in Chapter 1. Family Tree Maker opens to this view each time you re-open your program. This is the easiest and most logical place for you to enter basic information about each individual. This view represents three generations of a family group—a primary couple, the couple's children, and the couple's parents. It also includes buttons that let you easily click to relevant functions.

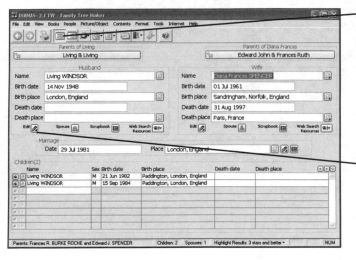

1. Click the **Family View** button on the main toolbar to access the Family View from anywhere in the program. You will go to the Family View of the individual you last selected. Chapter 3 will go in-depth on how to use the features in this view.

2. Click the **Edit** button to access the Edit Individual dialog box.

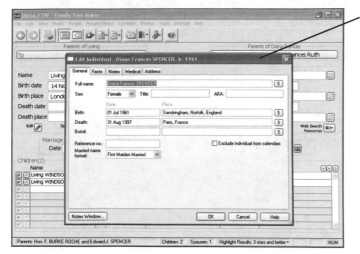

The Edit Individual dialog box can be accessed from several places: Family View, Pedigree View, and from several reports and charts. This dialog box lets you enter and view any details about a person other than relationship information. Click **Cancel**, **OK**, or the **X** button in the upper right-hand corner to close the dialog box.

3. Click the marriage **Edit** button to access the Edit Marriage dialog box.

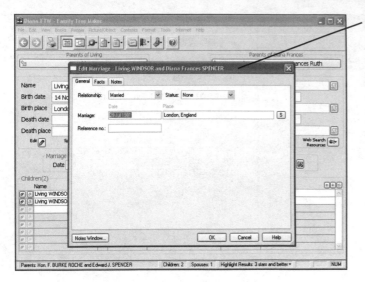

The Edit Marriage dialog box is similar to the Edit Individual dialog box but focuses on the details about the relationship between the couple rather than an individual. Click **Cancel**, **OK**, or the **X** button in the upper right-hand corner to close the dialog box.

4. Click one of the **Scrapbook** buttons.

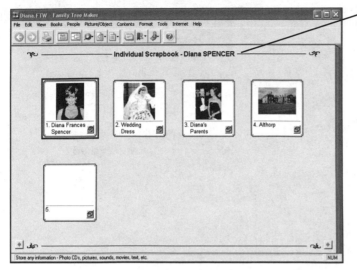

There is a Scrapbook for each individual and each marriage. The Scrapbook organizes any images or other multimedia objects you may want to associate with an individual or marriage. (The Scrapbook you are viewing will likely be empty because, unlike this example, you have probably have not saved any pictures to the Scrapbook yet.) Click the **Back** button on the toolbar. You will return to the last page you were on before you went to the Scrapbook.

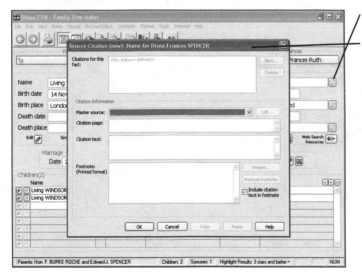

5. Click one of the **Source** buttons.

The Source-Citation dialog box lets you record details about where information was found and is especially useful when comparing conflicting information. Click **Cancel**, **OK**, or the **X** button in the upper right-hand corner to close the window.

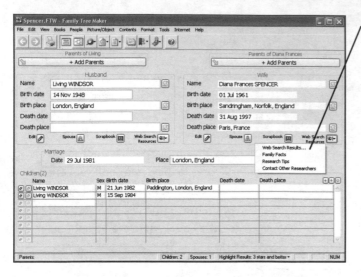

6. Click **Web Search Results** from the **Web Search Resources** button drop-down menu. If you are connected to the Internet, you'll be able to view a Web Search report, learn facts about surnames, and access research tips—all for the individual whose Web Search Resources button you clicked.

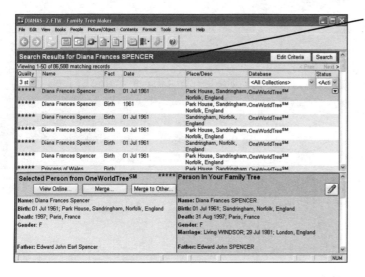

The Web Search report shows you search results for records that are available on Ancestry.com. If you find relevant records, you can merge your findings into your Family File. Click the **Back** button on the toolbar.

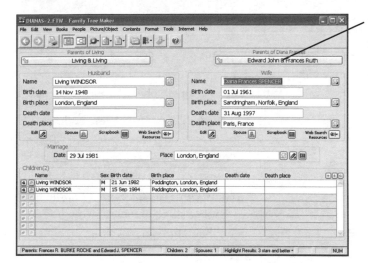

7. Click one of the **Parents** or **+Add Parents** buttons.

You will be taken to the Family View of the parents on whose name you clicked. The individual from whom you navigated will be listed in the Children fields. If you have not entered information about the parent yet, the Husband and Wife fields will be blank.

8. Click the blue arrow navigation button next to the child's name. You will be taken back to that child's Family View, with the child listed as the husband or wife.

NOTE

The parent and child navigation buttons provide one easy way to move to different Family Views. You will learn additional ways to navigate to individuals, including the Index of Individuals, in later chapters.

Exploring the Pedigree View

The Pedigree View is the second major work area in Family Tree Maker and provides a more comprehensive view of your Family File. The Pedigree View lets you see several generations at once and provides an easy way to navigate to each member of your family tree.

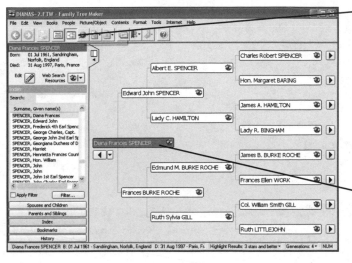

1. Click the **Pedigree View** button on the main toolbar to access the Pedigree View from anywhere in the program. The person you last selected in the Family View will appear in the primary or root position of the pedigree tree, and their ancestors will branch to the right. Chapter 5 will go in-depth on how to use the features in this view.

2. Right-click a name in the chart. A drop-down menu will appear with additional functions you can perform for that individual (e.g., Edit Individual, Move to Primary Position).

3. Click the node labeled **+Add Father** or **+Add Mother.** An Add Mother/Father of dialog box will open. This option will not be available if every node in your current Pedigree View already has a name entered. Click **Cancel** to close the dialog box.

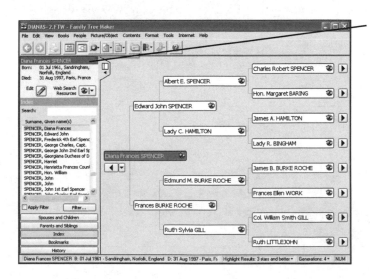

The Pedigree View Side Panel on the left side of the window will help you jump to the Pedigree Views of other individuals. It also provides more information about whichever individual in the tree is selected. The details at the top of the Side Panel stay the same, while the main section of the Side Panel changes according to which button you click: Spouses and Children, Parents and Siblings, Index, Bookmarks, and History.

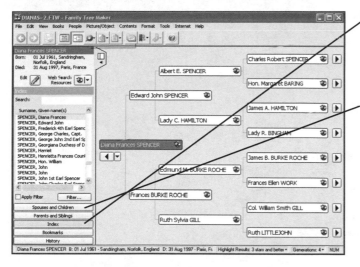

4. By default, the Index section should be expanded. If it is not, click the **Index** button to see how the Index section appears.

5. Click the **Spouses and Children** button. The Spouses and Children section will expand, and the Index section will collapse. As you click on each button in the Side Panel, the section will expand, and the one before it will collapse.

Exploring Tree Charts

Family Tree Maker offers a wide variety of family tree charts that you can customize with visually appealing backgrounds and then print. These charts let you quickly view the relationships between family members.

If you have only a couple of individuals in your tree, some of these charts will be very small, sometimes containing only one name. Some of the sample charts shown below have already been customized with special borders, images, etc., which you will learn to do in Chapter 8.

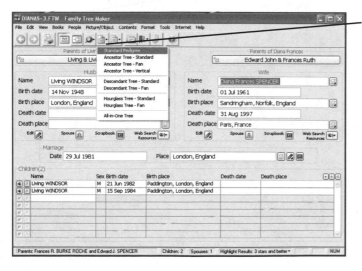

1. Click the **Tree Charts** button on the toolbar. A drop-down menu will appear listing several chart options.

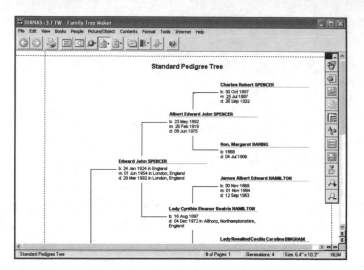

2. Click **Standard Pedigree**. The Standard Pedigree Tree will appear.

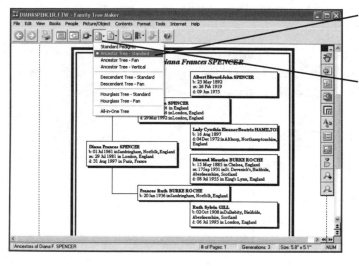

3. Click **Ancestor Tree - Standard** from the **Tree Charts** button on the toolbar. The Standard Ancestor Tree will appear.

4. Click the **Tree Charts** button on the toolbar again. Now try clicking some of the other charts available—the following diagrams show examples of each type of chart.

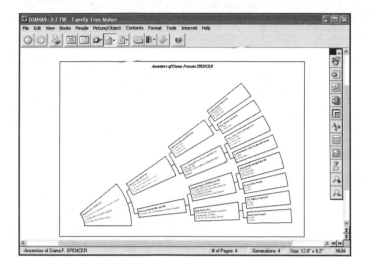

Ancestor Tree – Fan

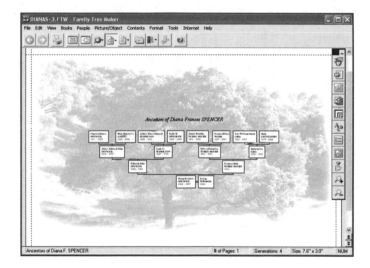

Ancestor Tree – Vertical (with the Tree Template as the background)

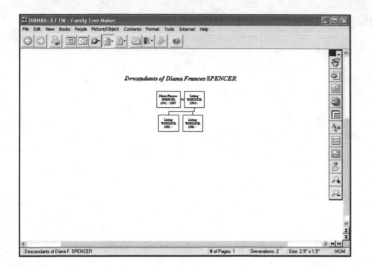

Descendant Tree – Standard

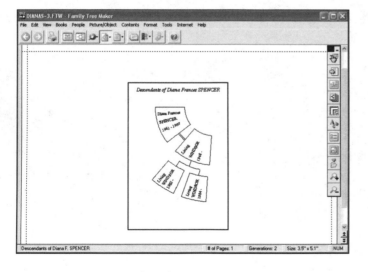

Descendant Tree – Fan

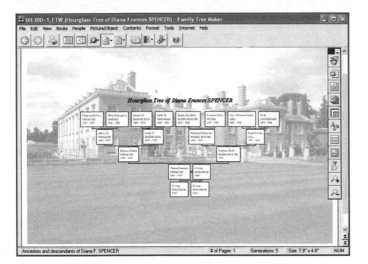

Hourglass Tree – Standard (with a Scrapbook photograph in the background)

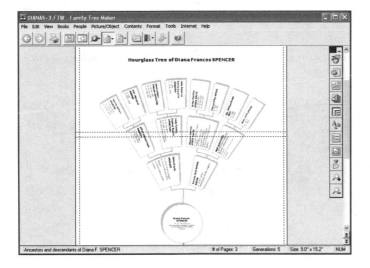

Hourglass Tree – Fan (using the Modern Template)

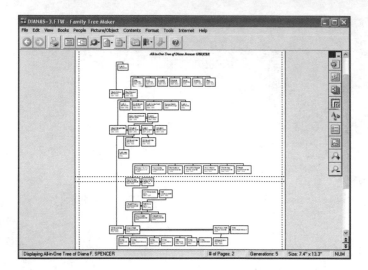

All-in-One Tree (with dotted lines show-ing how a larger chart would print on multiple sheets of 8 ½ x 11 paper)

Exploring Reports

Family Tree Maker offers a wide variety of reports to view or print. You can also create your own custom report.

Most of the reports you view at this point will have few details listed if you have not yet entered more than a couple names in Family View.

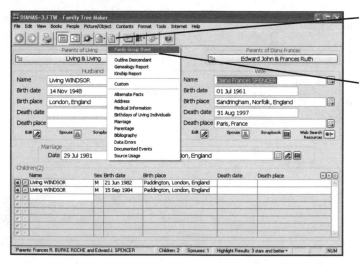

1. Click the **Reports** button on the tool-bar. A drop-down menu will appear list-ing several report options.

2. Click **Family Group Sheet**. The Family Group Sheet is one of the most commonly used reports by family histo-rians. Like the Family Tree Maker Family View, it includes information on three generations of a family.

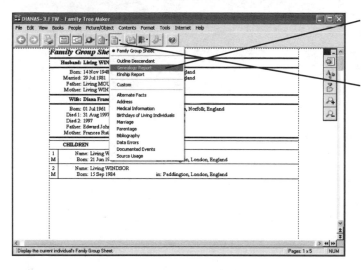

3. Click **Genealogy Report** from the **Reports** button on the toolbar. The Genealogy Report will appear.

4. Click the **Reports** button on the toolbar again. Now try clicking some of the other reports available. The Custom Report lets you choose the content as well as the formatting. For report examples and detailed instructions on creating custom reports, see Chapter 9.

PART II

Building Your Tree and Navigating in Family Tree Maker

3

Entering Information About a Family in Family View

Much of your time in Family Tree Maker will be spent entering the data you have uncovered about your family. At first, this information will focus on your small family group: yourself, your parents, and your children. As you continue, your focus will likely turn to your ancestral lines and other family groups, such as your grandparents and great-grandparents. Family Tree Maker helps you stay organized as you begin to enter information in Family View. In this chapter, you'll learn how to:

- Begin your Family File using Family View
- Enter information about individuals
- Enter events
- Enter information about a marriage
- Work with additional spouses
- View other family groups
- Add more details about an individual
- Add more details about a marriage

Beginning Your Family File Using Family View

In Chapter 1, you were introduced to the basics of entering information. This chapter covers how you enter information in Family View, including adding individuals, events, and related details. Before you begin, make sure you are in Family View.

Entering Information About Individuals

You might have entered names for a husband and wife in Chapter 1, but these steps will be quickly reviewed again.

> **TIP**
>
> Enter the last name in all-capital letters so you can distinguish first and middle names from last names at a glance, e.g., Diana Frances SPENCER. You will be able to enter nicknames, married names, etc., in the Edit Individual dialog box, which will be addressed later in this chapter.

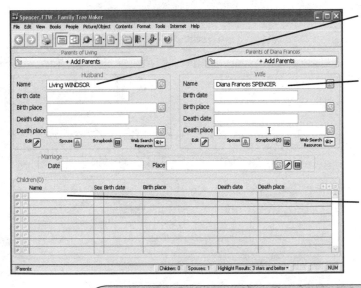

1. In the **Husband** section, enter the husband's name in the **Name** field (first name, middle name, and last name) .

2. In the **Wife** section, enter the wife's name in the **Name** field (first name, middle name, and maiden name). Always use maiden names for females. You can choose to display married names in charts and reports if you want.

3. In the **Children** section, enter the child's name in the **Name** field.

> **TIP**
>
> When entering children in Family View, Family Tree Maker will assume the child has the same surname as the father and add the surname automatically. You can ignore the suggested last name by continuing to type over the Fastfield.

Entering Events

The method for entering events is similar for husband, wife, and children, even though the fields for children may look a bit different from the fields for husband and wife.

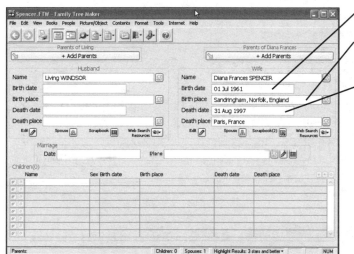

1. Enter a date in the **Birth date** field.

2. Enter a location in the **Birth place** field.

3. Enter a date in the **Death date** field.

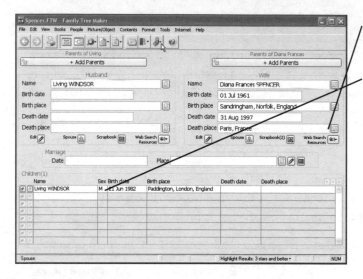

4. Enter a location in the **Death place** field.

5. In the **Sex** field, enter the child's gender, using "F" for Female, "M" for Male, or a "?" if unknown. Family Tree Maker assumes the Husband is male and Wife is female. (You can move the Husband or Wife to the child position of Family View and change the gender designation.)

NOTE

You can add as many children as you like, by pressing the Tab key at the end of each row to start a new entry. If you enter more than eight children, a scroll bar will appear on the right side of the Children fields, which you can use to navigate to any children not visible on the window. You can always check the parentheses in the "Children ( )" heading to see how many children are currently listed.

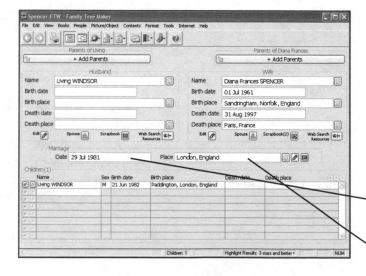

Entering Information About a Marriage

Family View displays the date and location of the couple's marriage. You will learn how to view and add additional information about marriages later in this chapter (see "Adding Details About a Marriage").

1. In the **Marriage** section, enter a date in the **Date** field.

2. Enter the marriage location in the **Place** field.

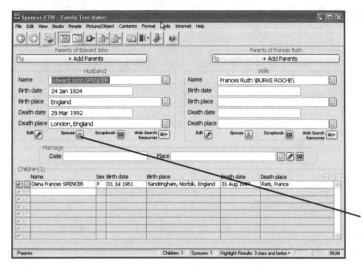

Working with Additional Spouses

The Family View allows only one spouse to be displayed at a time. However, there are times when a researcher needs to enter more than one spouse for an individual, for example if a widower remarries. Family Tree Maker lets you add multiple spouses.

1. Click the **Spouse** button in Family View, next to the individual who has another spouse. The Spouses of dialog box will open.

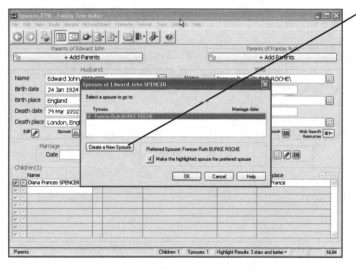

2. Click **Create a New Spouse**. A message box will open, asking if you want the new spouse to be associated with the children previously entered for an individual.

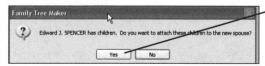

3. Click **Yes** if you want to create an association or **No** if you do not. You will be able to indicate the relationship between the child and each parent (e.g., step-parent, adopted, natural, etc.) in step 13. You will be taken to a new Family View with blank fields for the new spouse.

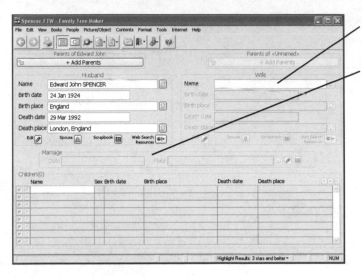

4. Fill in the blank fields about the spouse.

5. Enter the information you know about the marriage event. The marriage event fields will be gray until you add the name of the spouse.

Choosing a "Preferred" Spouse

If you enter more than one spouse, you need to indicate who is the "preferred" spouse. The preferred spouse is the spouse that the Family View, Pedigree View, charts, and reports will default to displaying. Usually, the logical selection is the spouse that had children in your family line.

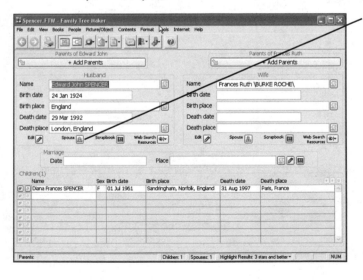

1. Click the **Spouses** button of the individual with multiple spouses in Family View. The Spouses of dialog box will open.

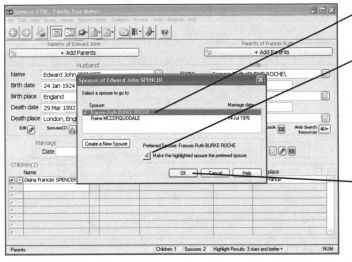

2. Click the name of the person who you want to be the preferred spouse.

3. Click the **Make the highlighted spouse the preferred spouse** check mark button. A check mark will appear on the left of the individual's name, in the Spouse section, to indicate the individual is the preferred spouse.

4. Click **OK** to save your changes and close the dialog box.

Viewing a Different Spouse

You can view the information and children of only one spouse at a time, so you may need to switch spouses when you want to work with a specific family. You will also need to change spouses if you want to add information about that particular marriage.

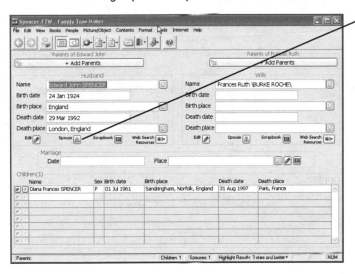

1. Click the **Spouses** button of the individual with multiple spouses. The Spouses of dialog box will open.

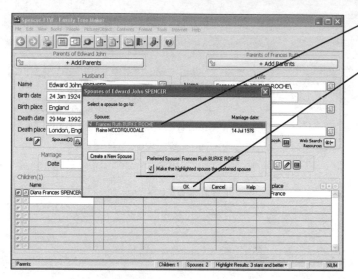

2. Click the name of the spouse whose marriage you want to view.

3. Click **OK**. The Spouses of dialog box will close, and you will return to the Family View with the alternate spouse you have selected. After viewing and making edits to the alternate spouse, if you leave this page, when you return, the spouse will revert back to the preferred spouse, and you will need to follow these steps again to view the alternate spouse.

TIP

Family Tree Maker will tell you how many children and spouses are known for the individual highlighted in the Family View, by indicating the number in parentheses .

Creating a Relationship Between Parents and Children

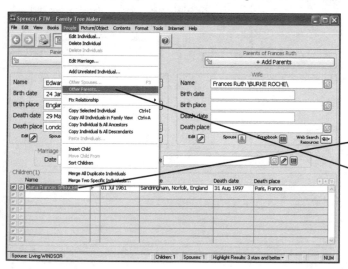

You can indicate the child's relationship to each parent. You must first move the chosen individual into the child position in Family View—the individual cannot be in the Husband or Wife position.

1. Click in the **Name** field for the child.

2. Click **Other Parents** from the **People** menu. The Parents of dialog box will open. The top field lists all sets of parents associated with a child.

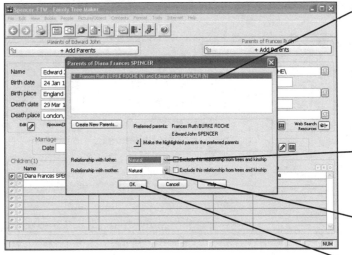

3. Click on a set of parents.

> **NOTE**
>
> If only set of parents is displayed, click the **Create New Parents** button to add additional parents.

4. Click the **Relationship with father** drop-down list to choose a relationship (natural, adopted, foster, etc.).

5. Click the **Relationship with mother** drop-down list to choose a relationship.

6. Click **OK** to save your changes and close the dialog box.

Viewing Other Family Groups

After you have entered information about a primary couple and their children, you may want to focus on a different family group. There are two main ways to navigate to a different family group:

Method 1: Use the Family View

1. Click the **Parents** button, which is marked with a blue arrow or click on a blue arrow next to the child whose Family View you want to see. If there are more than eight children in your list, you may need to scroll down until you find the desired child in the list.

The person selected will replace the person in the Husband or Wife field, and all of the other fields on the Family View will change in accordance with the information currently known about that child.

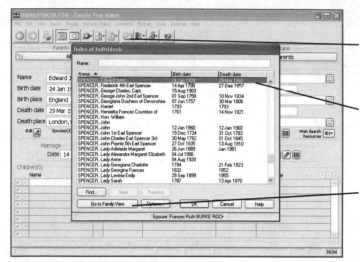

Method 2: Use the Index of Individuals

1. Click the **Index of Individuals** button in the toolbar. The Index of Individuals dialog box will open.

2. Make sure the name is highlighted. You can use the scroll bar to find the name or enter a name in the **Name** field.

3. Click **Go to Family View.** You will be taken to that individual's Family View, where that individual will be listed as the Husband or Wife.

TIP

You can also open the Index of Individuals dialog box by pressing the F2 key.

Adding More Details About an Individual

You can add more details about an individual through the Edit Individual dialog box. You can view and edit all the details you have entered into Family Tree Maker about an individual and add details that do not fit elsewhere, e.g., religion, education, hobbies.

You can access the dialog box through the Edit buttons, the People menu, or through certain charts and reports.

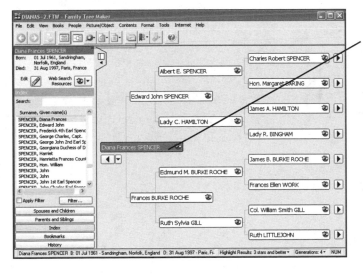

Method 1: Use the Family View

1. Click the **Edit** button near the husband, wife, or child. The Edit Individual dialog box for that individual will open.

TIP

If you want to see the Edit Individual dialog box for a different individual, go to their Family View first, by using the Index of Individuals button, then follow the above instructions. For example, for parents, click on their name to go to Family View, then click the **Edit** button from the Husband or Wife field.

Method 2: Use the Pedigree View

a. From the tree (not the Side Panel), double-click the individual whose Edit Individual dialog box you would like to see. The Edit Individual dialog box for that individual will open.

NOTE

Later on, you will learn about using Preferences to change your default settings. One of the default options you can choose is that if you double-click on a name, you will be taken to the individual's Family View instead of the person's Edit Individual dialog box.

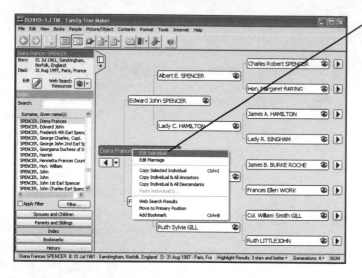

b. In the pedigree tree, right-click the individual and click **Edit Individual** from the drop-down menu. The Edit Individual dialog box for that individual will open.

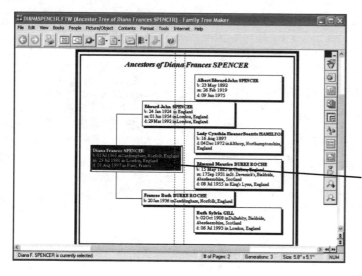

Method 3: Use a tree chart or report

NOTE

The Edit Individual dialog box can be opened from any of the tree charts and most of the textual reports.

1. Double-click the name of the person whose Edit Individual dialog box you would like to see.

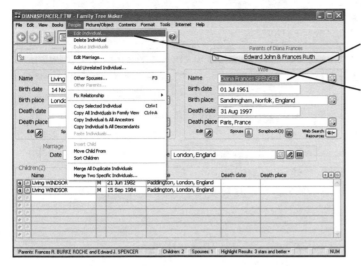

Method 4: Use the People menu

1. Click the name to select the individual.

2. Click **Edit Individual** from the **People** menu.

The Edit Individual dialog box contains five tabs:

- **General**—Name, sex, birth and death dates and places, and title of the individual
- **Facts**—A list of facts and events. You can enter general facts about the individual.
- **Notes**—Notes you want to add about the individual.
- **Medical**—Height, weight, cause of death, and other medical information.
- **Address**—Address information.

Using the General Tab

When you first open an Edit Individual dialog box, the view defaults to the General tab. The General tab contains all of the basic information about an individual including name, sex, and birth and death information.

NOTE

The reference number field on the General tab lets you enter any numbers or letters you choose—a combination of letters and numbers up to 11 characters. This reference system stems from the days when genealogy programs used numbers to find someone in the database. Today's software uses names, but some researchers still prefer to have reference numbers available. This is useful if you use a unique filing or pedigree refer-ence system. If you do not use such a system, leave the field blank. You can also have Family Tree Maker automatically create a reference number for each individual in the Reference Numbers tab of the Preferences dialog box (see Chapter 17).

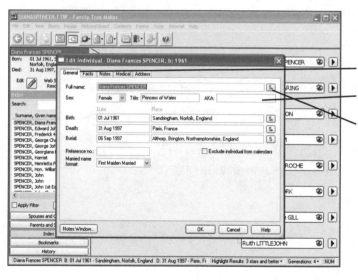

Adding a Nickname or Source for a Name

1. If necessary, click the **General** tab.

2. Enter a nickname in the **AKA** field.

3. Click **Sources** to add a source to the name. The Source-Citation dialog box will open. See Chapter 6 for more details about adding sources.

NOTE

When entering a title in the General tab, do not enter such items as Jr. or III. The titles entered here will be printed in front of the individual's name on reports (e.g., III George Hunt instead of George Hunt III or Jr. George Hunt instead of George Hunt Jr.). If your ancestor was a Jr. or a Sr., type this information into the Name field on the Family View, following a comma at the end of the name. When you are indexing your book, the comma becomes necessary in order to distinguish Jr. from the surname. Family Tree Maker auto-matically recognizes roman numerals such as III or IV, so no comma is necessary.

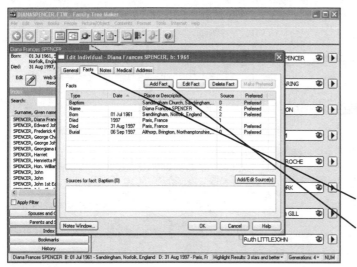

Using the Fact Tab

On the Fact tab, you can add and edit all facts and sources associated with an individual, except relationships between individuals, which are noted in the Edit Marriage dialog box.

Adding a Fact

1. Click the **Facts** tab.

2. Click **Add Fact**. The Add Fact dialog box will open.

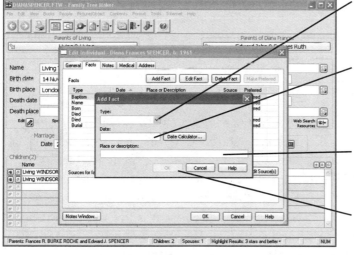

3. Click the **Type** drop-down list. A list of events will appear. For practice, choose **Occupation**.

4. Enter a date in the **Date** field if you have a date you associate with the Fact Type. In this example, it may be the hire date.

5. Enter a description in the **Place or Description** field. In this example, you might type "School teacher," or "Nanny."

6. Click **OK** to save your fact and close the dialog box. Your new fact should appear in the list in the Facts section.

TIP

You can add a source citation to this fact. Highlight the fact and click the Add/Edit Source(s) button. See Chapter 6 for more details about adding source citations.

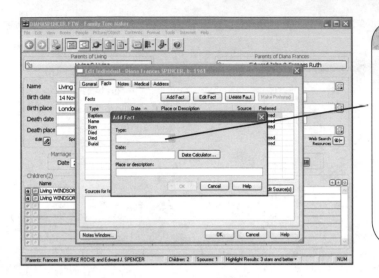

TIP

If you want to add a fact to the Facts tab that is not listed in the drop-down list, place your cursor in the Type field and type in your own fact name, e.g. Favorite Ice Cream, Awards Won, etc. Family Tree Maker will attempt to guess if you are trying to type in an existing fact, but ignore the suggestions and continue typing.

TIP

Click the Date Calculator button to help you determine an exact date or age if you know two of three things: the age of the person at the time of death, marriage, or other event; the birth date; or the date of some other event. See Chapter 17 for more information.

Adding an Alternate Fact

You may have conflicting information about the same event, e.g., two different birth dates, but you can record both facts. This is especially valuable if you are unsure which fact is correct. If you have multiple facts for the same event, you must click a "preferred fact," which is the fact that will be displayed in the various views, charts, and reports. Typically, this is the fact that you believe to be most accurate. Other facts for the same event are referred to as "alternate facts" in Family Tree Maker. You can add alternate facts and change their status to preferred fact at any time. Create the alternate fact by adding it with the Add Fact button of the Edit Individual dialog box Facts tab, just as you would when regularly adding a fact.

TIP

Alternate facts is one of the main reasons recording source information is so valuable.

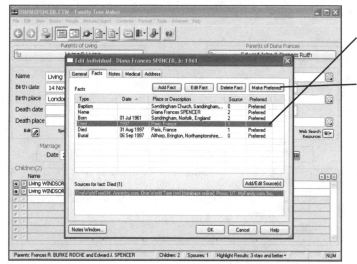

To make the fact preferred:

1. Click the alternate fact on the **Facts** tab.

2. Click **Make Preferred**. The Make Preferred button is gray once you click it, and the fact becomes preferred. The Preferred column shows which facts are preferred.

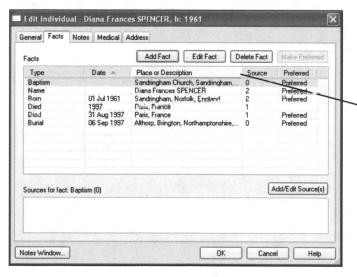

Resizing Columns

Although the columns on the Facts tab are automatically sized, you can override this setting.

1. Place your cursor over the **Type/Date/Place or Description/Source/Preferred** bar. Move your cursor until it changes from a single arrow to one that points both right and left at the same time.

2. Hold down the left mouse button and drag the column right or left to increase or decrease the width of the column.

Entering Information in the Notes Tab

You may have family stories or other lengthy notes you want to preserve for future generations. The Edit Individual dialog box Notes tab addresses this need. This window lets you
enter details in a narrative style.

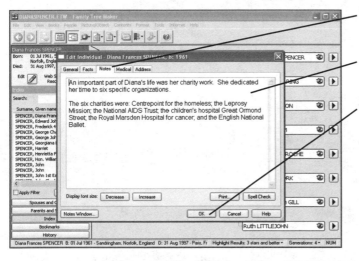

1. Click the **Notes** tab of the Edit
Individual dialog box.

2. Enter the text you want to include for
the individual in the text box.

3. Click **OK** to save your changes and
close the dialog box.

TIP

If you are typing information from another document on your computer into the Notes
tab, you can usually "copy and paste" the text so you don't have to re-type existing text.
For instance, if you are copying the text from a Word document into the Notes tab, highlight the text in the Word document, then press Ctrl+C to copy it. Then, go to the text box
of the Notes tab and press Ctrl+V to paste your copy into that document.

TIP

You should record source information in the Source-Citation dialog box, not the Notes
tab; otherwise, the information won't be included in reports.

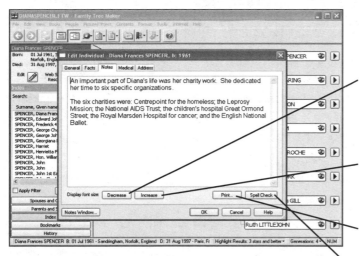

The Notes tab has four useful functions: Decrease, Increase, Print, and Spell Check.

- **Decrease**—Click the **Decrease** button if you want to decrease the size of the text. This will allow you to fit more words on a page.

- **Increase**—Click the **Increase** button to increase the size of the text. This will make the text easier to read.

- **Print**—Click the **Print** button to print the text.

- **Spell Check**—Click the **Spell Check** button if you want to check your work. The Spell Check dialog box will open and start checking this individual's notes for spelling errors.

  - If Family Tree Maker detects a potential spelling error, it displays the error in the **Not in dictionary** field.

  - Correct or ignore the word by using the Spell Check buttons. When a dialog box tells you that the spell check is complete, click **OK**. You can have Family Tree Maker ignore capitalized words, words with numbers, and known names. To customize spell check preferences, click **Preferences** from the **File** menu.

NOTE

If you close the Spell Check dialog box before the program has checked the entire Notes file, your spell check changes will not be saved.

> **NOTE**
>
> Family Tree Maker remembers the spell check you perform in a session, so if you attempt to spell check again, the spell checker will ignore the words you ignored in other spell checks of the file during the same session. When you close FTM and re-open the program, Family Tree Maker will check the words again. You will learn in Chapter 16 how to change your spell check preferences.

Printing Notes

Family Tree Maker lets you print a group of notes at one time. Make sure you are in Family View and that you close the Edit Individual dialog box before attempting to print a batch of notes. (You can also print individual notes by clicking the print button on the Notes tab.)

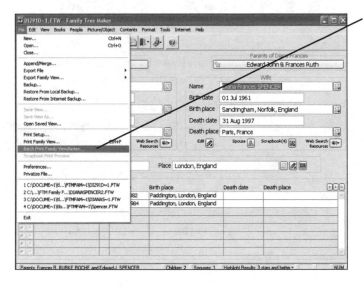

1. Click **Batch Print Family View/ Notes** from the **File** menu. The Batch Print dialog box opens.

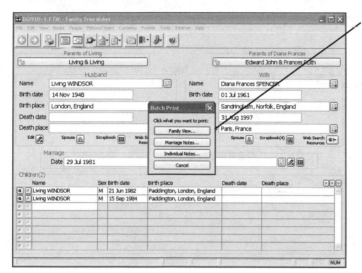

2. Click the button for the type of notes you want to print. The Individuals to Include in Batch Print dialog box will open.

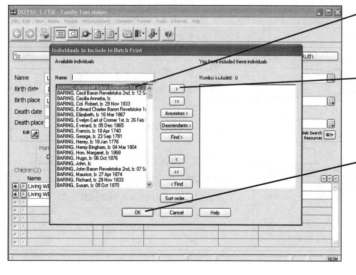

3. Click on a name in the **Available individuals** list to select the individual whose notes you want to print.

4. Click the **right angle bracket (>)** button to move the individual to the list of included individuals. You can select more than one individual if you want.

5. Click **OK**. The dialog box will close, and the Batch Print More About Individual dialog box will open.

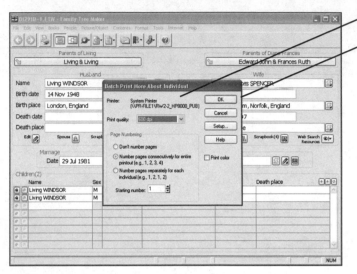

6. Change any print settings you want.

7. Click **OK**. The notes will print. (Make sure you have your printer on).

Resizing Notes

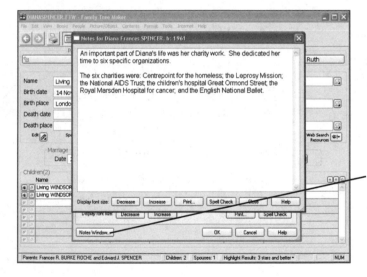

1. Click **Notes Window** to open the Notes for dialog box. This contains all the details you have entered in the Notes tab.

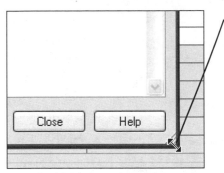

2. You may resize the Notes for dialog box to view all of your notes. Just place your mouse pointer on the lower right corner of the dialog box until the arrow turns into a double arrow, hold your left mouse button down, and drag the image right or left to increase or decrease the size of the box.

This dialog box also gives you the convenience of entering, comparing, and editing details in the Notes tab while viewing one of the other Edit Individual dialog box tabs. Just like in the regular Notes tab view, you can click the Increase and Decrease buttons to make the text larger and easier to read (Increase button) or smaller to fit more text (Decrease button). The Increase and Decrease buttons are for viewing convenience only and do not affect permanent settings or print jobs.

Entering Information in the Medical Tab

Knowing your family's health history can help you prevent and treat illnesses that run in family lines. The Medical tab helps you record basic medical details.

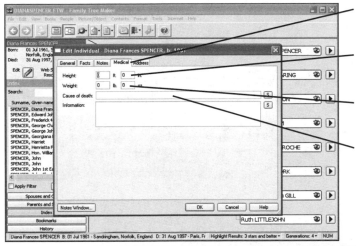

1. Click the **Medical** tab of the Edit Individual dialog box.

2. Enter the individual's height in feet and inches in the **Height** field.

3. Enter the individual's weight in pounds and ounces in the **Weight** field.

4. In the **Cause of Death** field, enter a cause of death if it is known, or leave the field blank if not applicable.

TIP

You can also use the metric system for measurements. You can change this through the Preferences dialog box found under the File menu.

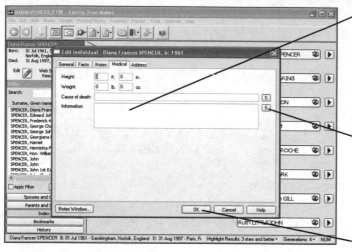

5. In the **Information** field, enter any details you feel are important about the individual's medical history, from long-term illnesses to simple things, such as "suffers from hay fever," "prescribed glasses at age 15," etc.

6. Click the **S** button to go to the Source-Citation dialog box to record where you obtained any information you entered. Source-Citation dialog boxes will be covered more thoroughly in Chapter 6.

7. Click **OK** to save your changes and close the dialog box.

Entering Information in the Address Tab

The Address tab is especially useful for recording the contact information of living relatives. However, it is also useful for researching records in an area where an ancestor was known to have lived.

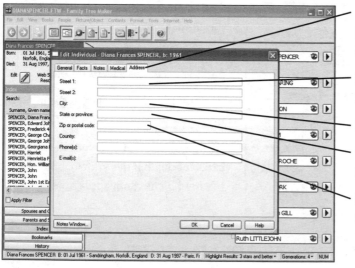

1. Click the **Address** tab of the Edit Individual dialog box. The Address window will be displayed.

2. Enter the street address in the **Street 1** and **Street 2** fields.

3. Enter the city in the **City** field.

4. Enter the state or province in the **State or province** field.

5. Enter the zip code or postal code in the **Zip or postal code** field.

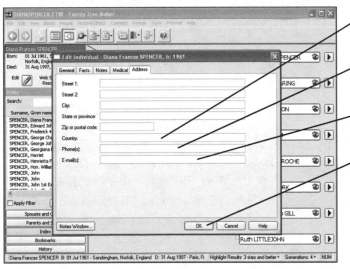

6. Enter the country in the **Country** field.

7. Enter a phone number in the **Phone(s)** field.

8. Enter the e-mail address in the **E-mail(s)** field.

9. Click **OK** to save your changes and close the dialog box.

Adding More Details About a Marriage

You can add more details about a marriage through the Edit Marriage dialog box, including engagement and marriage details, and other marriage-related facts. You can access the dialog box in two ways:

Method 1: Use the Family View

1. Click the **Edit** button located near the marriage information.

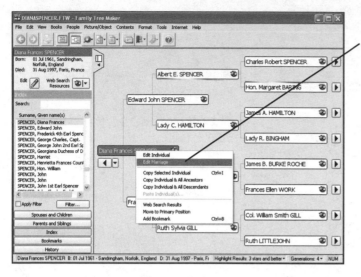

Method 2: Use the Pedigree View

1. Right-click the mouse button on an individual and click **Edit Marriage** from the drop-down menu.

The Edit Marriage dialog box contains three tabs: General, Facts, and Notes. The General tab contains basic information about the marriage (date, location). The Facts tab lets you add facts and source citations. The Notes tab functions exactly the same as the Notes tab of the Edit Individual dialog box, including increasing and decreasing the text size and spell check.

Choosing a Marriage Relationship Status

The Edit Marriage dialog box has two relationship measures and a referencing system.

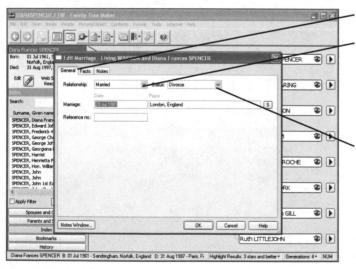

1. Click the **General** tab, if necessary.

2. The relationship for the couple will default to "Married." If you want to change this, use the **Relationship** drop-down list to choose from other options, e.g., friends, partners, unknown.

3. The status of the relationship will default to "None." If you want to change this status, click another option from the **Status** drop-down list.

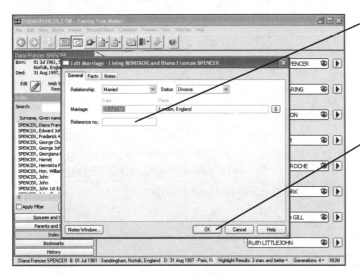

4. The **Reference no.** field lets you enter any numbers or letters you choose to keep track of marriages. This is the same function found under the General tab of the Edit Individual dialog box, discussed earlier in this chapter.

5. Click **OK** to save your changes.

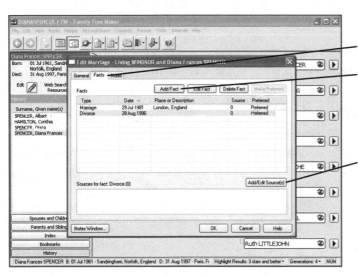

Adding a New Marriage Fact

1. Click the **Facts** tab.

2. Click **Add Fact**. The Add Fact dialog box will open.

NOTE

To add a source citation to the fact, click the fact, then click the **Add/ Edit Source(s)** button. See Chapter 6 for more details about adding source citations.

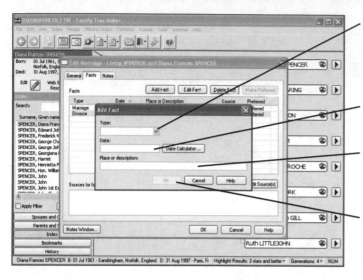

3. Click the **Type** drop-down list. A list of events will appear. Choose the type of fact you would like to add, e.g., engagement, separation.

4. Enter a date in the **Date** field, if a date is appropriate.

5. Enter descriptive information about the event (e.g., location) in the **Place or Description** field.

6. Click **OK**. The information will be added to the list of facts on the Edit Individual dialog box, and the Add Fact dialog box will close.

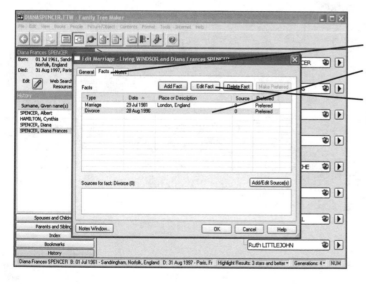

Editing a Marriage Fact

1. Click the **Facts** tab.

2. Click the fact you would like edit.

3. Click **Edit Fact**. The Edit Fact dialog box will open.

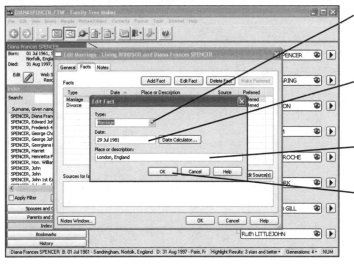

4. Click the **Type** drop-down list to change the type of fact, or, if the type of fact is correct, go to the next field.

5. Highlight the date in the **Date** field; type over it with the new date, or, if this is correct, go to the next field.

6. Change the information in the **Place or description** field if it is incorrect.

7. Click **OK** to save your changes.

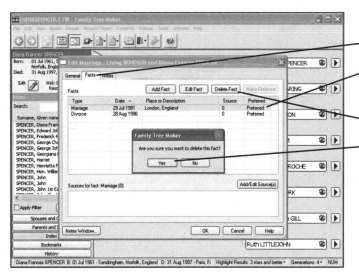

Deleting a Marriage Fact

1. Click the **Facts** tab.

2. Click the fact you would like to delete.

3. Click **Delete Fact**.

4. Click **Yes** when Family Tree Maker asks, "Are you sure you want to delete this fact?" Your fact will be removed from the Facts list.

4

Editing Your Family File

You may find errors in your entries or simply want to check for errors as you enter information, to make sure the details in your Family File are as accurate as possible. Being accurate now will save yourself and those who may inherit your research headaches in the long run and prevent incorrect facts from becoming accepted truths in your family history. In this chapter, you'll learn how to:

- Edit information in Family Tree Maker
- Find individuals in a Family File
- Fix relationships
- Delete individuals from a Family File
- Check a Family File for data errors
- Move information to another location
- Merge individuals
- Use the spell checker
- Use Find and Replace

Editing Information in Family Tree Maker

As you continue to enter information about your family, you will want to use the Family Tree Maker editing features to check and correct your work.

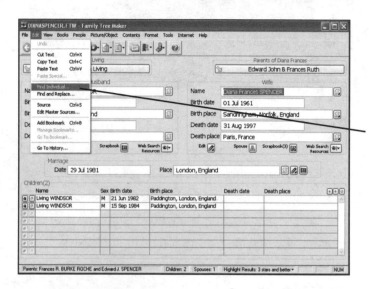

Finding Individuals in a Family File

You can quickly find a name in Family Tree Maker from the Family View.

1. Click **Find Individual** from the **Edit** menu. The Find Individual dialog box will open.

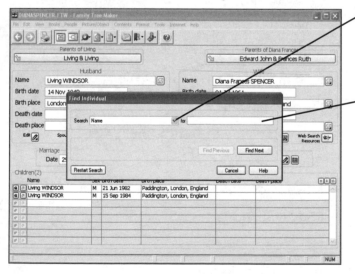

2. The **Search** drop-down list should default to Name; if not, choose this selection from the **Search** drop-down list.

3. Enter the name of the individual in the **for** field, then press **Enter** or click **Find next**. The Family View will switch to the individual you have selected.

TIP

You can also quickly find the individual using the Index of Individuals, or, if you are in the Pedigree View, you can use the Index section of the Side Panel to find an individual.

Fixing Relationships

As you continue your research, you might discover you were mistaken on a marriage entry or on a parent-child relationship. This is likely to occur when you come across multiple generations of individuals with the same name (for instance, you may have confused John Smith with his grandson, also named John Smith).

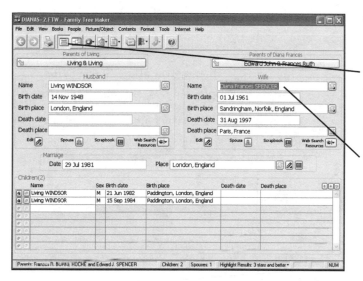

Changing a Marriage Relationship

1. Go to the **Family View** for the couple whose marriage is incorrect. To find an individual, use the Find Individual feature or the Index of Individuals.

2. Click in the **Name** field for the husband or wife that you want to detach.

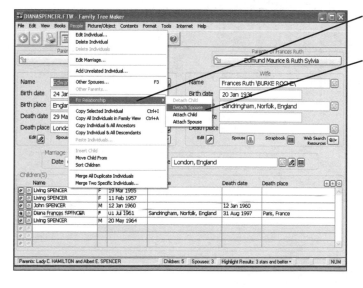

3. Click **Fix Relationship** from the **People** menu. A sub-menu will appear.

4. Click **Detach Spouse**. A message asks if you are sure you want to detach the spouse. If there are children associated with the couple, it also warns you that the children will no longer be associated with the individual being detached.

5. Click **Yes** to confirm the change.

Linking Children to Parents

You might discover you have entered an individual and his or her parents in the Family File, but you did not know they were related when you entered them. You can still link them together.

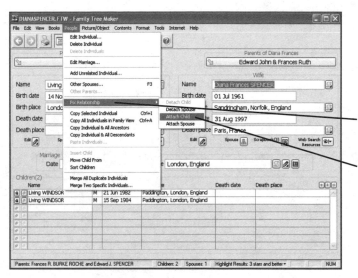

1. Go to the **Family View** for the parents to whom you want to link a child. To find an individual, use the Find Individual feature or the Index of Individuals.

2. Click **Fix Relationship** from the **People** menu. A sub-menu will appear.

3. Click **Attach Child**. A dialog box containing an index of individuals will open.

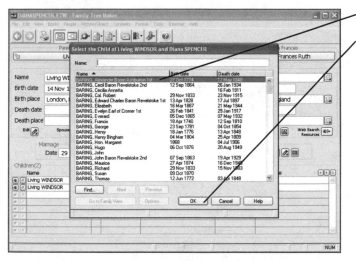

4. Click the child's name in the list.

5. Click **OK**. A message verifies that you want to attach the individual as a child of the parents in the Family View.

6. Click **Yes** to associate the child with the parents.

Detaching a Child from the Wrong Parents

If you have attached a child to the wrong parents, you can easily detach the child from the family. This will not delete the child from the Family File.

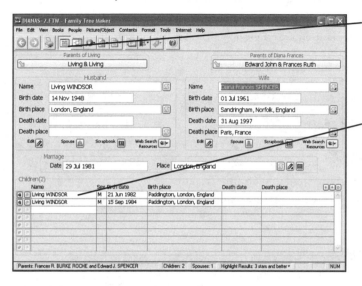

1. Go to the **Family View** for the parents for whom you want to detach a child. To find an individuals, use the Find Individual feature or the Index of Individuals.

2. In the **Children** section, click in the **Name** field for child you want to detach.

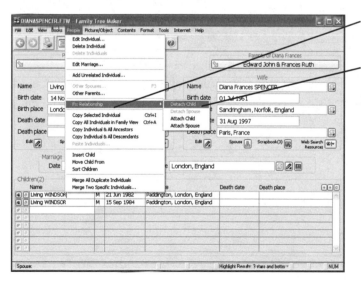

3. Click **Fix Relationship** from the **People** menu. A sub-menu will appear.

4. Click **Detach Child**. If the child has siblings, a message asks if you want to detach them as well. After you click **Yes** or **No**, another message ask you to confirm that you want to detach the child.

5. Click **Yes** to detach the child. A message explains how to reattach the child—if you change your mind.

Deleting Individuals from a Family File

If you find that you have entered the wrong individual in your Family File, you can completely delete the individual and their information from your file. Deleting an individual's name or information or removing an individual from a marriage does not remove the individual from the Family File. You can delete individuals from your file one at a time or as a group.

> ### CAUTION
>
> Deleting individuals from the Family File is permanent. You have one chance to bring the family members back after removing them, by using the **Undo** feature in the **Edit** menu *immediately* after the deletion. You should create a backup of your Family File before deleting anyone. You might want to save your backup file by another name. This way, if you do make a mistake, you will not lose valuable information.

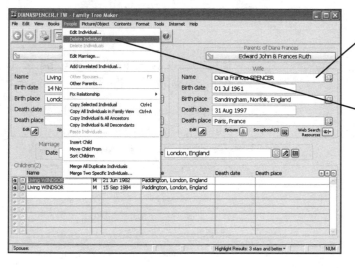

Deleting an Individual

1. Select the person you want to delete from either Family View or Pedigree View.

2. Click **Delete Individual** from the **People** menu. A dialog box will ask to confirm that you want to delete the individual.

3. Click **Yes** to delete the individual.

Deleting a Group of People

An easy way to delete a group of individuals is to use the tree charts. The group of individuals that you want to delete must be visible on the chart.

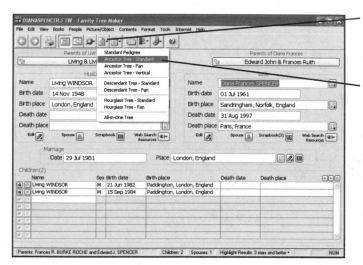

1. Click the **Tree Charts** button in the toolbar. A drop-down menu listing various tree charts will appear.

2. Click an appropriate chart that displays the people you want to delete.

TIP

You can also open a tree chart by clicking **Tree Charts** from the **View** menu, then clicking the chart from the sub-menu.

NOTE

Look at the primary person on the report. It is important to verify if that primary person and those related to that person and displayed on the report are the individuals you want to delete. If the person isn't the individual you want, you can use the Index of Individuals to select a new person. (Use the toolbar button to open the Index of Individuals dialog box. Select the correct individual in the list. Click OK.)

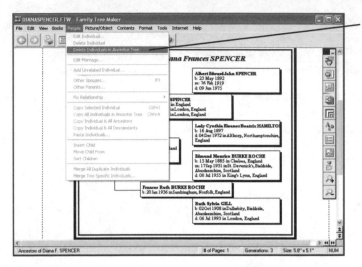

3. Click **Delete Individuals <chart name>** from the **People** menu. A message asks if you want to delete these individuals from your Family File.

> **NOTE**
>
> Remember that everyone who appears in the tree will be deleted.

4. Click **Yes** to delete all of the individuals in the chart from the Family File.

Checking a Family File for Data Errors

Family Tree Maker offers three different ways to check for errors: Data Entry Checking, the Find Error Command, and the Data Errors Report.

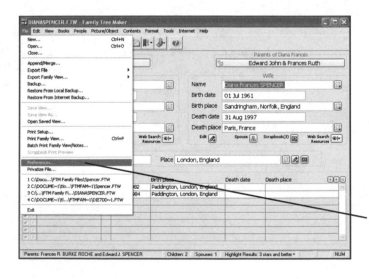

Enabling or Disabling Data Entry Checking

Family Tree Maker offers an error-checking feature that works automatically after you enable it in the preferences. It will check for errors as you enter information and alert you if it detects a possible error, such as an illegal character (e.g., *, &, #).

1. Click **Preferences** from the **File** menu. The Preferences dialog box will open.

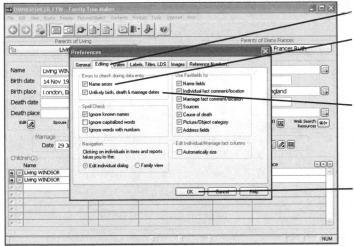

2. Click the **Editing** tab.

3. Click the **Name errors** check box to have Family Tree Maker check for name errors.

4. Click the **Unlikely birth, death & marriage dates** check box to have Family Tree Maker check for date errors in those areas.

5. Click **OK** to save your changes and close the dialog box.

NOTE

When you type in a date that doesn't coincide with the other dates for an individual or family, Family Tree Maker will open a Data Entry Error message box to point out the problem, e.g., "death date is before birth date."

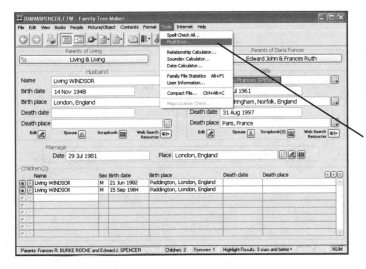

Using the Find Error Command

You can have Family Tree Maker search your entire file for errors and address them one at a time.

1. Click **Find Error** from the **Tools** menu. The Find Error dialog box will open.

TIP

If the Find Error menu item is grayed out, you may need to change to a different window, like Family View.

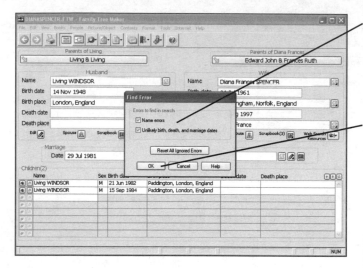

2. Click the errors for which you want to search. You can search for **Name errors** and/or **Unlikely birth, death, and marriage dates** by clicking the appropriate check box.

3. Click **OK**. Family Tree Maker will search your Family File for errors. When an error is found, you will have the following options:

> ### NOTE
>
> If you previously searched for errors and chose to ignore some of the potential problems found by Family Tree Maker, the **Reset All Ignored Errors** button will allow you to view them again.

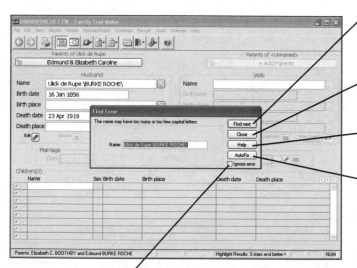

a. Find next—Moves you to the next error and saves any changes you have made.

b. Close—Closes the dialog box and stops checking for errors.

c. Help—Shows the Family Tree Maker Help for this topic.

d. AutoFix—Family Tree Maker fixes the error based on what it thinks is most logical (if the AutoFix feature is not disabled).

e. Ignore Error—Family Tree Maker ignores the error indefinitely. You can always choose to view previously ignored errors again by opting to reset all ignored errors at the beginning of the Find Error process.

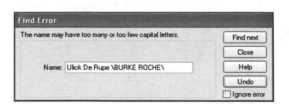

TIP

If you click AutoFix mistakenly, or if the change made by Family Tree Maker is not correct, click **Undo**. The AutoFix button turns into the Undo button immediately after you fix an error, giving you an opportunity to change your mind. If you use the Undo feature, you will not move to the next error until you click the **Find next** button. The Undo button appears only after you fix an error.

Working with the Data Errors Report

The Data Errors Report lists all potential errors that Family Tree Maker identifies in your Family File, including missing and illogical dates, individuals with no relations, duplicate individuals, and unrecognized characters or symbols.

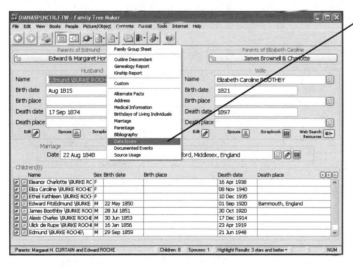

1. Click the **Reports** button on the toolbar and select **Data Errors** from the drop-down menu.

TIP

You can also go to the **View** menu, click **Reports**, then **Data Errors**.

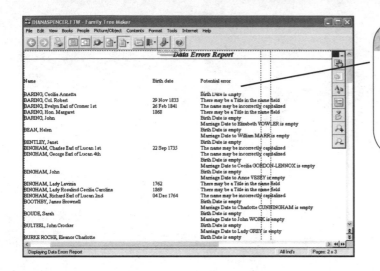

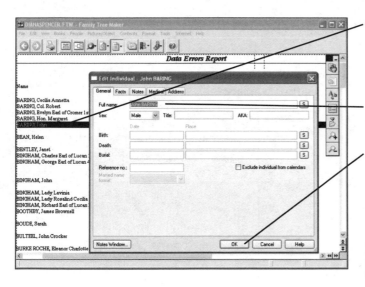

2. Double-click the individual to edit his or her information. The Edit Individual dialog box for the individual will open.

3. Correct the error in the Edit Individual dialog box if known.

4. Click **OK** to close the Edit Individual dialog box and return to the next error in the Data Errors Report.

Moving Information to Another Location

Family Tree Maker lets you use the standard Windows Copy and Paste functions to move text from field to field. For this to work, you must be in a field where text can be selected, for example, Family View.

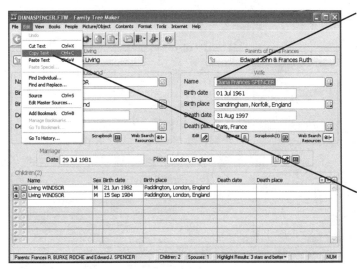

1. Place the mouse in front of the first character you want to select, hold down the left mouse button, and drag the mouse until you reach the last character you want to cut or copy. The selected text will be highlighted. In some windows, you cannot drag your mouse over a select amount of characters but clicking once will still allow you to select the text.

2. Click **Copy Text** from the **Edit** menu. (Or, select **Cut Text** to remove the text item from the field. The selected text will be removed from the field, but you will still be able to copy it to a new location.)

3. Go the field where you want to place the information.

4. Click **Paste Text** from the **Edit** menu. The text you just copied or cut will be moved to the new field.

Merging Individuals

Family Tree Maker offers a method to merge individuals that looks not only at the name of the individuals, but also at additional information, such as family relationships and dates of events.

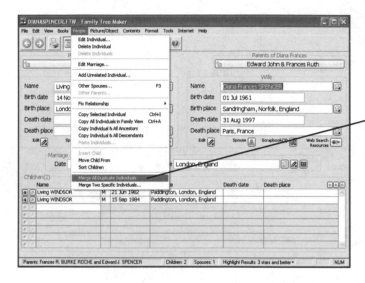

Merging Duplicate Individuals

You must be in Family View for the Merge Duplicates options to be enabled.

1. Click **Merge All Duplicate Individuals** from the **People** menu. A message reminds you to back up your file before you merge duplicate individuals.

> **TIP**
>
> You should make it a practice to back up your Family File before you make any major changes. For more on backing up files, see Chapter 15 "Working with Other Family Files."

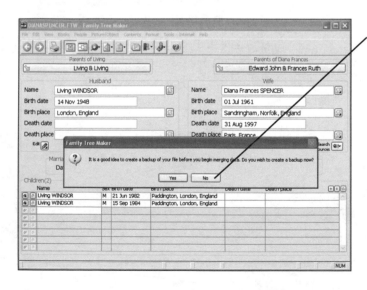

2. Click **No** if you do not want to back up your file at this time. The Merge All Duplicate Individuals dialog box will open.

> **NOTE**
>
> If Family Tree Maker cannot find duplicates, a message tells you that none were found.

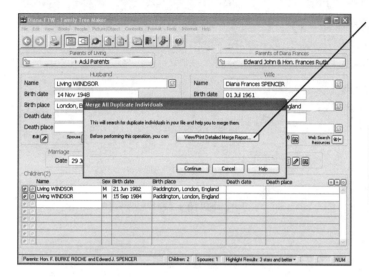

3. Click **View/Print Detailed Merge Report**. The Merge Individuals and Sources Report window (labeled Merge Individuals Report) will open.

> ## TIP
>
> You can click on a line in the list to obtain additional information regarding differences between two possible duplicates.

4. Click **Close**. The Merge All Duplicate Individuals dialog box will reopen.

> ## NOTE
>
> If you have a particularly lengthy list of potential duplicates, it is a good idea to print out this report before going ahead with the additional steps. This way you have a printed record of the duplicates Family Tree Maker merged.

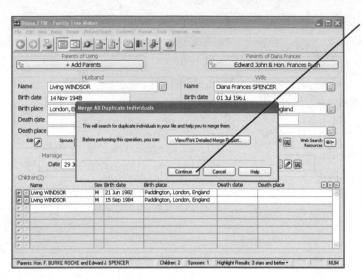

5. Click **Continue**. The Merge All Duplicate Individuals dialog box will close and the Likely Matches dialog box will open with all matches selected for merging.

> **NOTE**
>
> Family Tree Maker uses the check boxes next to the potential duplicates to select them for action.

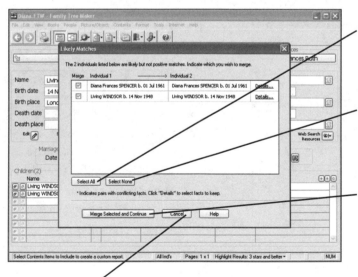

6. Choose from the following options:

a. Click **Select All**. The check box next to each pair of likely matches will be selected. Click **Details** for more information (see steps 7 and 8).

b. Click **Select None**. The check box next to each pair of likely matches will be empty. Click **Details** for more information (see steps 7 and 8).

c. Click **Merge Selected and Continue**. Family Tree Maker merges the likely pairs that have a check in their check box. Click **Close** when the operation is complete.

d. Click **Cancel**. A message asks if you want to cancel. Click **Yes**. The Likely Matches dialog box will close, and the merge will be canceled.

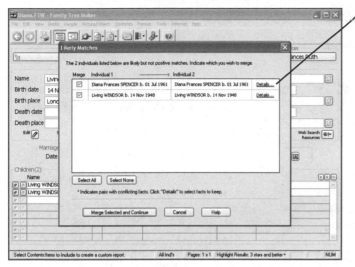

7. Click **Details**. The Merge Individuals dialog box will open.

Use the Merge Individuals dialog box to compare information between the two names before completing the Family Tree Maker merge.

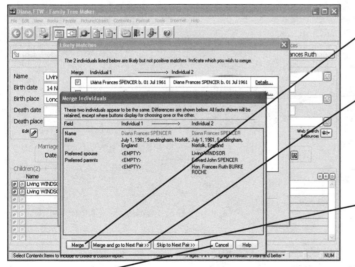

8. Choose one of the following options:

a. Click **Merge**. The individuals will be merged, and the Likely Matches dialog box will close.

b. Click **Merge and go to Next Pair**. The individuals will be merged, and the details for the next pair of individuals in the Likely Matches dialog box will be shown.

c. Click **Skip to Next Pair**. The individuals will not be merged, and the details for the next pair of individuals in the Likely Matches dialog box will be shown.

d. Click **Cancel**. The individuals will not be merged, and the Merge Individuals dialog box will close.

Merging Two Specific Individuals

Instead of checking for duplicate individuals, you can also merge two specific individuals that you know have duplicate information.

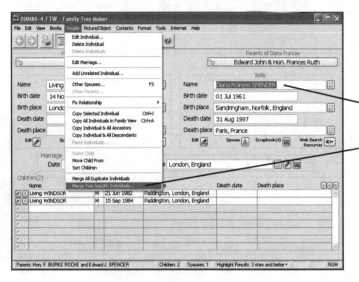

1. Go to the **Family View** for an individual whom you want to merge. To find an individual, use the Find Individual feature or the Index of Individuals.

2. Click in the **Name** field for the individual who has duplicate information.

3. Click **Merge Two Specific Individuals** from the **People** menu. The Select the individual dialog box will open.

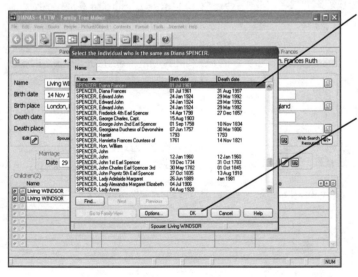

4. Click the duplicate individual from the list, using the scroll bar to move up and down the list, or typing in the last name, a comma, a space, and then first name.

5. Click **OK**. Family Tree Maker will open a dialog box verifying the information.

6. Click **Yes**. The Merge Individuals dialog box will open.

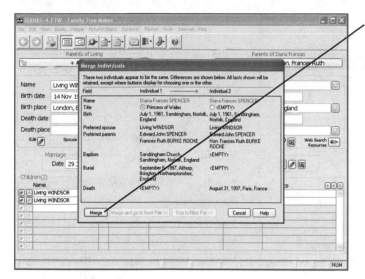

7. Click **Merge** to complete the merge.

Using the Spell Checker

Use the spell checker to catch spelling errors in your Family File. Family Tree Maker spell checks your Books and your Edit dialog boxes separately.

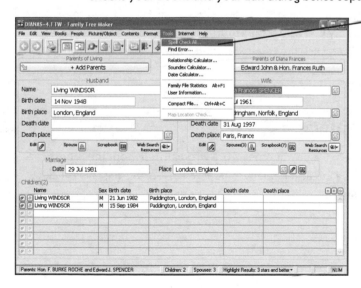

1. Click **Spell Check All** from the **Tools** menu. The Spell Check dialog box will open. Family Tree Maker highlights the first word not found in the Family Tree Maker dictionary.

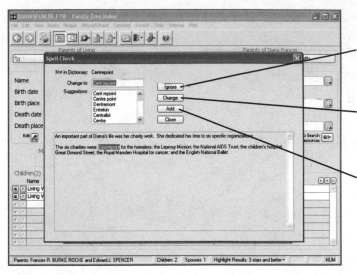

2. Choose one of the following options:

a. Ignore—Ignores the word and moves to the next word that spell checker finds.

b. Change—Replaces the highlighted word with the word listed in the Change to field.

c. Add—Places the highlighted word in the dictionary so Family Tree Maker recognizes the word as an acceptable word and does not consider it misspelled. You may want to do this with certain names that appear frequently in your notes since the spell checker will not automatically recognize surnames and city names.

TIP

If the dictionary does not supply you with an appropriate choice, you can type the word in the **Change to** field and then click the **Change** button. Family Tree Maker will make the change.

Using Find and Replace

You may have inadvertently spelled a city or other word wrong throughout the Family File. You can use Family Tree Maker's Find and Replace feature to correct this mistake quickly and easily over the entire Family File, rather than looking for each occurrence of the same error.

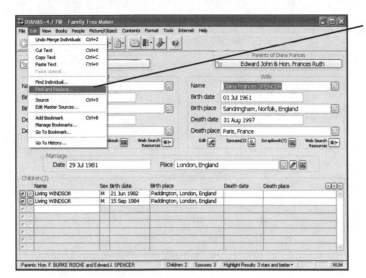

1. Click **Find and Replace** from the **Edit** menu. The Find and Replace dialog box will open.

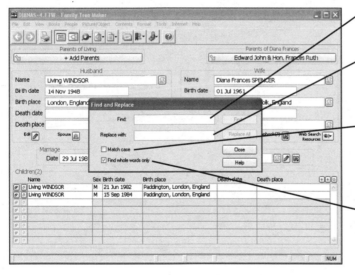

2. Type the word or name that you want to change in the **Find** field.

3. In the **Replace with** field, type the word or name you would like to use in place of the word in the Find field.

4. Click the **Match case** check box if you want Family Tree Maker to find only words that match exactly (upper and lower case letters).

5. Click the **Find whole words only** check box if you want Family Tree Maker to find only matching words (for example, if you asked for "Will," Family Tree Maker would not show results for "William").

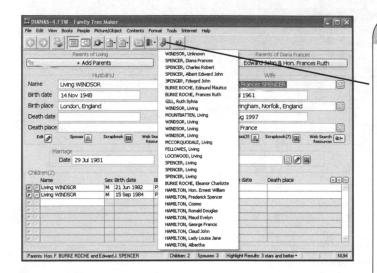

NOTE

You can view your most recently edited individuals by viewing your editing history. Click the **History** button from the toolbar for a drop-down menu of recently edited individuals, or click **Go To History** from the **Edit** menu to see a history dialog box of the last thirty individuals you have edited. In either case, the individual you select will become the primary individual in whatever window you have open (e.g., if you Go To History from Family View, you will go to that individual's Family View).

5

Navigating and Editing in Pedigree View

Pedigree View, the second main view in Family Tree Maker, complements Family View by allowing you to view, browse, and edit up to seven generations of your family tree at a time, so you can take a comprehensive look at your progress on your family tree, quickly establish relationships between individuals, and organize your research with the various functions of the program. In this chapter, you'll learn how to:

- Open Pedigree View
- Navigate in Pedigree View
- Use the Pedigree View Side Panel
- Edit in Pedigree View

While Family View focuses on a single-family unit, Pedigree View offers you a more comprehensive view of your family tree, allowing you to view three to seven generations at once. You can navigate within the tree, view details about individuals, check for Web Search results regarding each individual, edit and add details, and more. The Side Panel provides additional navigation and details about an individual and his/her immediate family. This chapter will cover the various features in Pedigree View.

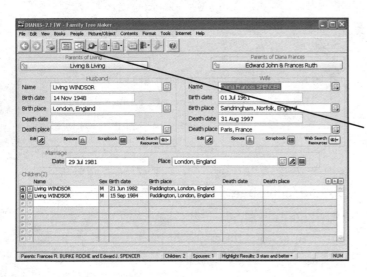

Opening Pedigree View

Method 1: Use the Pedigree View button

Click the **Pedigree View** button on the toolbar.

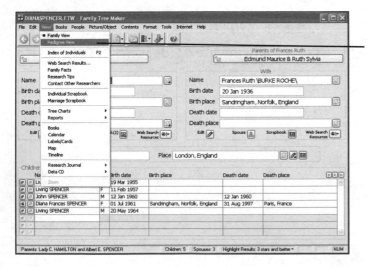

Method 2: Use the View menu

Click **Pedigree View** from the **View** menu.

Navigating in Pedigree View

> **NOTE**
>
> Family Tree Maker has a standard pedigree chart that is not navigable, which should not be confused with the Pedigree View.

Understanding Navigation Arrows

• **Solid navigational arrows** indicate that more ancestors are available to view in the pedigree tree that do not fit in the allotted number of generations displaying in the current chart.

The arrows pointing to older generations are located to the right of the pedigree.

The arrow pointing to the left under the primary individual will shift the tree to the descendants of that person.

By default, Family Tree Maker will move down through your tree via the same path you traversed up your tree. If you haven't previously navigated to the descendants of the primary person, Family Tree Maker will automatically go to the child with descendants. If more than one child has descendants, Family Tree Maker will then look at the previous generation. If Family Tree Maker still can't determine the most probable path, the program will display a drop-down list of children for you to choose. At any time, you can click the drop-down arrow below the primary individual to choose a child of the primary person rather than waiting to see which path Family Tree Maker will choose by default.

• **Empty or white navigational arrows, or arrows that are gray**, indicate that the next generation has not yet been entered into the Family File.

• **Down arrow** lists all the descendants of the root individual. Click on a name from the list to make the child the new primary individual.

> **NOTE**
>
> The drop-down list of descendants will display only the children of the individual's preferred marriage if the individual has more than one spouse in the Family File.

Changing the Primary or Root Individual

Since Pedigree View shows only the direct ancestors of the primary individual, you may want to switch the primary individual to view a different ancestor line, or you may want to switch primary individuals to view ancestors further up the ancestral line.

Even though a family member in your Family File is not in the current line in your Pedigree View, you can still view family members in the Side Panel (covered later in this chapter).

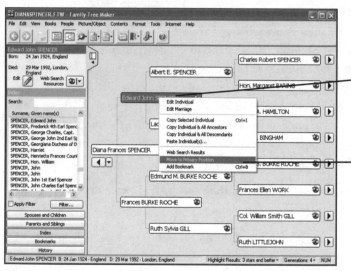

To move an individual in the current tree display to the position of primary individual:

1. Right-click the node listing the individual you want to be the primary individual from the tree. A menu will appear either above or beneath the node.

2. Click **Move to Primary Position**. Animation will indicate how the individuals are shifting within the tree as the individual is moved to the Primary position.

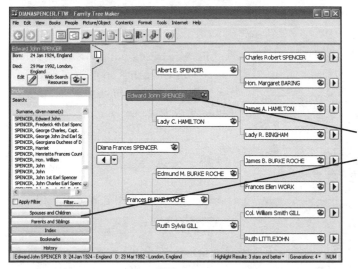

If the individual you want to see become the primary individual is not in the current tree but is an immediate family member (i.e., a spouse, sibling, or child of an individual in the current view):

1. Click the individual in the chart.

2. Click **Spouses and Children** or **Parents and Siblings** from the Side Panel, depending on what is appropriate. The button will expand in the Side Panel.

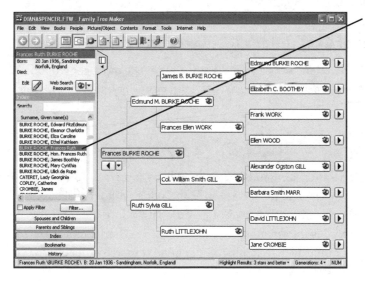

3. Click once on the desired individual. The individual will become the primary individual in the tree.

You can also go to any individual in your Family File by using the Index option in the Side Panel:

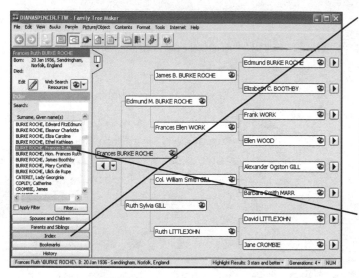

1. Click the **Index** button in the Side Panel. This will bring up a list of all the individuals you have entered into Family Tree Maker.

> **TIP**
>
> You can also look for a name in the Index by typing the name in the **Search** field.

2. Click once on the desired individual. The individual will become the primary individual in the tree.

Changing the Number of Generations Displayed in Pedigree View

You can view three to seven generations in Pedigree View at a time. The more generations you add, the smaller the names will appear in the chart, but the more ancestors you will be able to view at once.

> **NOTE**
>
> If you choose the seven-generation option, the names will be too small to be legible. However, you can use your mouse to "hover" over the node without clicking to view bubble help, which will provide the name, birth, and death information for the individual if you have entered this information in your Family File. The six and seven generation views are useful for quickly determining where more research is needed, or where there are holes in your family tree.

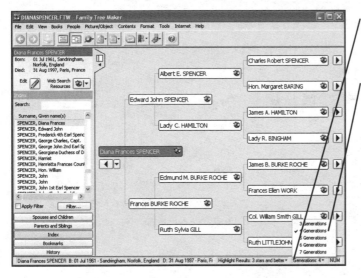

1. Click the **Generations** drop-down list in the status bar at the bottom right section of the screen.

2. Click the number of generations you would like the chart to display. The Pedigree View chart will change to reflect the number of generations you chose.

Ranking Web Search Results in Pedigree View

Family Tree Maker uses a five-star ranking system to indicate the probability of a data match to an individual in your Family File. The greater the number of stars, the more relevant the search result. A small Web Search Resources button will appear next to each name in the chart node if an individual meets a search criteria that you set. You can change your Web Search criteria at any time. (Learn more about Web Search in Chapter 11.)

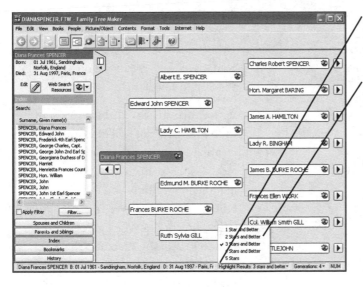

1. Click the **Highlight Results** drop-down list in the status bar at the bottom right section of the screen.

2. Click the number of stars you would like (i.e., the quality level of the match) before Family Tree Maker displays the Web Search icon on an individual's node. A check mark will appear next to the item you chose.

The Pedigree View will show Web Search result icons wherever search results for an individual have met these conditions.

Using the Pedigree View Side Panel

The Side Panel offers both navigational shortcuts as well as useful contextual information about the individuals in the tree.

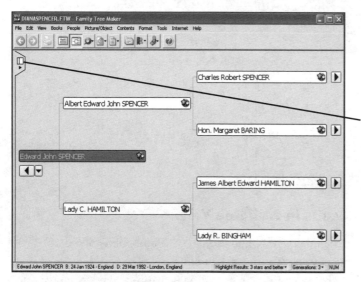

Opening and Closing the Side Panel

The Side Panel is expandable and contractible.

Click the tab at the top left of the Pedigree View to open or close the Side Panel.

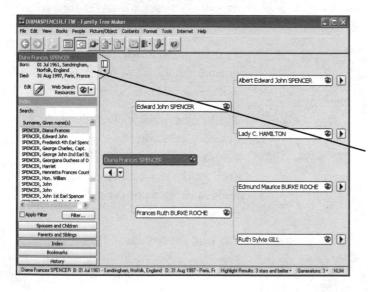

Exploring the Side Panel

The Side Panel contains six major sections specific to the selected individual (which does not need to be the primary/root individual, click once on a name in the tree to select the individual):

1. Details—Located at the top of the Side Panel, Details will display the basic information about the selected individual, such as birth and death information. In addition, you can click the Edit button to open the Edit Individual dialog box or the Web Search Results button to visit the Web Search page. This section remains visible as long as the Side Panel is expanded.

NOTE

If the birth and death fields are blank, but the christening and/or burial dates have been entered (see Chapter 3), these dates will appear in the details section in place of the birth and death dates. Since initiations into a religion can occur later in life, Family Tree Maker uses the "christening" fact to represent a beginning of life date, while the baptism fact can be used if it occurred later in life.

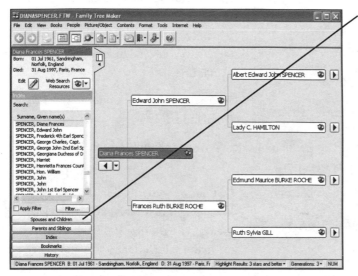

2. Spouses and Children—This section contains a list of the spouse(s) and children of the selected individual for both reference as well as easier navigation. To view basic information about any of these individuals, select one of the names (scroll over without clicking) in the list, and a pop-up will appear listing details. If you click on the name, the name will be moved to the root position in the tree.

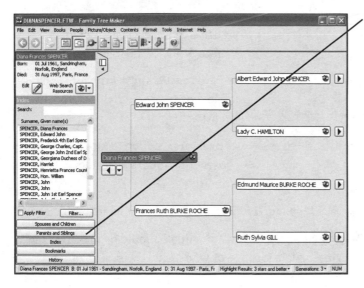

3. Parents and Siblings—This section contains the list of parents and siblings of the selected individual. To view basic information about any of these individuals, scroll over one of the names with your mouse. If you click on the name, the name will be moved to the root position in the tree.

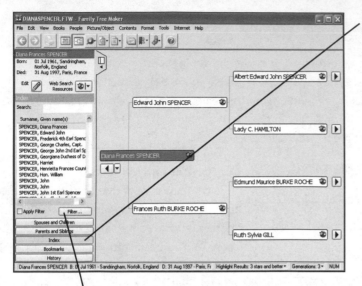

4. Index—This section contains a list of all of the individuals in your file. Just click on a name to jump to the pedigree tree of anyone in the list. You can use the scroll bar to move down the list, or you can type a name in the search box (last name, space, first name) to jump to a particular person. You can also filter this list to show a subset of individuals, which can be useful if your file is very large and you want to focus on a particular line.

To create and apply a filter in the Side Panel Index:

a. Click the **Filter** button in the Side Panel (only visible when in Index mode). The Individuals to Include dialog box will open.

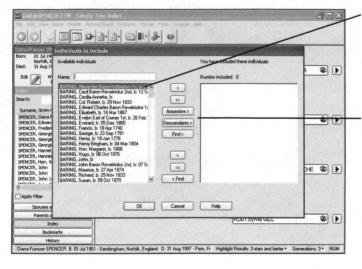

b. Click an individual in the left list (Available individuals) and then click the **right angle bracket (>)** button to move the selected individual to the right list.

c. If you want to move multiple individuals at once, click an individual and then click one of the following buttons:

• **Right double angle bracket (>>)** button to move every individual from the left list to the right list.

• **Ancestors>** button to move all of the chosen individual's ancestors to the right list.

• **Descendants>** button to move all of the individual's descendants to the right list.

• **Find>** button to specify a category type in which all individuals should be moved to the right list, e.g., all individuals born in a certain location or who are all the same gender.

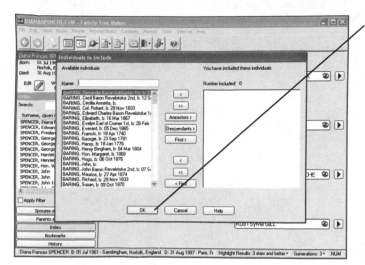

d. Click **OK** when the right list is populated with the set of individuals you want to appear in the Index. The dialog box will close, and only the individuals you have selected will appear in the Index.

TIP

You can always turn the filter off by removing the check mark from the **Apply Filter** box (click inside the box) if you want to see the entire list again.

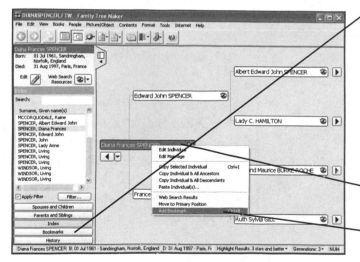

5. Bookmarks—This section contains a list of all individuals you have specifically bookmarked as individuals you want to be able to find quickly in your Family File. Click on a name to jump to the Pedigree View of anyone in the list.

To bookmark an individual in Pedigree View:

a. Right-click on a name in Pedigree View.

b. Click **Add Bookmark** from the drop-down list.

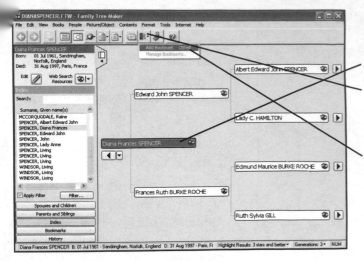

To bookmark an individual from any-where in your Family File:

a. Click the name so it is selected.

b. Click the **Bookmarks** button from the toolbar. A drop-down menu will appear.

c. Click **Add Bookmark**. The name will be added to your bookmark list.

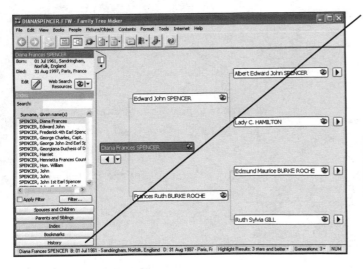

6. History—This section lists the individuals you have edited most recently in your Family File. If you click on a name in the list, the name will be moved to the root position in the tree.

NOTE

An individual will automatically be added to your History list if you open his or her Edit Individual dialog box and click **OK**. If you do not make changes, click **Cancel** to avoid having the individual added to your History list.

Editing in Pedigree View

Adding New Individuals in Pedigree View

If an empty node (no information entered about the individual) follows directly after a completed node (information has been entered about the individual) in Pedigree View, the node will be labeled **+Add Father** or **+Add Mother**. There are two recommended ways to add this information.

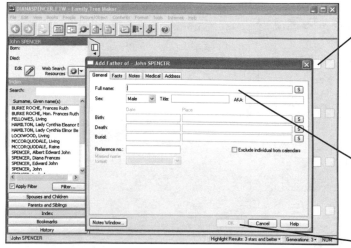

Method 1: Click an empty node

1. Click the **+Add Father** or **+Add Mother** node. The Add Mother of dialog box or the Add Father of dialog box will open. These function the same as the Edit Individual dialog box discussed in Chapter 3.

2. Enter the father's or mother's name in the **Full name** field, in the same order you would enter the information in the Name field of Family View.

3. Click **OK** to add the information and close the dialog box.

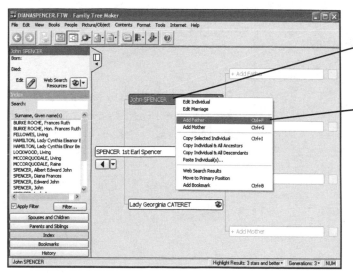

Method 2: Right-click an individual

1. Right-click the individual for whom you would like to add a father or a mother.

2. Click **Add Father** or **Add Mother** from the drop-down menu. Fill in the Edit Individual dialog box with details about the new individual the same way as in Method 1.

Adding or Editing Details About Individuals in Pedigree View

You can add or edit details about an individual by opening the Edit Individual dialog box you learned about in Chapter 3. There are a few ways to open the Edit Individual dialog box from Pedigree View, including the method you just learned to open the father's and mother's Edit Individual dialog box.

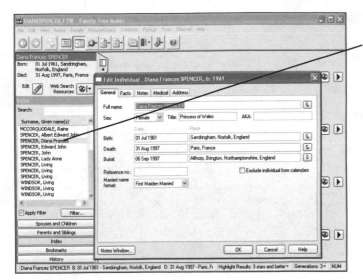

Method 1: Double-click the individual

Double-click the individual you would like to edit. The individual's Edit Individual dialog box will open. Click **Cancel** to close the Edit Individual dialog box.

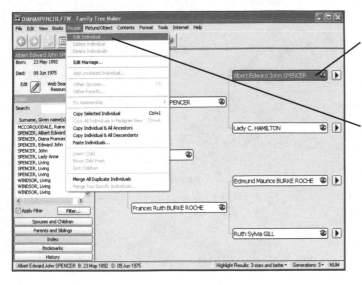

Method 2: Use the People menu

1. Click once on the individual you would like to edit. The node will be highlighted, indicating it has been selected.

2. Click **Edit Individual** from the **People** menu. The Edit Individual dialog box will open. Click **Cancel** to close the Edit Individual dialog box.

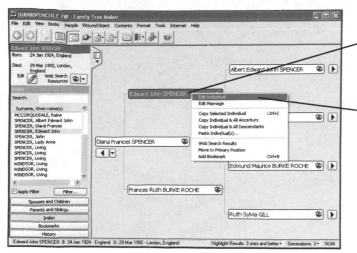

Method 3: Right-click the individual

1. Right-click the individual you would like to edit. A drop-down menu will appear.

2. Click **Edit Individual**. The individual's Edit Individual dialog box will open. Click **Cancel** to close the Edit Individual dialog box.

6

Documenting Sources

Citing the sources of your family history information is one of the most important aspects of your research. Citing sources helps you keep track of the records you have used, which helps you avoid wasting time revisiting sources. In this chapter, you'll learn how to:

- Understand master sources and source citations
- Create a master source
- Merge master sources
- View the use of master sources
- Create a source citation
- Add additional source citations
- Copy information between sources
- Attach an image to a source
- Display and print source information in reports

With Family Tree Maker, you can cite sources for the names of individuals and specific events. You can also cite multiple sources for each fact. This lets you compare conflicting information, keep track of which sources you have researched, and compare notes with other researchers. When possible, you should cite a source for every name and fact you enter.

Understanding Master Sources and Source Citations

Family Tree Maker lets you create both "Master" sources and source citations, which saves you time and lets you avoid typing in the same source information multiple times. For example, you may want to cite a particular book as a source for several different pieces of information. The basic information about the book (title, author, publication information) is the same for every citation, but you may have found information in several places throughout the book.

- The Master Source dialog box stores unchanging facts, such as the author, title, and publication information for a book, so you can quickly recall them when entering information in the Source-Citation dialog box, rather than typing the same fact over and over.

- The Source-Citation dialog box lets you record individual source citation details for each fact and individual you enter.

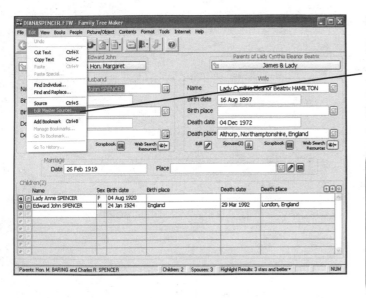

Creating a Master Source

1. Click **Edit Master Sources** from the **Edit** menu. The Master Sources dialog box will open.

> **NOTE**
>
> You can also create a Master Source from the Source-Citation dialog box, which will be covered later in this chapter. Click the **Master Source** drop-down list and choose **New Master Source**. Complete the source fields and click **OK**.

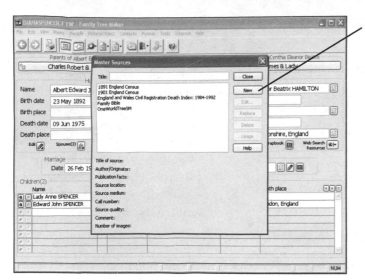

2. Click **New**. The New Master Source dialog box will open.

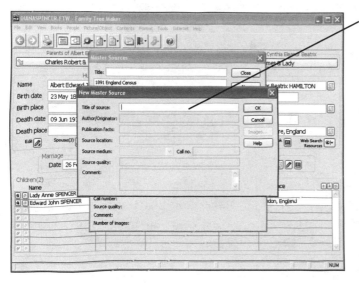

3. Enter the title of the source in the **Title of source** field. The rest of the fields will be activated, and the cursor will move to the Author/Originator field.

After you enter your first Master Source, the next time you open the Master Source dialog box, it will pre-populate with that information.

NOTE

In most cases, the title of the source will print out in italics when source citations are included on reports.

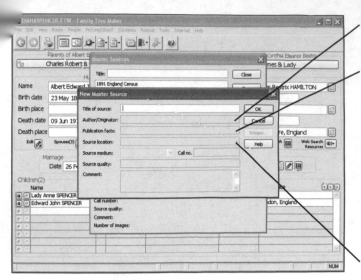

4. Enter the author's name in the **Author/Originator** field.

5. Enter the publication information in the **Publications facts** field.

NOTE

Publication information includes the place of publication, the name of the publishing company, and the copyright date, e.g., Provo, Utah: MyFamily.com, Inc., 2006.

6. Enter a location in the **Source location** field.

NOTE

The source location is wherever the original source exists, so you can return to it if you need to revisit the original. This could be a library, archive, county courthouse, or cousin's residence, for example.

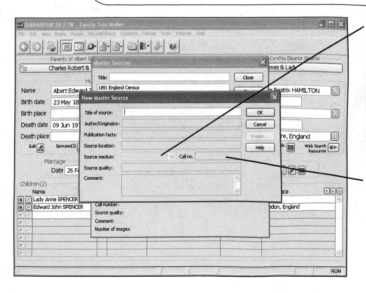

7. Click the type of media from the **Source medium** drop-down list.

NOTE

Including the source media type will help you later if you want to view the source again.

8. Enter the call number, if one exists, in the **Call no.** field.

NOTE

The call number is the number assigned to the source in the repository where it was found. This could be a microfilm number, a Dewey Decimal system number, or some other numbering system unique to a particular library or archive.

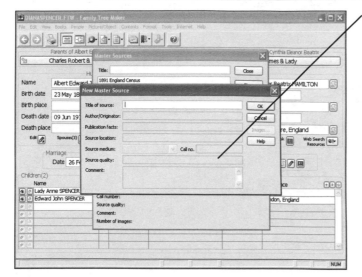

9. Enter the quality of the source in the **Source quality** field.

NOTE

The quality of the source is one reference to the reliability of the source. You can use this field to note both the legibility of the source as well as its potential accuracy (i.e., primary source, secondary source, family legend, etc.).

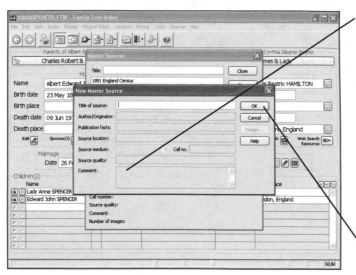

10. Enter your comments in the **Comment** field.

NOTE

Use the Comment field to record any additional thoughts about the source and information. This information will not print on your reports; it is for your personal reference.

11. Click **OK** to save your changes and close the New Master Source dialog box.

12. Click **Close** to close the Master Sources dialog box.

Merging Master Sources

You might have created multiple names for sources that contain the same information.

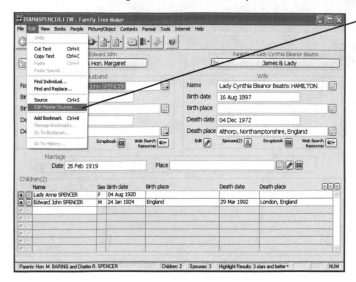

1. Click **Edit Master Sources** from the **Edit** menu. The Master Sources dialog box will open.

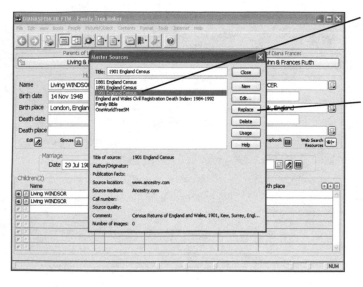

2. Click the source that you want to replace in the list of master sources. You can use the scroll bar to move up and down the list.

3. Click **Replace**. The Replace Master Source dialog box will open.

NOTE

If you want to see which facts are associated with the master source before you replace it, click the **Usage** button.

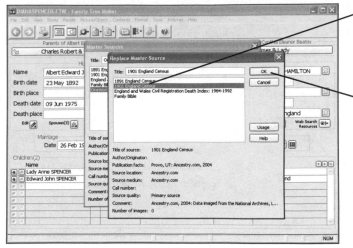

4. Click the source that you want to keep in the list of master sources. You can use the scroll bar to move up and down the list.

5. Click **OK**. A dialog box will ask you to confirm that you want to replace the source.

6. Click **Yes**. All the facts associated with the original source will now be associated with the remaining source.

7. Click **Close** to close the Master Sources dialog box.

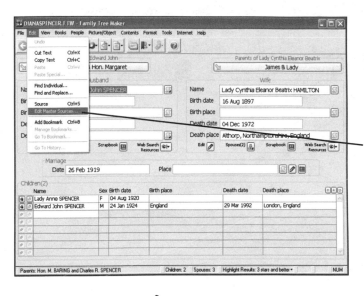

Viewing the Use of Master Sources

You can view the individuals and facts that are associated with a specific master source.

1. Click **Edit Master Sources** from the **Edit** menu. The Master Sources dialog box will open.

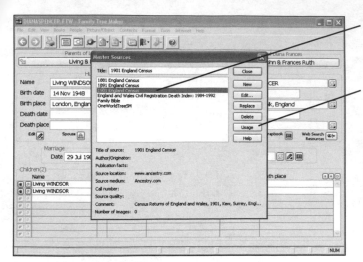

2. Click a source from the list of master sources. You can use the scroll bar to move up and down the list.

3. Click **Usage**. The Source Usage dialog box will open.

NOTE

You can also print a Source Usage report that shows how all of your master sources are being used, see Chapter 10.

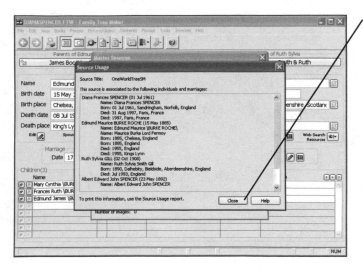

4. When you finish viewing the information, click **Close**. The Source Usage dialog box will close.

5. Click **Close** to close the Master Sources dialog box.

Creating a Source Citation

The Source-Citation dialog box is where you will select the appropriate master source for the information you are citing. You can enter source information when you enter the data and details for each ancestor in Family View.

1. Choose one of the following options to open the Source-Citation dialog box:

a. Click the **Source/Citation** button next to the field for which you want to add a source citation, for example, the source citation for an individual's name.

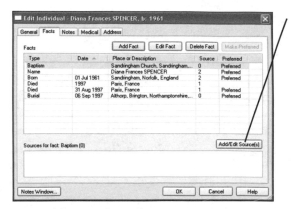

b. In the Edit Individual dialog box or Edit Marriage dialog box, highlight the appropriate fact on the Facts tab and click **Add/Edit Source(s)**.

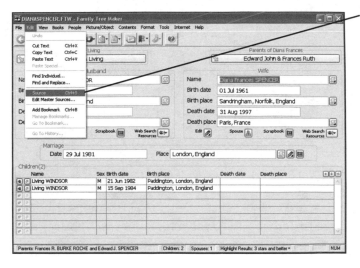

c. Click **Source** from the **Edit** menu or press **Ctrl+S**. The source citation will be attached to the highlighted field or the last field in which you were working.

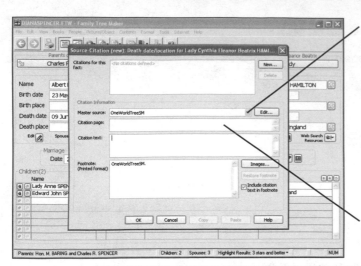

2. Click a source from the **Master source** drop-down list.

3. Enter the citation's page number in the **Citation page** field if applicable.

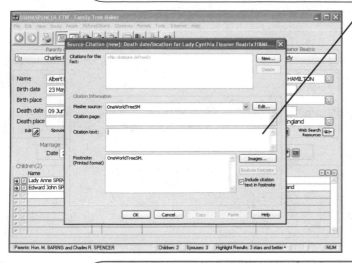

4. Enter the citation information in the **Citation text** field if desired. The citation text might be additional identifying information. For instance, when citing a census record, you would want to include the enumeration district, supervisor's district, dwelling number, and family number for the specific house of your ancestor on that census page.

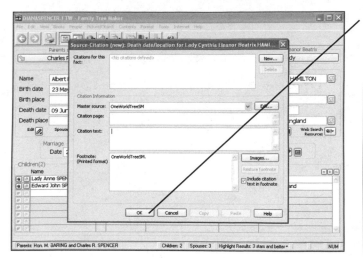

5. Click **OK** to save your changes and close the Source-Citation dialog box.

NOTE

Notice that the Source button has changed to indicate that you have cited a source for that fact. When no source had been added, the source button was a blank sheet of paper. Now, the Source button has a small black triangle in the lower right corner of the button and there appears to be writing on the sheet.

Adding Additional Source Citations

You can add more than one source citation for the same fact.

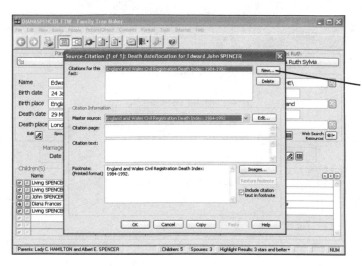

1. Open the Source-Citation dialog box for the fact for that you want to add an additional source citation to.

2. Click **New**. The citation fields will become blank, but you will not lose the source information you already entered.

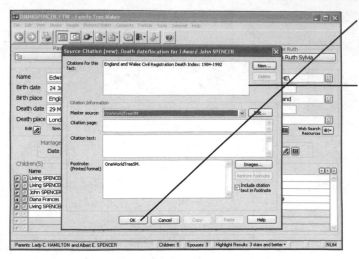

3. Enter the new source information and then click **OK**. The Source-Citation dialog box will close.

The **Citations for this fact** field shows how many sources have been entered for the fact. Click each master source in the field to toggle between the sources.

Copying Information Between Sources

Several individuals in your Family File might have the same citation information for a fact. For example, an entire family might appear on the same census record. Instead of entering the information (enumeration district, dwelling number, etc.) manually for each person, you can copy and paste all the citation information and relevant images.

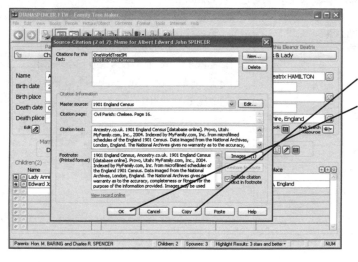

1. Open the Source-Citation dialog box for the individual and fact that you want to copy information from.

2. Click **Copy**.

3. Click **OK** to close the Source-Citation dialog box.

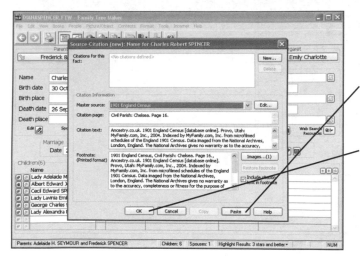

4. Open the Source-Citation dialog box for the individual and fact that you want to copy information to.

5. Click **Paste**. The citation fields are completed with the information from the previous Source-Citation dialog box.

6. Click **OK** to save your changes and close the dialog box.

Attaching an Image to a Source

Family Tree Maker lets you attach images to your sources in a manner similar to how you attach images to charts, reports, and the scrapbook. Scrapbooks are the main area in which you will work with images, as will be covered in a later chapter.

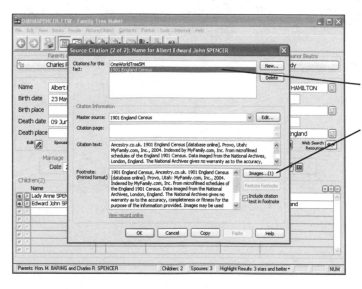

1. Open the Source-Citation dialog box for that fact for which you want to add an image.

2. Highlight a master source in the **Citations for this fact** field, if necessary.

3. Click **Images**. The View Picture dialog box will open.

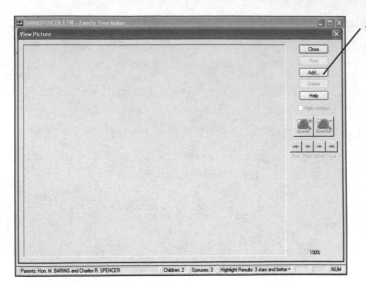

4. Click **Add**. The Get Image From dialog box will open.

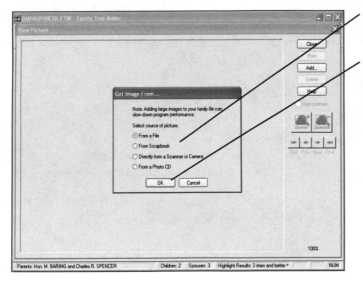

5. Click the appropriate source of the picture.

6. Click **OK**. Family Tree Maker will open a window or launch the appropriate program.

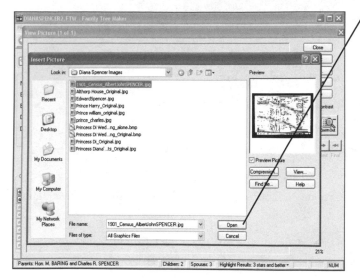

7. Click the image that you want and click **Open**. The Edit Picture dialog box will open.

8. Click **OK**. The image will be added to your source.

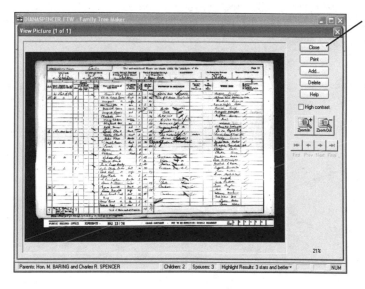

9. Click **Close** to close the View Picture dialog box.

10. Click **OK** to close the Source-Citation dialog box.

Displaying and Printing Source Information in Reports

You can display and print your source information in select reports:

• The Bibliography report lists all sources you have entered into your Family File (see Chapter 9).

• The Documented Events report lists all events for which you have entered source information (see Chapter 9).

• The Source Usage report lists each master source and the individuals and facts associated with that source (see Chapter 9).

• You can choose to enter source information at the bottom of each Genealogy Report (see Chapter 8) by selecting Options from the Contents menu and clicking the appropriate Source Information radio buttons.

You can print source information from one of the reports listed below by clicking the **Print** button on the toolbar while the report is open and clicking **OK** from the Print dialog box.

Using Family Tree Maker's Scrapbook

You can add images to your Family File to link to individuals and to enhance charts, reports, and more. Family Tree Maker helps you organize your images into Scrapbooks for each individual. In this chapter, you'll learn how to:

- Access a Scrapbook
- Add images and other multimedia objects
- Enter information about Scrapbook objects
- Rearrange Scrapbook objects
- Copy objects into other Scrapbooks
- Enhance images
- Search for Scrapbook objects
- Share Scrapbooks

Each individual and each marriage in your Family File has a Scrapbook in which you can store photographs, documents, video, sound files, and other multimedia files.

You can view these images in the Scrapbook separately or as a slide show, or you can use these images to enhance charts, reports, and other areas of Family Tree Maker. To use individual images in charts and the family group sheet, it is necessary to have the picture in the person's Scrapbook. (You will learn how to use your Scrapbook images in charts, reports, and on your personal Internet home page in following chapters.)

NOTE

When you insert a picture or other object into a Family Tree Maker Scrapbook, the original is not moved from its location. You should always maintain that original picture or multimedia file in case you want to use it outside of Family Tree Maker. Multimedia objects are embedded into your Family File and cannot be retrieved as separate files.

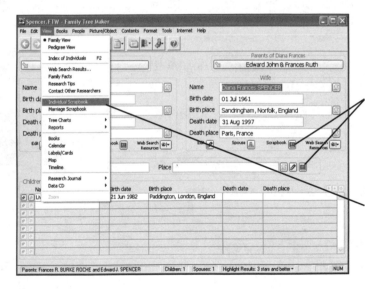

Accessing a Scrapbook

1. Go to the Family View of the individual or marriage.

2. Click the **Scrapbook** button next to the individual or marriage. The Scrapbook will open.

TIP

You can access a Scrapbook from other windows, including charts, reports, and the Pedigree View, without returning to Family View. Select the individual, then click **Individual Scrapbook** or **Marriage Scrapbook** from the **View** menu. If the menu item is gray, the Scrapbook is not available in that window.

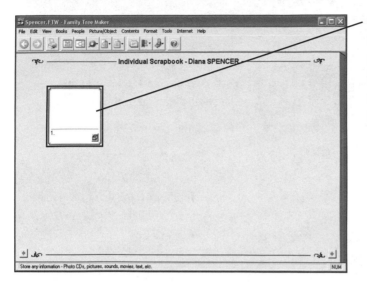

The empty, numbered frame in the Scrapbook represents where the first image will go. Every time you fill in one frame with an object, a new blank frame will appear. Each frame can hold an image, sound clip, or another object.

Adding Images and Other Multimedia Objects

Adding Images

The easiest way to save an image to a Scrapbook is from a disc or from a location on your computer. You can also insert a picture from a scanner, digital camera, or photo CD.

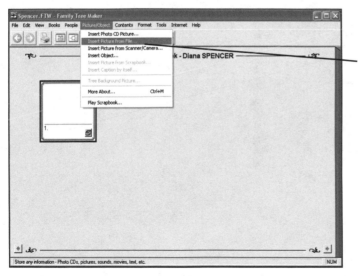

1. Access the Scrapbook that you want to add an image to.

2. Click **Insert Photo CD Picture** or **Insert Picture from File** from the **Picture/Object** menu, depending on where you have your picture stored. The Insert Picture dialog box will open.

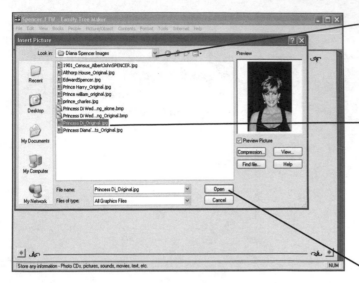

3. Click the **Look in** drop-down list to locate the folder where you have saved your images. When you have found the correct folder, click on it, and the picture file should appear in the list box.

4. Click the desired image.

NOTE

You can preview the image you have selected by clicking the Preview Picture check box.

---

5. Click **Open**. An Edit Picture dialog box will open with a view of the picture.

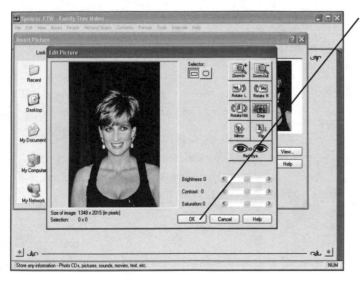

6. Click **OK**. The Edit Picture dialog box and the Insert Picture dialog box will close.

(You will learn later in this chapter how to use the Edit Picture dialog box to enhance your picture.)

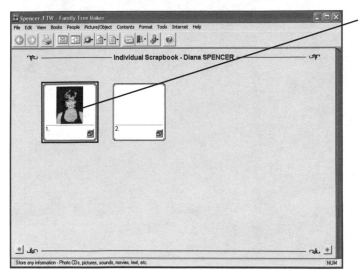

Your image will appear in the frame, which means it has been properly saved to the Scrapbook.

> ### TIP
>
> You can also scan the picture directly into the Scrapbook. Click **Insert Picture from Scanner/Camera** from the **Picture/Object** menu. Images can take up a lot of file space, so you may want to set your resolution to a maximum of 200 dpi (dots per inch). At this resolution, the image size will be large on your computer screen, but it will be blurry if you try to print it.

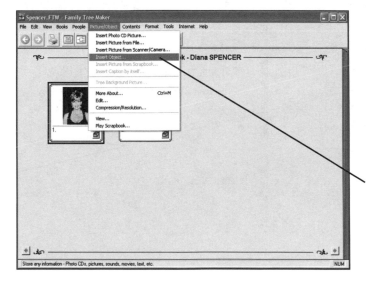

Adding Sound and Video Clips

You can add sound and video clips to a Scrapbook similarly to how you added an image.

1. Access the Scrapbook that you want to add sound or video clips to.

2. Click **Insert Object** from the **Picture/Object** menu. The Insert Object dialog box will open.

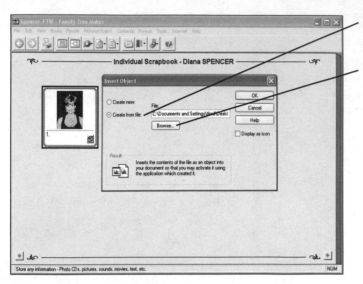

3. Click the **Create from file** radio button.

4. Click **Browse**. The Browse dialog box will open.

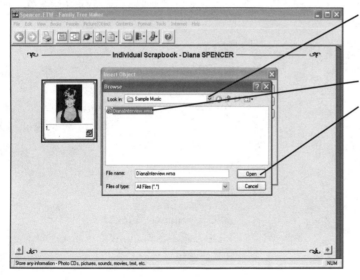

5. Click the **Look in** drop-down list to locate the folder where you have saved the files.

6. Click the desired file.

7. Click **Open**. The Browse dialog box will close. You will be returned to the Insert Object dialog box.

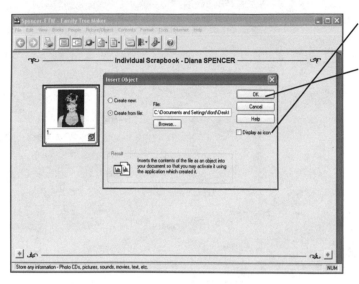

8. In the Insert Object dialog box, click the **Display as icon** check box.

9. Click **OK**. The Insert Object dialog box will close.

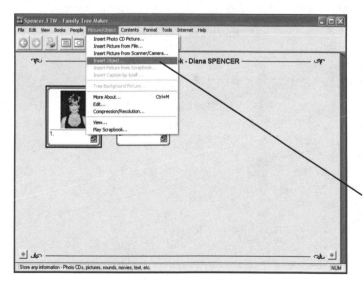

Launching Programs in a Scrapbook

Family Tree Maker lets you launch programs from a Scrapbook using Object Linking and Embedding (OLE). You might want to do this so you can open a word processing file to display a detailed family story.

1. Click **Insert Object** from the **Picture/Object** menu. The Insert Object dialog box will open.

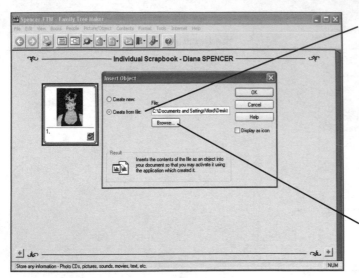

2. Click the **Create from file** radio button.

TIP

If you click the **Create new** radio button, you can select an object type from the list that appears. Then click **OK**, and the program will start if it is installed on your computer.

3. Click **Browse**. The Browse dialog box will open.

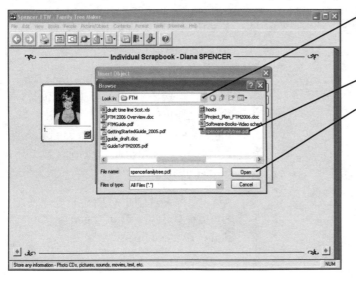

4. Click the **Look in** drop-down list to locate the folder where you have saved the file.

5. Click the desired file.

6. Click **Open**. The Browse dialog box will close. You will be returned to the Insert Object dialog box.

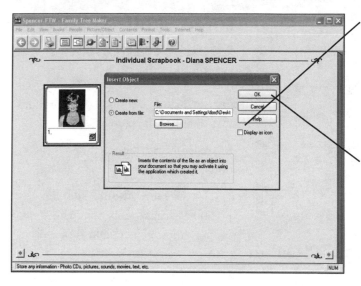

7. Click the **Display as icon** check box if you want to display the object as a description or icon rather than showing an image of the object. You can change the appearance of the icon by clicking **Change Icon**. Family Tree Maker will insert an icon in the Scrapbook.

8. Click **OK**. The Insert Object dialog box will close.

NOTE

Displaying an object as an icon makes it easier to identify multi-media objects such as sound and video files. The object will behave the same way whether you choose to display it as an icon.

TIP

When you save images to a Scrapbook, the Scrapbook button in Family View changes to show that Scrapbook items have been added for the individual. First, a black triangle will appear in the bottom right corner of the button. Second, a number in parentheses following the word "Scrapbook" will indicate the number of images or objects added to the Scrapbook.

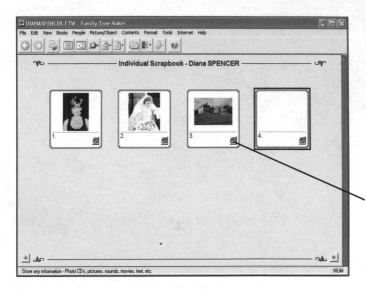

Entering Information About Scrapbook Objects

You can include a caption at the bottom of each object frame in a Scrapbook.

1. Access the Scrapbook for an individual or marriage.

2. Click the **More About** button for the selected Scrapbook item. The More About Picture/Object dialog box will open.

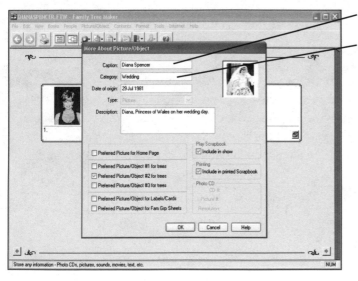

3. Enter a caption in the **Caption** field.

4. Enter a category in the **Category** field.

TIP

Plan ahead before you use the Category field. Family Tree Maker lets you categorize your Scrapbook objects, making them easier to search and add to charts. For example, you may want to name a category for events (e.g., weddings), a time frame (e.g., baby photos), or a photo type (e.g., portraits).

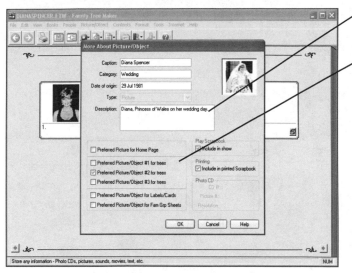

5. Enter a description for the object in the **Description** field.

6. Click the check box(es) for your preferred selections. These options allow you to determine which images appear in charts, family group sheets, labels, and your home page. For example, if you select **Preferred Picture/Object #1 for trees** and then create a tree chart using pictures designated as Preferred Picture/Object #1 for trees, this picture will appear next to the person in the chart. See Chapter 8 for more information on creating tree charts.

NOTE

Remember that only images will print, not sounds, video, and OLE objects.

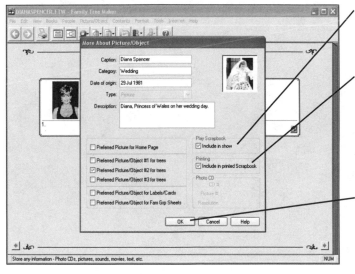

7. Click the **Include in show** check box for objects you want to display when you play the Scrapbook as a slide show.

8. Click the **Include in printed Scrapbook** check box if you want the object to be printed when you print the Scrapbook. You may not want to include multimedia objects such as sound files since they will only print as icons.

9. Click **OK** to save your changes and close the More About Picture/Object dialog box.

Rearranging Scrapbook Objects

Although images and objects display in the order they were inserted into the Scrapbook, you can rearrange the order.

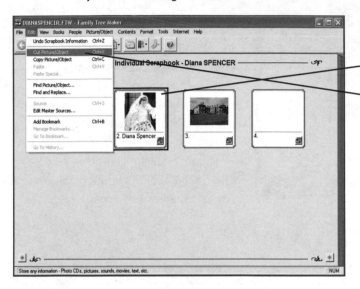

1. Access the Scrapbook for an individual or marriage.

2. Click the object you want to move.

3. Click **Cut Picture/Object** from the **Edit** menu. The object will be removed from the Scrapbook and placed on the clipboard.

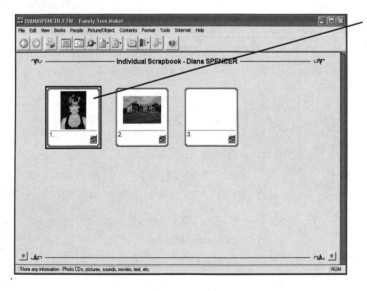

4. Click the frame where you want to place the object.

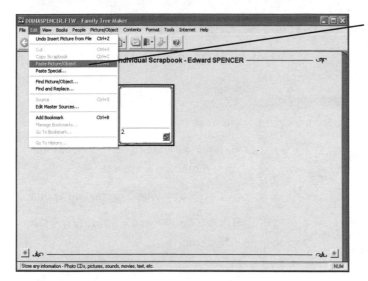

5. Click **Paste Picture/Object** from the **Edit** menu.

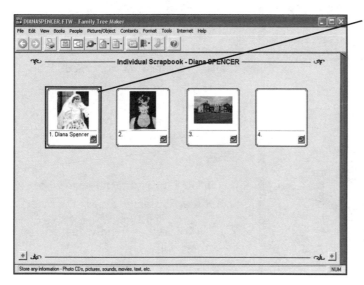

The object will be pasted in the new position, and the object you have replaced will move one space to the right.

Copying Objects into Other Scrapbooks

You can copy a Scrapbook object from the Scrapbook of one individual to that of another individual.

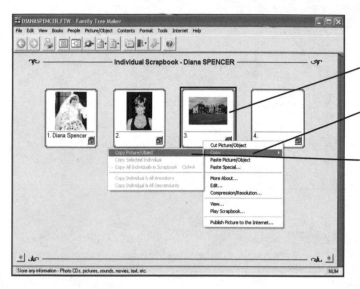

1. Access the Scrapbook for an individual or marriage.

2. Right-click the object you want to copy. A menu will appear.

3. Click **Copy**. A sub-menu will appear.

4. Click **Copy Picture/Object** from the sub-menu.

> **NOTE**
>
> Rather than right-clicking on an object you want to copy, you can also click once on the object, then click **Copy** from the **Edit** menu.

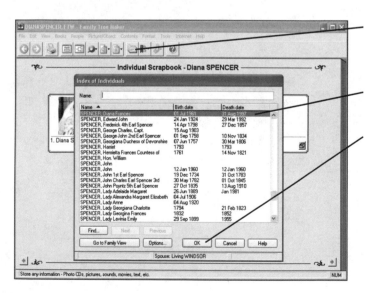

5. Click the **Index of Individuals** button. The Index of Individuals dialog box will open.

6. Click the individual name in whose Scrapbook you want to paste the object.

7. Click **OK**. The new individual's Scrapbook will open.

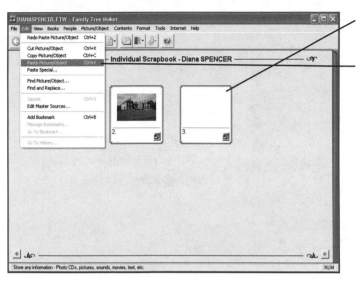

8. Click the frame where you want to place the object.

9. Click **Paste Picture/Object** from the **Edit** menu.

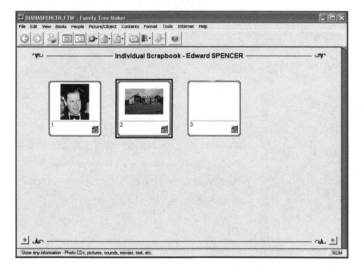

The copied object will be placed into the Scrapbook.

Enhancing Images

As mentioned earlier in this chapter, you can enhance images that you add to a Scrapbook. Using features built into Family Tree Maker, you can rotate, crop, mirror, and flip images; adjust color and brightness; and remove red eye.

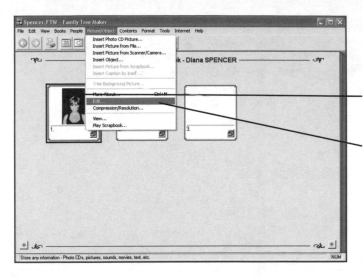

Cropping an Image

You may want to trim the edges of your picture to make it more attractive.

1. In a Scrapbook, click the image you want to crop.

2. Click **Edit** from the **Picture/Object** menu. The Edit Picture dialog box for the image you selected will open.

TIP

This is the same dialog box that opens when you first save an image into a Scrapbook. You can edit the image at that point or reopen it for editing like you are doing now.

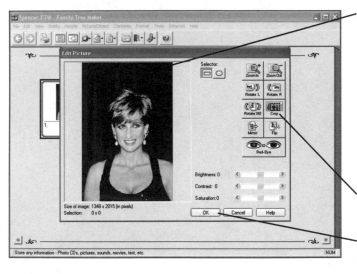

3. In the Edit Picture dialog box, click and drag your mouse over the portion of the image you want to keep. Everything outside the dotted lines of the box will be removed. If you are not happy with where you have drawn the box, you can click on the picture again and click and drag your mouse to re-draw the box.

4. Click the **Crop** button. The image will be cropped.

5. Click **OK** to save your changes or **Cancel** to close the dialog box without saving any changes.

Adjusting the Color and Brightness of the Image

You may be able to enhance your picture by lightening or darkening it. For example, you might want to darken an old photo that has faded to see if it will bring out some of the details in the image.

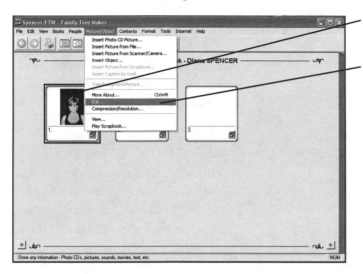

1. In a Scrapbook, click the image you want to enhance.

2. Click **Edit** from the **Picture/Object** menu. The Edit Picture dialog box for the image you selected will open.

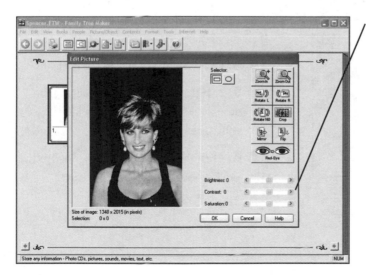

3. Use the **Brightness**, **Contrast**, and **Saturation** slider bars to change the appearance of the image. (To do this, click the right and left arrows for each bar or use your mouse to drag the square in the middle to the left or right.)

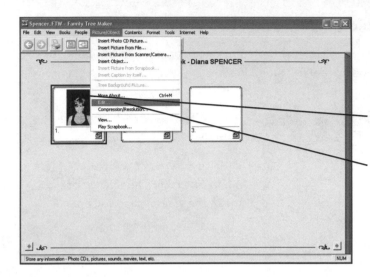

Correcting Red Eye

Use this feature to correct the red-eye effect that may have occurred in your photographs.

1. In a Scrapbook, click the image you want to enhance.

2. Click **Edit** from the **Picture/Object** menu. The Edit Picture dialog box for the image you selected will open.

> **TIP**
>
> You can also access an individual's Edit Picture dialog box by right-clicking the image and selecting **Edit** from the menu that appears.

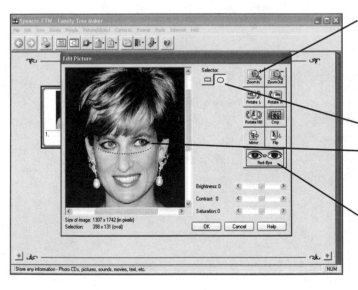

3. Click the **Zoom In** button as many times as you need to in order to bring the eyes into a close focus. Slide the scroll bars if necessary until the eyes come into view.

4. Click the **oval selector** button.

5. Select the eye area by dragging the mouse over the image. An oval selector will appear over the eyes.

6. Click the **Red-Eye** button. The Red Eye Removal dialog box will open.

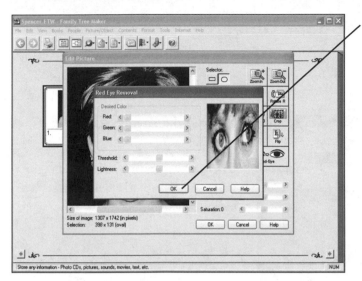

7. Click **OK** to let Family Tree Maker automatically fix the red eye. In most cases, you will not need to make any adjustments to the color selection yourself.

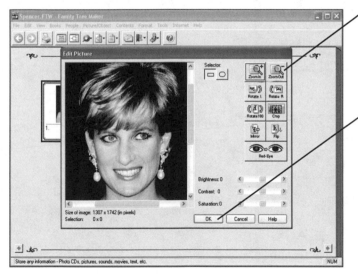

8. Zoom back out to see the effect. If you are not satisfied with the results, you can manually adjust the colors using the color slider bars in the Red Eye Removal dialog box.

9. Once you are satisfied with your changes, click **OK** to save your changes and close the Edit Picture dialog box.

Searching for Scrapbook Objects

You may reach a point where you have so many objects stored in your Scrapbook that you have difficulty finding a particular item quickly. You can use the Find feature to speed your search.

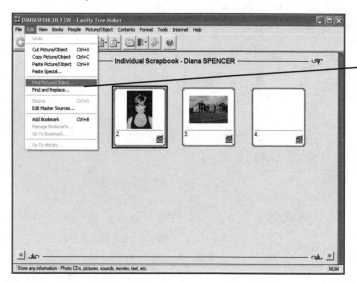

1. Access the Scrapbook for an individual or marriage.

2. Click **Find Picture/Object** from the **Edit** menu. The Find Picture/Object dialog box will open.

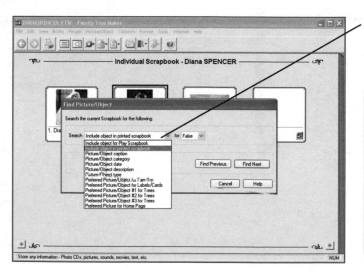

3. Click the **Search** drop-down list to choose the search type you want to use.

> ### TIP
>
> If you are searching for a regular image in your program, you will probably want to choose Picture/ Object type in the Search box and Picture in the second box. Another common choice is to search on the Picture/Object caption field, for a word you have typed into the caption.

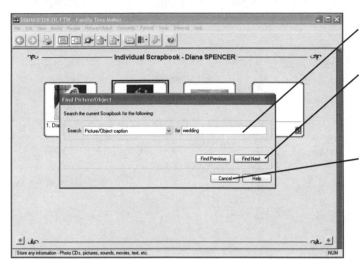

4. In the **for** field, enter the term for which you want to search.

5. Click **Find next**. The dialog box will stay up, but Family Tree Maker will highlight the first frame that matches that description.

6. If Family Tree Maker finds the object you are seeking, click **Cancel** in the Find Picture/Object dialog box to close the dialog box. If not, click **Find Next** to search for the next possible match.

Sharing Scrapbooks

You can share your Family Tree Maker Scrapbooks with others through slide shows or by printing copies of Scrapbook images.

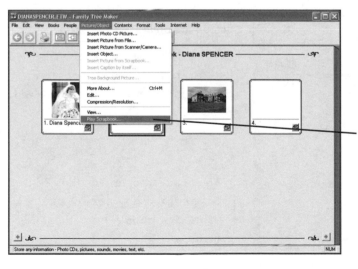

Playing a Scrapbook in a Slide Show

You can display a Scrapbook's images in a slide show on your computer—sounds and OLE objects will not play.

1. Click **Play Scrapbook** from the **Picture/Object** menu. The Play Scrapbook dialog box will open.

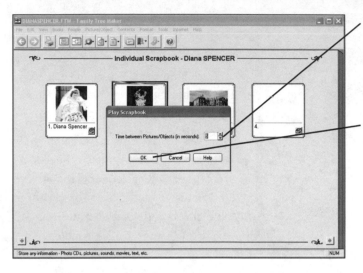

2. Click the **up** and **down arrows** to increase or decrease the time between objects being displayed. Or, highlight the number in the field and type a new number over the existing number.

3. Click **OK**. The Scrapbook slide show will play.

Printing Scrapbooks

To print a Scrapbook, make sure you have accessed an individual's Scrapbook and have the printer turned on.

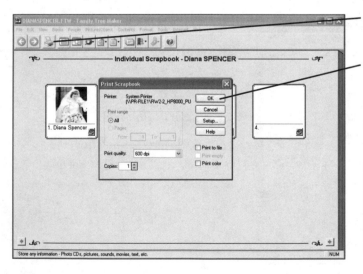

1. Click the **Print** button. The Print Scrapbook dialog box will open.

2. Click **OK** in the Print Scrapbook dialog box. The dialog box will close and the Scrapbook images and captions will print.

NOTE

You can also open the Print Scrapbook dialog box by clicking **Print Scrapbook** from the **File** menu.

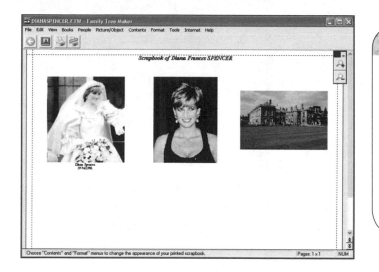

TIP

You can click **Scrapbook Print Preview** from the **File** menu to view how the Scrapbook will print. When you are done viewing the preview page, you can use the Back button or Back to Scrapbook button in the toolbar to return to the Scrapbook, or you can use the other buttons to print the page and adjust the print setup.

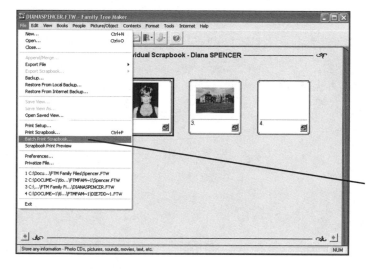

Batch Printing Scrapbook

You can print all the Scrapbook images from all the individuals in your Family File at once. Make sure you have accessed a Scrapbook—it does not matter which individual's Scrapbook or if the individual even has an image in their Scrapbook.

1. Click **Batch Print Scrapbook** from the **File** menu. The Individuals to Include in Batch Print dialog box will open.

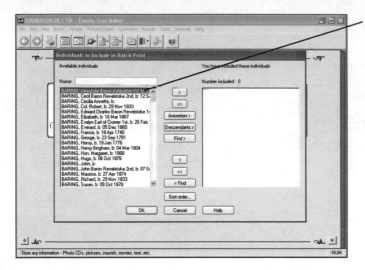

2. Move the individuals whose Scrapbooks you want to print to the **Number included** list. To do this, click a name in the **Available individuals** list, then click one of the following:

a. The **right angle bracket (>)** button to move one individual to the Number included list.

b. The **right double angle bracket (>>)** button to move every individual to the Number included list.

c. The **Ancestors>** button to move all the ancestors of the selected individual to the Number included list.

d. The **Descendants>** button to move all the descendants of the selected individual to the Number included list.

3. Click **OK**. The Batch Print Scrapbook dialog box will open.

4. Click **OK** again to begin printing.

PART

III

Creating and Printing Charts and Reports

Creating and Printing Tree Charts

After you enter information about your family into Family Tree Maker, you will likely want to display the information in a tree, chart, or graph. Family Tree Maker offers a number of different trees that will show the ancestors, descendants, or both for a selected individual. In this chapter, you'll learn how to:

- View a tree chart
- Customize and format a tree chart
- Use templates
- Add photographs and images to tree charts
- Print tree charts
- Save a tree chart in PDF format

In Chapter 2, you learned how to display the different tree charts available in Family Tree Maker. Once you have entered information for your family, you can customize and print these charts.

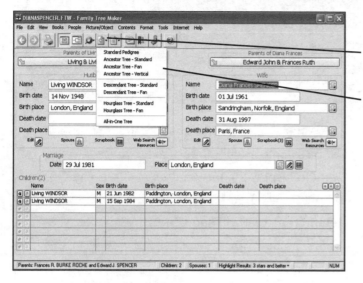

Viewing a Tree Chart

1. Click the **Tree Charts** button in the toolbar. A drop-down menu will appear.

2. Click the tree you want to display from the drop-down menu.

Here's a quick review of each of the tree types:

• **Standard Pedigree Tree**—Displays direct-line ancestors of an individual, with blank spaces showing for ancestors where details have been left out. This is the standard tree among genealogists.

• **Ancestor Tree**—Standard, Fan, and Vertical. Displays direct-line ancestors of an individual. This chart uses boxes rather than the plain lines of the standard pedigree tree, and allows for more personalization.

• **Descendant Tree**—Standard, Fan. Displays descendants of an individual.

• **Hourglass Tree**—Standard, Fan. Displays both ancestors and descendants of an individual with ancestors above and descendants below in a shape similar to the hourglass.

• **All-in-One Tree**—Displays every individual that has been entered into the Family File. You can click the Options button to select if you want to show unconnected step-family trees and/or unrelated trees.

Customizing and Formatting a Tree Chart

You can change the amount of information that is displayed in a tree, as well as text style, box shape, size, background color, and borders of the chart. You can also use templates to change the overall appearance of a tree.

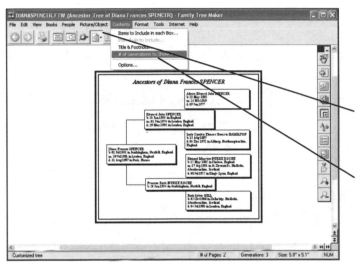

Changing the Number of Generations Displayed in a Chart

You can decide how many generations you want to appear in a chart.

1. Click the **Tree Charts** button and select a chart from the drop-down menu.

2. Click **# of Generations to Show** from the **Contents** menu. The # of Generations to Show dialog box will open.

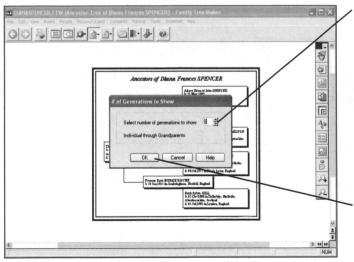

3. Click the up and down arrows to select the number of generations you would like to appear in the chart.

> ### TIP
>
> Instead of using the up and down arrows to select the number of generations, you can also highlight the number and type in a new number.

4. Click **OK**. The dialog box will close, and the chart will change to show no more than the number of generations you have selected.

Changing the Formatting

Family Tree Maker lets you change the format of the chart. For example, a fan chart can show the ancestors in a semi-circle around the root individual or in a complete circle around the root individual. The formatting options differ between the Fan and Pedigree Charts because of the differences between the types of charts.

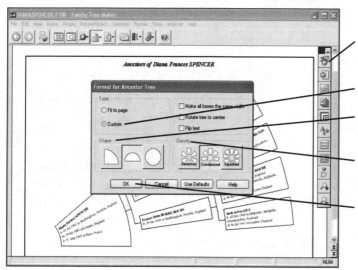

Formatting a Fan Chart

1. Click the **Format** button. The Format for Ancestor Tree dialog box will open.

2. Click the **Custom** radio button.

3. Click the **Shape** of the Fan Chart you prefer.

4. Click the **Density** of the Fan Chart you prefer.

5. Click **OK**. The Format for Ancestor Tree dialog box will close, and your changes will be displayed.

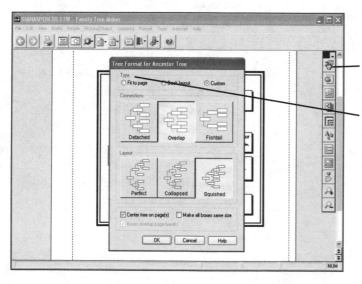

Formatting a Standard Tree

1. Click the **Format** button. The Tree Format for Ancestor Tree dialog box will open.

2. Click the **Type** of Ancestor Tree you want to display.

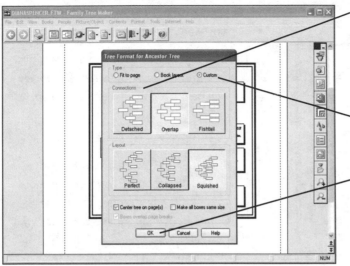

3. Click the **Connections** you want to use in the chart. The chart's boxes will be moved closer together or farther apart, depending on the type of connections you select.

4. If you want to change the Layout, click the **Custom** radio button, then click the type of layout you would like.

5. Click **OK**. The Tree Format for Ancestor Tree dialog box will close, and your changes will be displayed.

TIP

When you select the Book layout or Custom type, you can choose to have each tree centered on the page.

TIP

Click the **Zoom Out** button to see more of the tree. Click the **Zoom In** button for a larger view of a portion of the tree.

Rearranging the Standard Ancestor Chart

If you do not like where Family Tree Maker has placed an individual on a pedigree chart, you can move the individual box for that person or a complete lineage, using your mouse and the keyboard. This can be done only in standard ancestor and standard descendant trees.

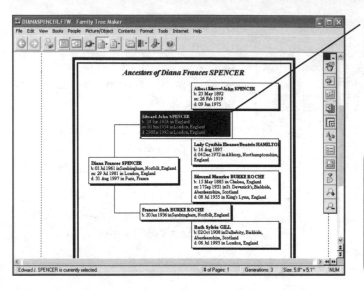

1. Click the individual whose lineage you want to move on a chart.

2. Drag the mouse to the new location. The individual or the selected lineage will be moved elsewhere on the chart.

NOTE

Remember that when you are dragging the mouse, you need to hold down the left mouse button or the left mouse button and the CTRL key while you are dragging the lineage or individual to a new location.

Including Siblings on Trees

You can use any of the Ancestor Tree formats or the Standard Hourglass Tree to add siblings to your tree.

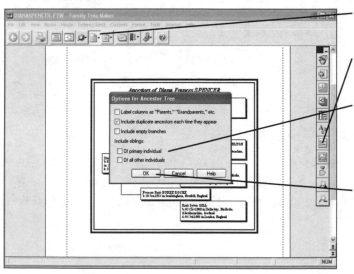

1. Click the **Tree charts** button and click a chart from the drop-down menu.

2. Click the **Options** button. The Options for Tree dialog box will open.

3. Click the **Include siblings** check box for the siblings you want to add to the tree. A check mark will appear in the selected box.

4. Click **OK**. The Options for Tree dialog box will close.

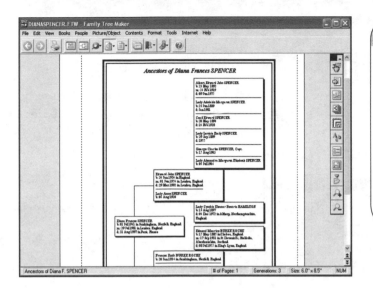

NOTE

Notice how the changes affect the overall look of the Ancestor Tree, especially if you have elected to include the siblings for everyone on the tree. Even when you select this option, the siblings will be left out if there is not enough space for them when you print, unless you have chosen a custom layout.

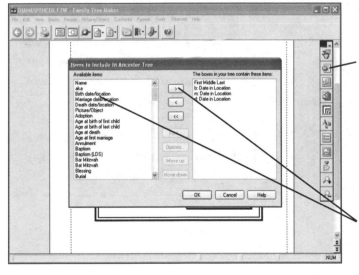

Including and Excluding Items in a Tree Chart

1. Click the **Items to Include** button in the vertical toolbar. The Items to Include in Ancestor Tree dialog box will open. The items in the right-hand list are the items that will appear in the tree, while the items in the Available items list on the left are the items you can select to include in the tree.

2. Click an item in the **Available items** list. Then, click the **right angle bracket** (**>**) button. A dialog box containing options for that item will open.

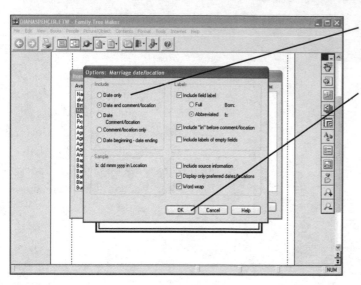

3. Click the radio buttons and check boxes to select the options you would like to include in the chart.

4. Click **OK**. The dialog box will close and the item will be added to the boxes in your tree.

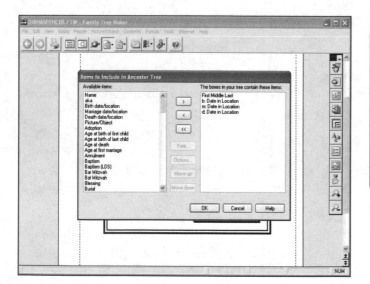

TIP

If you decide you want to change one of the options you selected, or want to change specific options or font details, click the item in the right-hand box item list of the Items to Include dialog box, then click the **Font** or **Options** buttons, whichever selection is appropriate.

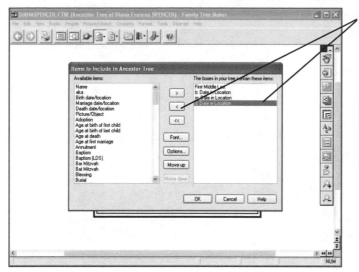

5. To exclude an item, click an item in the right-hand list. Then, click the **left angle bracket (<)** button.

> ## TIP
>
> Use the left double angle bracket (<<) button to move all items from the right list to the left list at once.

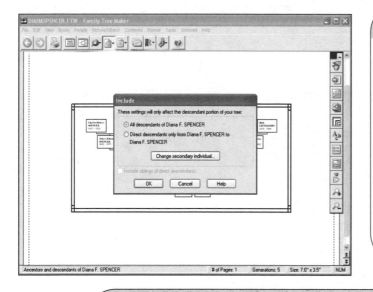

> ## NOTE
>
> In the Descendant and Hourglass Tree Charts, you can also choose whether to include all descendants or only direct descendants, as well as the siblings of direct descendants. Click **Individuals to Include** from the **Contents** menu, then make your selections. If you make a mistake, click **Undo** from the **Edit** menu (or press **Ctrl+Z**) to revert to the previous chart.

> ## NOTE
>
> You can add titles and footnotes to your tree chart; click **Title & Footnote** from the **Contents** menu. The Title and Footnote Tree dialog box will open. Type in the information and then click **OK**. Your footnote will be included.

Adding Empty Branches

You can add empty branches to your Ancestor trees, Vertical trees, and Hourglass trees.

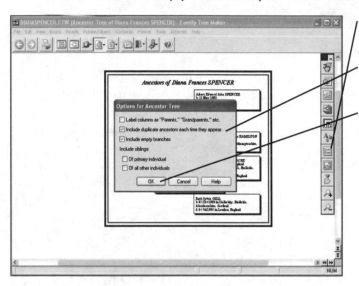

1. Click the **Options** button in the vertical toolbar. The Options dialog box will open.

2. Click the **Include empty branches** check box.

3. Click **OK**.

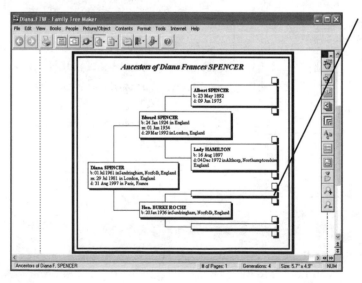

The Options dialog box will close and the tree will change to show the empty branches.

Changing the Font

You can change the appearance of the text in your charts to make the charts appear more formal, or more fun, etc., by selecting a different font.

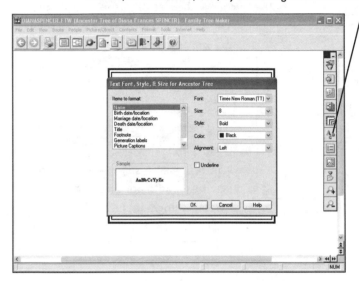

1. Click the **Text Font, Style, & Size** button in the vertical toolbar. The Text Font, Style, & Size dialog box will open. The complete name of the dialog box will depend on the tree or report that you have selected.

NOTE

When you print the chart, the vertical toolbar will not be printed. You can click the minimizing button at the top of the toolbar to minimize the vertical toolbar.

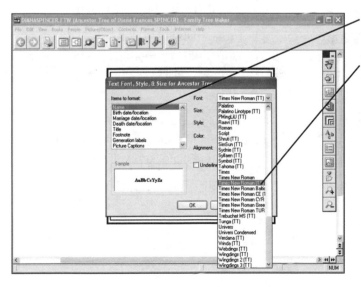

2. Click an item in the **Items to format** list.

3. Click the **Font** drop-down list and click the font you want to use.

The Sample box shows you how the font you have selected will appear in the chart.

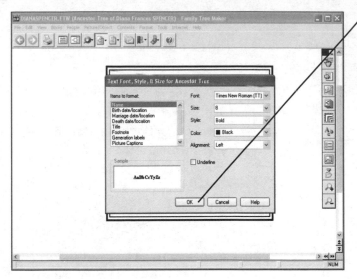

4. Click **OK** if you like the way the font looks in the Sample box and any other selections you have made. You can also change the size of the text (font size), style, color, and alignment in the same way you changed the font. The Text Font, Style, & Size dialog box will close, and the changes to the font will be displayed.

TIP

You can see a sample of each font in the Sample box by using the keyboard arrows to move through the list of fonts.

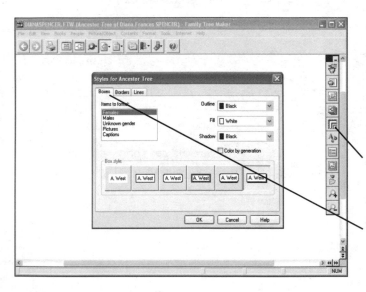

Adding Boxes, Borders, Lines, and Background Colors

You can beautify and personalize your tree charts by changing the box styles, borders, and background colors of your tree.

1. Click the **Box, Line & Border Styles** button in the vertical toolbar. The Styles for Tree dialog box will open.

2. Click the **Boxes** tab if the dialog box does not already default to this tab.

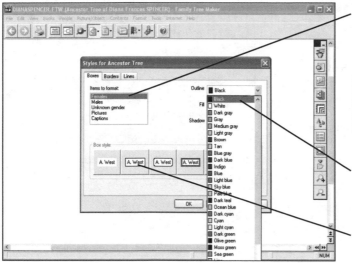

3. Click an item in the **Items to format** list.

TIP

You can hold down the **Ctrl** key and click on each item to select more than one item at a time.

4. Click the drop-down lists to select the colors for the outline, fill, and shadow.

5. Click a box style.

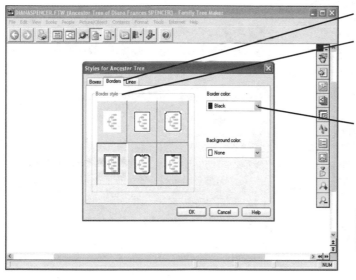

6. Click the **Borders** tab.

7. Click a **Border style**. The first style indicates no border at all. The style you select will appear indented to show that it has been selected.

8. Click the **Border color** drop-down list and click the color you want for your border.

NOTE

If you select the "No border" style, the border color will not show.

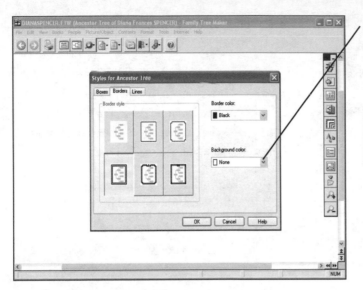

9. Click the **Background color** drop-down list and click the color you want for the background.

TIP

Choose "None" for your background color if you do not want to use a color background.

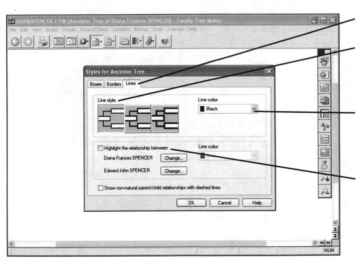

10. Click the **Lines** tab.

11. Click a **Line style**. The style you select will appear indented to show that it has been selected.

12. Click the **Line color** drop-down list and click the color you want for your border.

13. Click the **Highlight the relationship between** check box if you want to emphasize the relationship between two individuals in the tree.

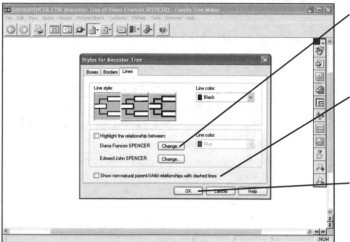

14. Click **Change** to select each of the two individuals you would like to compare, and click a color from the **Line color** drop-down list.

15. Click the **Show non-natural relationships** check box if you want to show a dotted line for non-natural parent/child relationships.

16. Click **OK**. The Styles for Tree dialog box will close, and the changes will be displayed.

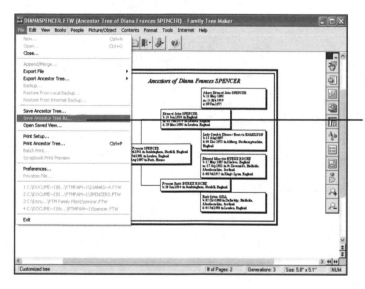

Saving Your Customized Tree Chart

Now that you've customized your chart, be sure to save your changes.

1. Click **Save [type of] Tree As** from the **File** menu. The Save View As dialog box will open.

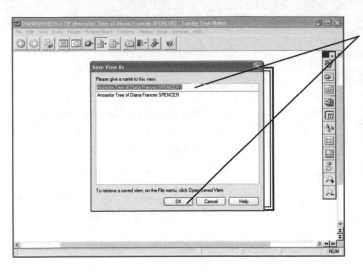

2. Type a name for your new tree, then click **OK**. You have now saved the customized tree chart.

NOTE

To open a saved tree chart, click **Open Saved View** from the **File** menu.

Using Templates

Family Tree Maker has several templates you can choose from with creative borders and other artwork.

NOTE

If you have spent a lot of time customizing a tree chart, make sure to save your customized chart before using templates, so you do not lose your work.

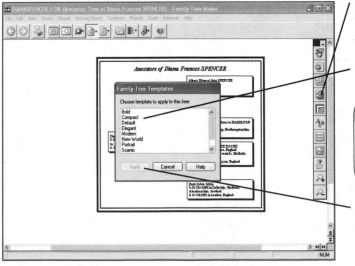

1. Click the **Tree Templates** button. The Family Tree Templates dialog box will open.

2. Click the template you want to use.

NOTE

Be sure to see all template options by using the scroll bar on the right of the list.

3. Click **Apply**. The selected template will be applied to the family tree chart.

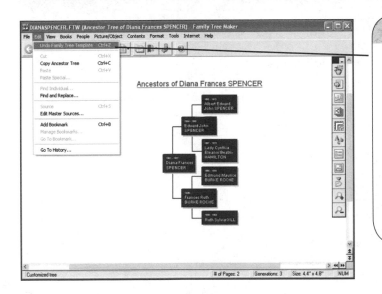

If you do not like the look of the template, and you have not done anything else, such as zooming in or out to view the template better, you can click **Undo** from the **Edit** menu or press **Ctrl+Z** to quickly undo the template change you made to the chart. Or, you can return to the Family Tree Templates dialog box to select a different template.

Adding Photographs and Images to Tree Charts

You can include background images in any of your tree charts. You can also add individual photographs to family group sheets within the boxes of any of the tree charts except for the fan charts. To add a background image to a tree chart, the file must be somewhere on your computer. However, to add an individual picture to a family group sheet or tree chart, the photograph must have already been added to a Scrapbook (see Chapter 7) in your Family File for the individuals included in the chart.

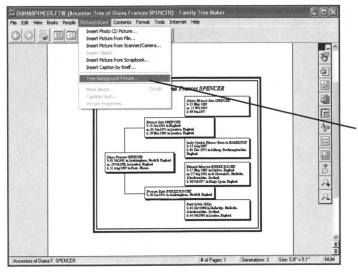

Adding a Background Image

1. Click the **Tree Charts** button and click the tree chart to which you want to add a background image.

2. Click **Tree Background Picture** from the **Picture/Object** menu. The Background Picture dialog box will open.

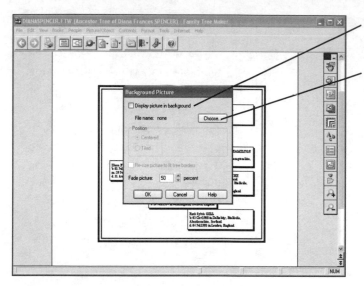

3. Click the **Display picture in background** check box.

4. Click **Choose** to select an image or photo. Another dialog box with a list of directories will open.

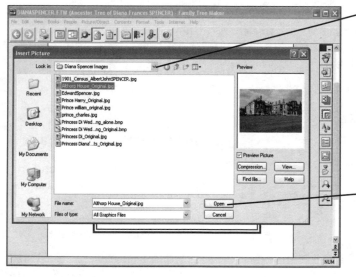

5. Click the **Look-in** drop-down list if your photograph or image is not located in the default directory and you want to switch to a different directory.

TIP

To preview the image, click the Preview Picture check box.

6. Click **Open** when you have selected the desired photograph or image. The Edit Picture dialog box will open.

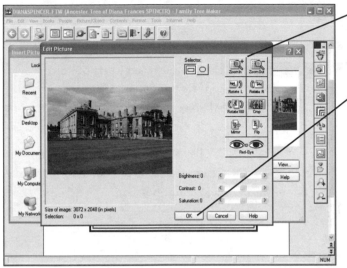

7. Click buttons in the Edit Picture dialog box, such as cropping, rotating, and adjusting the image quality, to make your selection.

8. Click **OK**. The file name you have selected should now appear in the **Background Picture** dialog box.

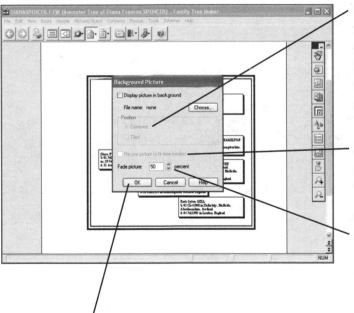

9. Click an image position. If you want the image to be centered in the background, click the **Centered** radio button. If you want a series of the same image to fill the background, click the **Tiled** radio button.

10. Click the **Re-size picture to fit tree borders** check box if you have a large picture and need to adjust the size to fit within the tree chart.

11. Click the **Fade picture** up or down arrows to adjust the intensity of the image—at 100 percent, the image will appear as it does normally, while a smaller percentage will fade the image so the chart text is easier to read.

12. Click **OK** when you are done adjusting the image selection, position, and color intensity. The Background Picture dialog box will close, and the image will display in the background.

Adding Individual Images

You can add individual photographs or images to family group sheets or tree charts:

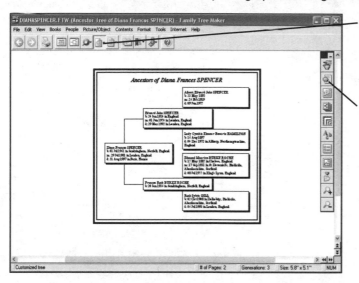

1. Click the **Tree Charts** button or **Reports** button and click the tree chart or family group sheet to which you want to add pictures.

2. Click the **Items to Include** button on the vertical toolbar. The Items to Include dialog box opens.

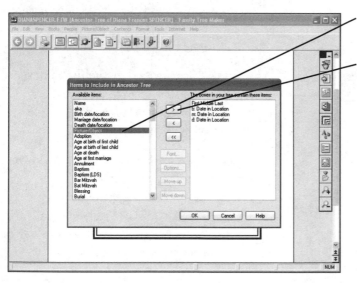

3. Click **Picture/Object** in the **Available items** list.

4. Click the **right angle bracket (>)** button to move the item to the right-hand list. The Options: Picture/Object dialog box will open.

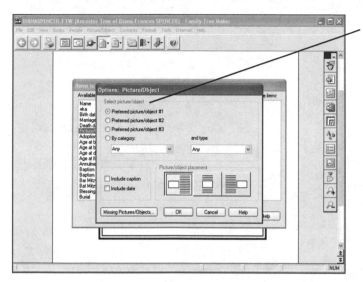

5. Click the radio button for the preference number or category of photograph you want to add to the group sheet or chart.

NOTE

When you add a photograph to a Scrapbook, you can assign a preferred number to the photograph. This lets you choose which photographs you want to include in different charts more quickly. For example, you may want to always use a particular photograph of an individual for that person's family group sheet but a different photograph for a tree chart. When you create the chart, choose which set of preferred photographs to use. Similarly, you can opt to create categories of photographs (e.g., wedding, baby pictures, photos for pedigree charts) and use a category when adding photos to a chart. For more information on Scrapbooks, see Chapter 7.

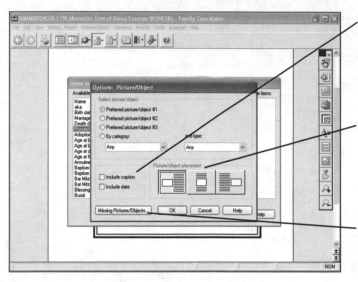

6. Click the **Include caption** and **Include date** check boxes if you want to include the caption or date you attributed to the photograph when you added it to the Scrapbook.

7. Click a **Picture/Object Placement** for how you want to position the text next to the photograph. The placement you select will appear indented to show that it has been selected.

8. Click **Missing Pictures/Objects** if no picture exists in the Scrapbook for the individual. The Missing Pictures/Objects dialog box will open.

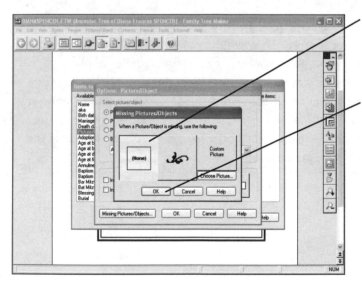

9. Click **None** to leave the area blank, click an image, or select a different image from a file anywhere on your computer by clicking **Choose Picture**.

10. Click **OK** to accept your Missing Pictures/Objects options. The Missing Pictures/Objects dialog box will close.

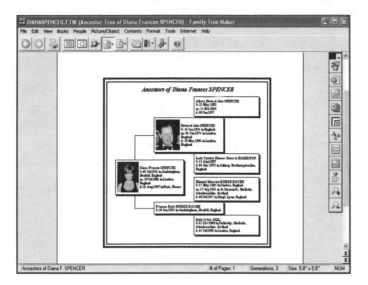

11. Click **OK** to accept the changes you made to the chart. The dialog box will close, and the changes will appear in your chart.

Printing Tree Charts

When you are done customizing your chart, you may want to print it. First, you will need to understand various aspects of print setup.

Resizing a Tree Chart

Depending on what tree chart you have open, you may have noticed dotted lines running vertically and horizontally across the page. These lines represent the margins of standard 8 ½" x 11" sheet of paper. If those dotted lines cross through a part of your tree, you may want to change the formatting to fit the tree on one page or use the book layout option to include continuation indicators for multiple pages. You can also export a large tree to PDF format and have it printed on large paper by a copy/printing store. You can also tape pages together if you prefer to use your own printer.

TIP

You can turn the lines off if you do not want to view them on your computer screen. Click **Show Page Lines** from the **Format** menu. Click the same option again to turn the lines back on.

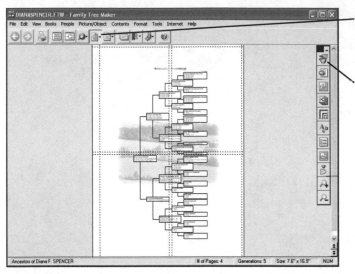

1. Click the **Tree Charts** button and select a chart from the drop-down menu.

2. Click the **Format** button on the vertical toolbar. The Tree Format dialog box will open. The options available through this dialog box will vary depending on the type of tree you have selected.

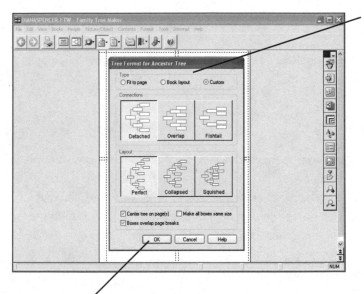

3. Click the formatting options you want for your tree. If you choose the **Fit to page** option but the number of individuals to show is too large to fit all of the desired information, Family Tree Maker will verify that you want it to modify the amount of information shown in order to fit the tree. The **Book layout** option (available for all non-fan charts except for the All-in-One tree) will spread the tree over multiple pages with continuation indicators. The **Custom layout** option lets you choose your own layout regardless of the number of pages the chart takes.

4. Click **OK**. The dialog box will close and the format will change.

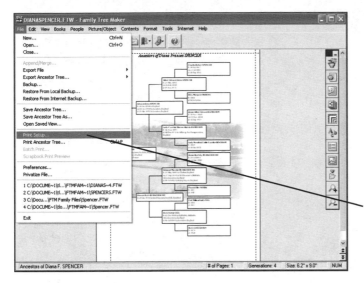

Changing Print Setup Options

You can make a tree shorter or narrower by changing the type of content on the tree; various ways to change content were mentioned above. You can also change margins and print orientation. Changes you make to the print setup will change the settings only for the type of chart with which you are working.

1. Click **Print Setup** from the **File** menu. The Print Setup dialog box will open.

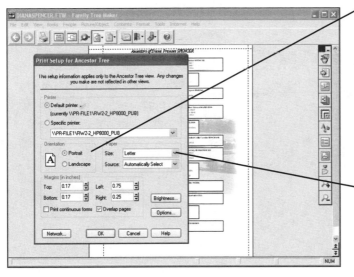

2. In the **Orientation** section, click the **Portrait** radio button if you want your document to print with the short edge of the paper at the bottom (the way a letter normally prints). This is the default setting. Click the **Landscape** radio button if you want your document to print with the long edge of the paper at the bottom.

3. Click the **Paper Size** drop-down list to change the size of the paper if your printer is capable of printing larger sheets of paper. Otherwise, leave the selection at letter size, which is a standard 8 ½" x 11" sheet of paper.

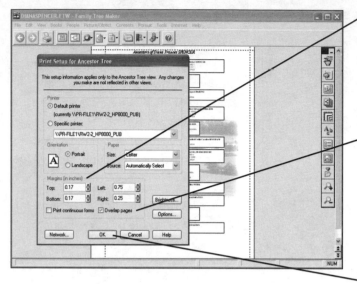

4. In the **Margins** section, click the drop-down lists to change the margin size on your page. By default, each page prints with 1-inch margins at the top, a quarter inch of margin on the left and right, and .17-inch margin at the bottom.

5. Click the **Print continuous forms** check box if you use an older printer with the continuous sheets on perforated paper. This lets the chart print across the perforations. Click the **Overlap pages** check box if you use a laser printer that feeds single sheets at a time.

6. Click **OK** to save your changes and close the dialog box.

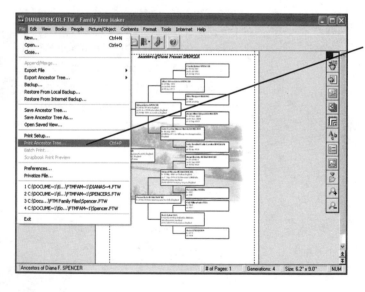

Printing a Chart

1. Click **Print Tree** from the **File** menu. The menu item name will reflect the tree you have open, e.g., Print Descendant Tree.

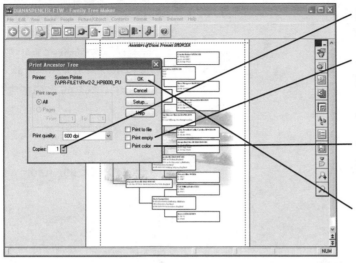

2. Enter the number of copies you want to print in the **Copies** field.

3. Click the **Print empty** check box to print an empty report. Printing an empty report is an excellent way to create forms for a research trip.

4. Click the **Print color** check box to print the report in color, if you have a color printer.

5. Click **OK** to send the report to the printer.

Saving a Chart in PDF Format

You can share your tree charts with others even if they do not own the Family Tree Maker program. Do this by using the Portable Document Format (PDF) that can be viewed using Adobe Reader, which is available as a free download from the Adobe website.

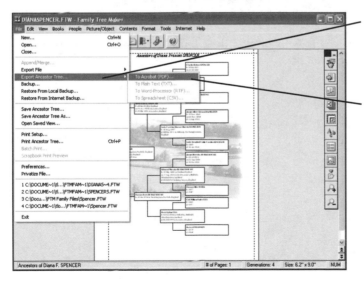

1. Click **Export Tree** from the **File** menu. The name will vary slightly depending on which tree you have open. A sub-menu will appear.

2. Click **To Acrobat (PDF)**. The Export Tree dialog box will open.

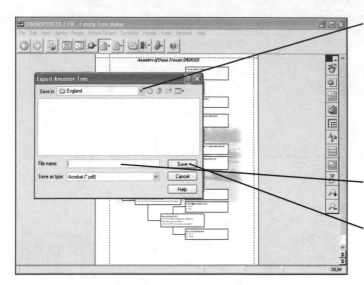

3. Click the **Save in** drop-down list to choose where you want to save your file or use the Family Tree Maker default location. Be sure to make a note so you can find the file later. This is also a good time to save the PDF directly to a disk if you want to share your report with someone.

4. Type a new name in the **File name** field.

5. Click the **Save** button. A message reminds you that you need the Adobe Reader to view the file.

6. Click **OK**.

7. Click **OK** when the export is complete.

8. If you did not choose to save the PDF to a disk in step 3, you can do so now, or you can attach the PDF to an e-mail to send to others.

NOTE

Remember that when sharing this with others, they must have the Adobe Reader installed on their system to read the file.

9

Creating Genealogy and Research Reports

You may want to share more in-depth reports with family members and fellow researchers. Genealogy and research reports are full of details and are the best format to use for this purpose. In this chapter, you'll learn how to:

- View a genealogy report
- Choose a report formatting style
- Format a report
- Create endnotes
- Create a bibliography
- Create a report of facts with sources
- Create a source usage report
- Create a research journal

In Chapter 2, you learned how to display the different genealogy reports in Family Tree Maker. Genealogy reports in Family Tree Maker are generally narrative reports. This chapter covers three narrative-style reports, as well reports that are created specifically to keep track of research—endnotes, bibliographies, and the Family Tree Maker Research Journal.

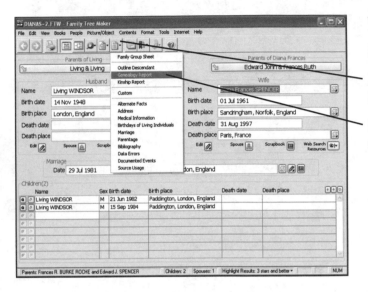

Viewing a Genealogy Report

1. Click the **Reports** button in the toolbar. A drop-down menu will appear.

2. Click **Genealogy Report**. A Genealogy Report will open.

Choosing a Report Formatting Style

You can change the style and numbering system that is used for a report.

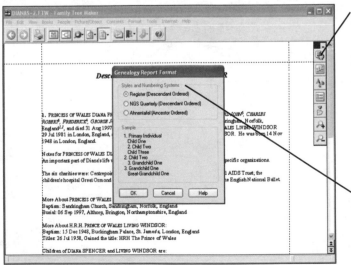

1. Click the **Report Format** button on the vertical toolbar.

NOTE

You can also click **Genealogy Report Format** from the **Format** menu. The Genealogy Report Format dialog box will open.

2. Click the **Style and Numbering System** you would like to use for the report.

Here's a description of each of the format styles. In addition, the Sample section in the Genealogy Report Format dialog box shows how each style will appear and be numbered.

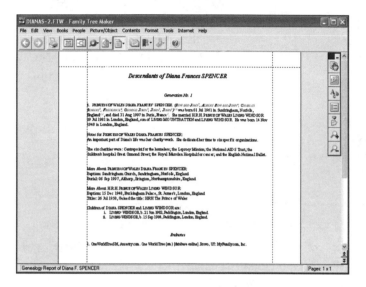

Register Format

The Register format report is the format accepted by the New England Historic Genealogical Society, the oldest genealogical society in the United States. The Register format dates back to 1870 and is used to show someone's lineage. This report lists individuals and details about a family beginning with a particular ancestor and moving to descendants.

NOTE

The Register format assigns an identifying number to those who have offspring.

NGSQ Format

Like the Register format, the NGS Quarterly format lists information about a family starting with an ancestor and moving forward in time to that individual's descendants. This is the preferred genealogical report of the National Genealogical Society. The format dates back to 1912.

NOTE

The NGSQ format assigns a number to each individual and assigns a plus sign to those with offspring.

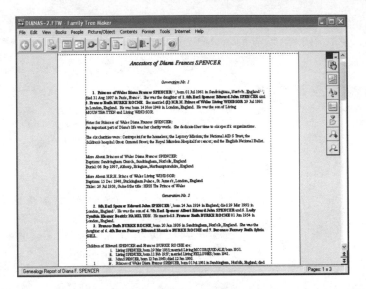

Ahnentafel Format

The Ahnentafel format is ancestor-ordered, meaning that it starts with one individual and moves backward in time to that individual's ancestors; the opposite of the other two reports. This format is used less frequently because it records two family lines in the same report.

NOTE

The Ahnentafel format assigns the first individual the number 1. His or her father is number 2 and his or her mother is number 3. Men are always even numbers, and women are always odd numbers (the exception being when a man is the first individual).

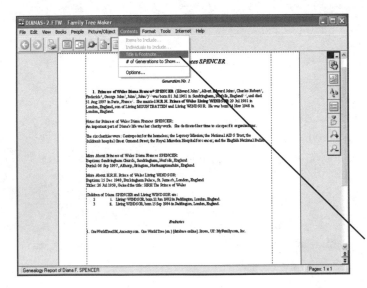

Formatting a Report

In addition to choosing a formatting style, you can format other areas of the report as well.

Changing Title and Page Numbering

You can change the default settings for title and page numbers.

1. Click **Title & Footnote** from the **Contents** menu. The Title & Footnote for Genealogy Report dialog box will open.

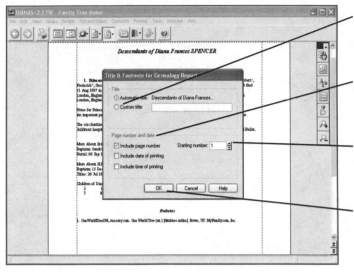

2. Click the **Custom title** radio button and enter the title you would like displayed in the report.

3. In the **Page Number and date** section, click the options that you want to use for the report.

4. Click the **Starting number** up and down arrows to change the starting page number.

5. Click **OK** to save your changes and close the Title & Footnote for Genealogy Report dialog box.

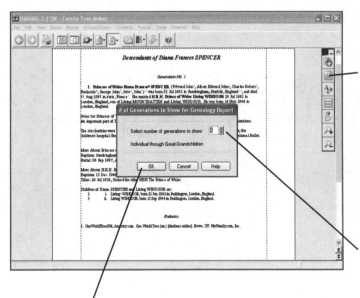

Changing the Number of Displayed Generations

1. Click the **Number of Generations** button in the vertical toolbar.

NOTE

You can also click **# of Generations to Show** from the **Contents** menu. The # of Generations to Show dialog box will open.

2. Click the up and down arrows to select the number of generations you would like to appear in the report.

3. Click **OK**. The # of Generations to Show for Genealogy Report dialog box will close, and the number of generations you have chosen will show on the chart.

Including Notes and Other Options

You can select additional notes you recorded in other areas of the Family File to include in your printed reports.

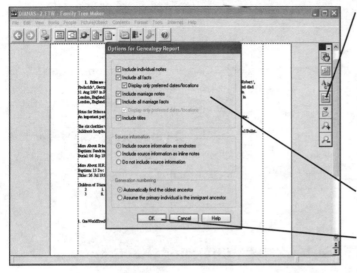

1. Click the **Options** button on the vertical toolbar.

> ### NOTE
>
> You can also click **Options** from the **Contents** menu. The Options for Genealogy Report dialog box will open.

2. Click the check boxes and radio buttons for the options you want.

3. Click **OK**. The Options for Genealogy Report dialog box will close.

> ### TIP
>
> Family Tree Maker turns on some of the options by default. You may want to check your report to verify if you want those default options to show.

Creating Endnotes

You can print source information at the end of a report as endnotes. Before following these steps, make sure your genealogy report is still open.

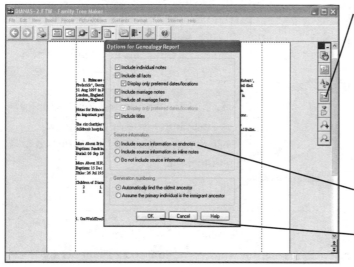

1. Click the **Options** button on the vertical toolbar.

NOTE

You can also click **Options** from the **Contents** menu. The Options for Genealogy Report dialog box will open.

---

2. Click the **Include source information as endnotes** radio button.

3. Click **OK**. The Options for Genealogy Report dialog box will close. You can use the scroll bar to go to the bottom of the report to view the source information.

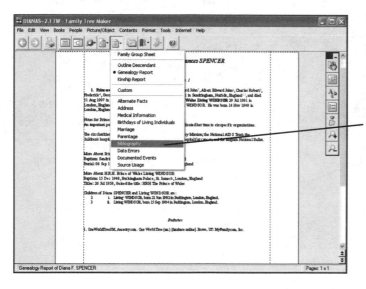

Creating a Bibliography

The bibliography report lists all the sources you used in your research.

1. Click **Bibliography** from the **Reports** button drop-down menu. A Bibliography report will be generated.

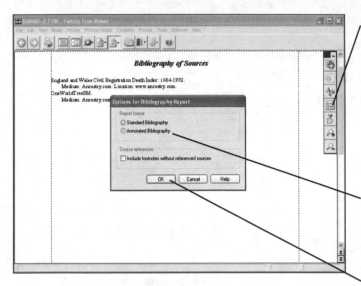

2. Click the **Options** button in the vertical toolbar.

3. Click the **Annotated Bibliography** radio button if you do not want to use the default setting for Standard Bibliography.

4. Click **OK**.

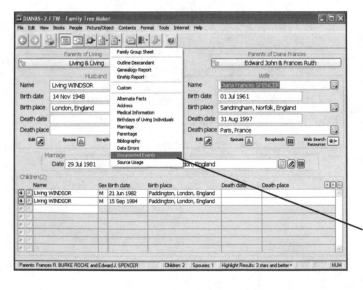

Creating a Report of Facts with Sources (Documented Events Report)

The Documented Events Report lists all of the events for which you have source information. Conversely, you can choose to show all of the events for which you do not have source information.

1. Click **Documented Events** from the **Reports** button drop-down menu. The Documented Events report will open.

NOTE

If you already have a custom report open, you can click **Document Events** from the **Format** button in the vertical toolbar.

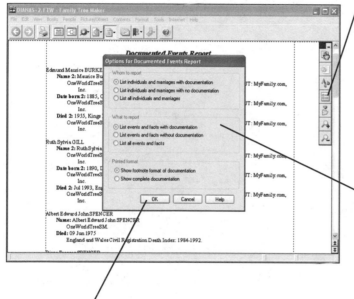

2. Click the **Options** button on the vertical toolbar.

NOTE

You can also click **Options** from the **Contents** menu. The Options for Documented Events Report dialog box will open.

3. Click the radio buttons to select which type of individuals to display (those with sources or those without sources or all), what information to display (events with or without sources or all), and how to display the source information.

4. Click **OK**. The Options for Documented Events Report dialog box will close.

Creating a Source Usage Report

The Source Usage report includes each "master" source you have created and lists the individuals and facts associated with that source. This report helps you determine which recorded facts are supported by sources. It can be useful in keeping track of the sources you've researched and lets you compare notes with other researchers. You can choose whether to include individuals and facts for sources or only individuals.

NOTE

If you have not assigned a master source to any facts in Family Tree Maker, the report will include the fact and the message "Not associated with any facts."

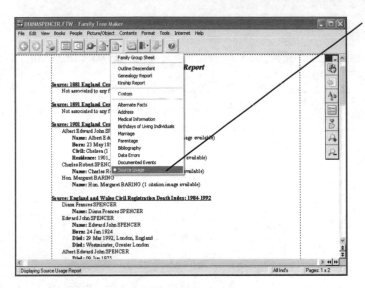

1. Click **Source Usage** from the **Reports** button drop-down menu. A Source Usage report will be generated.

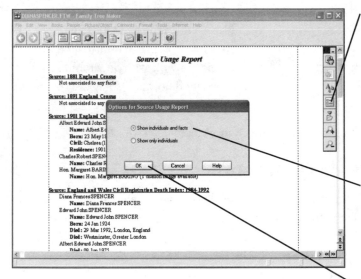

2. Click the **Options** button on the vertical toolbar. The Options for Source Usage Report dialog box will open.

NOTE

You can also click **Options** from the **Contents** menu to open the Options for Source Usage Report dialog box.

3. If you want to include only individuals in the report, click **Show only individuals**; if you want to include individuals and the facts associated with them, click **Show individuals and facts**.

4. Click **OK** to save your changes and close the dialog box.

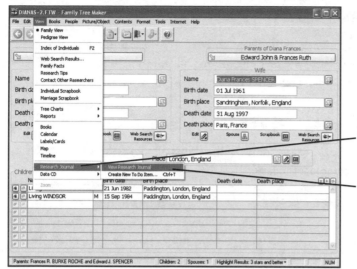

Creating a Research Journal

The Research Journal lets you track your research and make notes on to-do items within Family Tree Maker.

1. Click **Research Journal** from the **View** menu. A sub-menu will appear.

2. Click **View Research Journal**. The Research Journal will open.

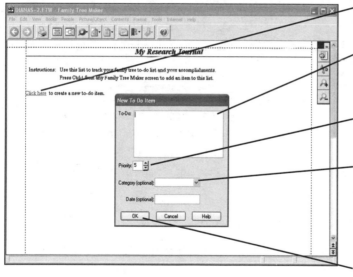

3. Click the **Click here** link. The New To-Do Item dialog box will open.

4. Enter your to-do item in the **To-Do** field, e.g., "Look for Aunt Marge in 1930 census."

5. Click the up and down arrows to choose a numbered priority for the task.

6. Enter or click a category in the **Category** field. Suggested category topics can be the type of research (e.g., Census or Church Records) or family group (e.g., Smiths, Jones, or Lees).

7. Click **OK**. The New To-Do Item dialog box will close.

Viewing Done or Not Done Items

The Research Journal is your road map of the research you have done and the research that still must be accomplished. There will be times when you will want to see it all, and other times when you will want to see only what you have done or what is left to do.

> **NOTE**
>
> You can use the Done check boxes to keep track of the status of your tasks. Click a task's Done check box when you complete the task.

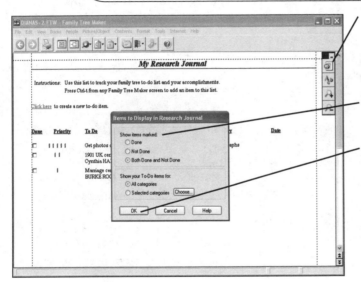

1. Click the **Items to Display** button on the vertical toolbar. The Items to Display in Research Journal dialog box will open.

2. Click a **Show items marked** radio button.

3. Click **OK**. The Items to Display in Research Journal dialog box will close.

> **NOTE**
>
> The Research Journal will reflect the changes in the items listed based on whether the To-Do item has been done or is still pending.

Viewing Items for a Specific To-Do Category

Another way to affect the format of the Research Journal is through the To-Do categories. Usually based on resources or repositories, the To-Do categories let you narrow the focus of the report to just those entries for the selected category or categories.

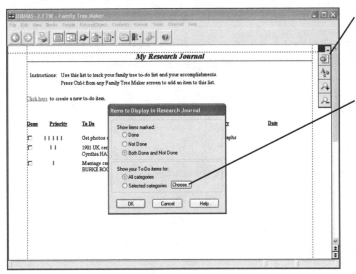

1. Click the **Items to Display** button on the vertical toolbar. The Items to Display in Research Journal dialog box will open.

2. Click **Choose**. The Categories to Include dialog box will open. This dialog box resembles and functions the same as the Individuals to Include dialog box.

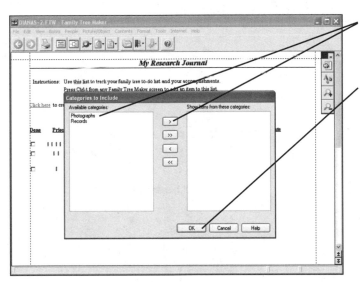

3. Click on items you want to include in the Available categories list and click the **right angle bracket (>)** button.

4. Click **OK** to save your changes and close the dialog box.

5. Click **OK** in the two dialog boxes. The Categories to Include dialog box will close, then the Items to Display in Research Journal dialog box will close, and the Research Journal will reflect your changes.

TIP

If you want to delete a To-Do item that you have created, click the item so that it is high-lighted and then press the **Delete** key.

Adding a To-Do Item Anytime

While the Research Journal report is useful, you do not have to go to the Research Journal to add a new to-do item. You can add a new to-do item any time you want. This feature is most useful when adding new research.

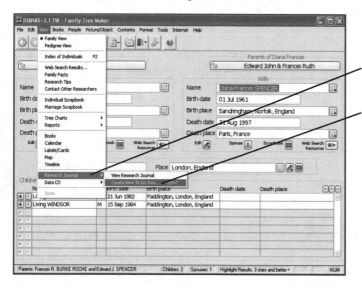

1. Click the **Family View** button. The Family View will appear.

2. Click **Research Journal** from the **View** menu.

3. Click **Create New To Do Item** from the sub-menu. The New To Do Item dialog box will open.

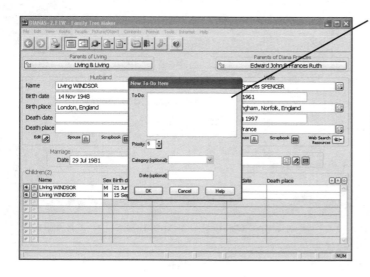

4. Enter your to-do item in the **To-Do** field. The next time you open the Research Journal the additional to-do items will be listed.

TIP

You can also press **Ctrl+T** to open the New To Do Item dialog box.

5. Click **OK** to save your changes and close the dialog box.

10

Creating Specialty and Custom Reports

In addition to its many trees and genealogy reports, Family Tree Maker also includes a number of other reports that let you understand the information you have in your database and how the individuals might be related. In this chapter, you'll learn how to open a report and view and format:

- Family Group Sheets
- Outline Descendant and Kinship reports
- Alternate Facts reports
- Address, Medical Information, and Living Individual reports
- Marriage and Parentage reports
- Data Errors reports
- Timelines, maps, calendars, mailing labels and cards
- Custom reports

Family Tree Maker offers a variety of specialty reports, such as kinship reports, data errors, timelines, maps, address reports, birthday lists, mailing labels, and calendars. You can also create your own custom report. In this chapter, we'll cover the different types of specialty reports and what you can do to customize these reports (options differ by report), as well as how to generate your own custom report.

Opening a Specialty Report

The specialty reports available in Family Tree Maker include text reports that are likely to be of interest to you as well as more graphical reports such as maps, timelines, and calendars. All of the textual reports can be accessed through the Reports button on the toolbar or the View menu. The more graphical reports are available through the View menu.

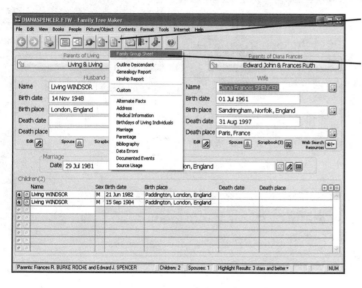

1. Click the **Reports** button on the toolbar.

2. Click the report you would like to view. The report will open. These same steps are used to open and view all of the reports covered in this chapter.

Family Group Sheets

A family group sheet is one of the most commonly used reports in genealogy. It is a detailed report about a single family (primarily the parents and children of a family although it also includes the names of the main couple's parents), including names, birth information, death information, marriage information, notes, and sources. You can also add images for each individual. Family Tree Maker lets you make many customizations to the family group sheet, including what information to include, how the page is laid out, what titles and footnotes to use, and how the text appears in size, color, and shape.

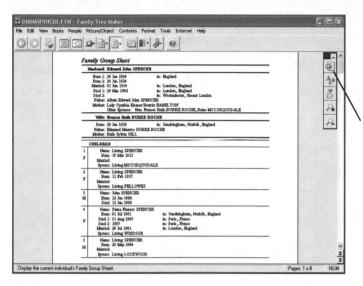

Choosing Items and Options to Include

You can customize the items you include in your family group sheets.

1. Open a family group sheet and click the **Items to Include** button from vertical toolbar. The Items to Include in Family Group Sheet dialog box will open.

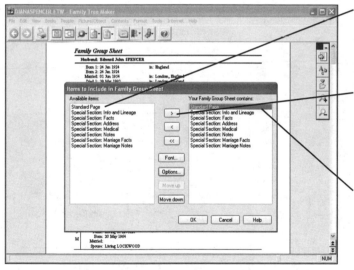

2. Click on an item in the **Available items** list to select the item that you want to include on your family group sheet.

3. Click the **right angle bracket (>)** button to move the item to the **Your Family Group Sheet contains** list. You can select more than one item if you want.

Make sure **Standard Page** is included in the **Your Family Group Sheet contains** list.

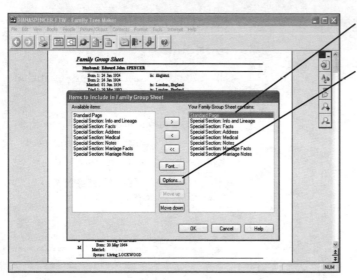

4. Click **Standard Page** in the **Your Family Group Sheet contains** list.

5. Click **Options**. (The Options button is grayed out until you click on an item in the right-hand list.) The Options: Standard Page dialog box will open.

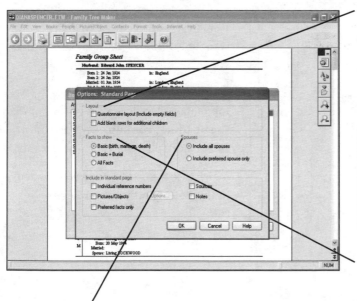

6. Click the **Layout** check boxes if you want to include headings for which you have not yet entered information (e.g., a blank Died row) and blank rows for children that have not yet been added.

TIP

You might want to use the Layout options if you want to create a blank group sheet to take with you on a research trip or to send to family members.

---

7. Click the **Facts to show** radio buttons to specify which details you want to appear in the family group sheet.

8. Click the **Spouses** radio buttons to specify if you want all spouses to appear in your group sheet or just the preferred spouse.

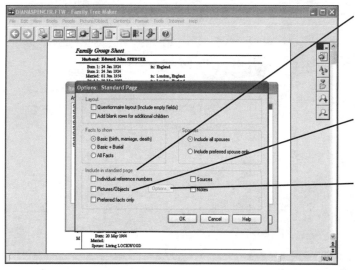

9. Click the **Include in standard page** check boxes to indicate which of the listed items you would like to appear in your group sheet. The Pictures/Objects check box has additional options.

10. If you want your scrapbook images to appear on the family group sheet, click the **Pictures/Objects** check box.

11. Click **Options**. The Options: Pictures/Objects on Family Group Sheet dialog box will open.

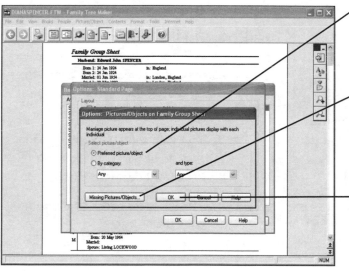

12. Click the radio button to indicate if you want to display images that are preferred or that fall within a certain category or type.

13. Click **Missing Pictures/Objects**. The Missing Pictures/Objects dialog box will open. Select an image you want to show if no image is available—either None, a flourish, or a custom picture.

14. Click **OK** to save your changes and close each dialog box.

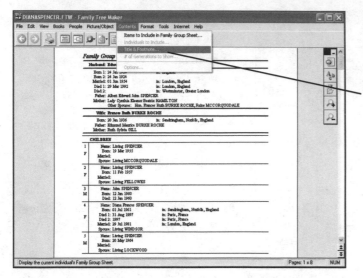

Adding Titles and Footnotes

You can add titles and footnotes to your family group sheets.

1. Click **Title & Footnote** from the **Contents** menu. The Title & Footnote dialog box will open.

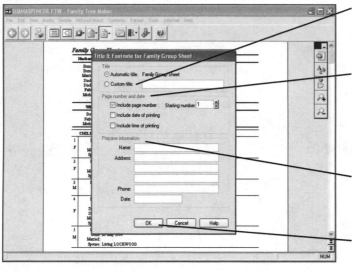

2. Click the **Custom title** radio button to change the default title (Family Group Sheet), and enter the new title.

3. Click the **Page number and date** check boxes if you want to add a page number (also, select which number you would like to be the starting number), date, and/or time.

4. Enter your contact information that you want to be part of the footnote in the **Preparer information** fields.

5. Click **OK** to save your changes and close the dialog box.

Creating Separate Page Family Group Sheets

If you choose to include additional information for each person (e.g., notes, medical information, etc.) you can have that information appear on separate pages for each individual.

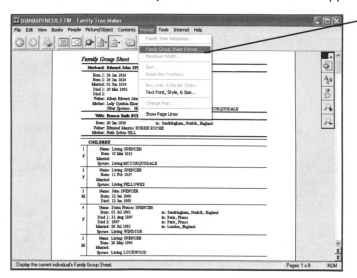

1. Click **Family Group Sheet Format** from the **Format** menu. The Family Group Sheet Format dialog box will open.

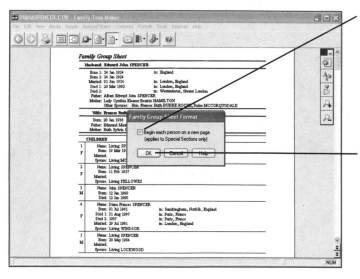

2. Click the check box if you want each person in your group sheet to appear on a separate page. This applies to any special sections you have added to your group sheet from the "Choosing Items and Options to Include" instructions in the previous section.

3. Click **OK** to save your changes and close the dialog box.

Choosing Text Font, Style, and Size for a Family Group Sheet

You can determine how to format particular items in your family group sheet, such as font, font size, style, and color.

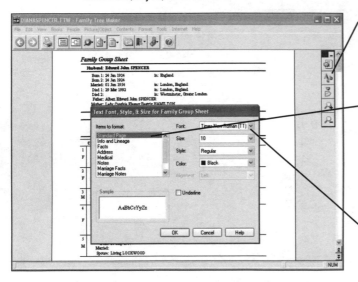

1. Click the **Text Font and Style** button from the vertical toolbar. The Text Font, Style, & Size for Family Group Sheet dialog box will open.

2. In the **Items to format** box, click the item for which you would like to apply a new style. You can click on and format one item at a time or hold down the Ctrl key and click on multiple items to format several items at once.

3. Click the **Font** drop-down list to choose a font. You can view how your changes will look in the Sample box.

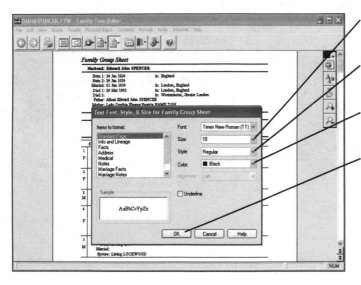

4. Click the **Size** drop-down list to choose a font size.

5. Click the **Style** drop-down list to choose a font style.

6. Click the **Color** drop-down list to choose a font color.

7. Click **OK** to save your changes and close the dialog box.

Outline Descendant Reports

This report starts with an ancestor and outlines each generation of descendants. In Outline Descendant Report, you can change the formatting of the report, select which items and individuals to include in the report, select the number of generations to show in a report, select titles and footnotes, select relationship options, and even select border styles.

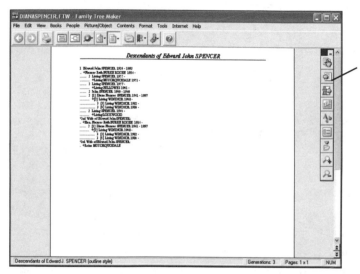

Formatting the Outline Descendant Report

1. Click the **Report Format** button from the vertical toolbar. The Tree Format for Outline Descendant Tree dialog box will open.

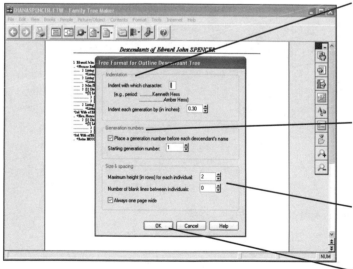

2. In the **Indention** section, click the character and spacing you want to use. For example, if you select "-," Family Tree Maker will use "----" instead of the default, "….." By default, Family Tree Maker indents with an ellipses.

3. Click the check box in the **Generation Numbers** section, if you want to include a generation number before each descendant's name.

4. Click the height of the row and the number of blank lines between individuals in the **Size & Spacing** section.

5. Click **OK** to save your changes and close the dialog box.

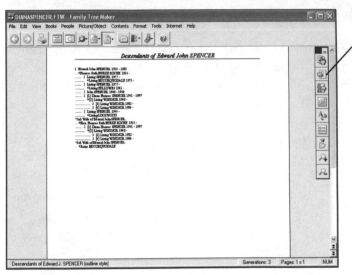

Choosing Items to Include

1. Click the **Items to Include** button from the vertical toolbar. The Items to Include in Outline Descendant Tree dialog box will open.

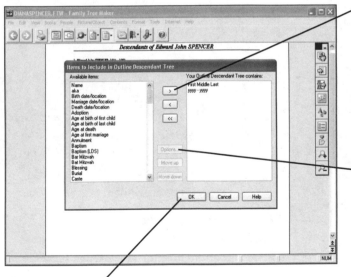

2. Select which items to include, following the same steps as the Items to Include dialog box in Family Group Sheets. (Click on an item in the **Available items** list, then click the **right angle bracket** (>) button to move the item to the **Your Outline Descendant Tree contains** list.)

When you move an item to the right list, the Options dialog box may open. If not, you can click the item in the right list, then click **Options**. That way, you can make specific selections on each item you choose to include in the Outline Descendant Tree.

3. Click **OK** to save your changes and close the dialog box.

Choosing Individuals to Include

You can select whether to include all descendants or only direct descendants in the Outline Descendant Tree.

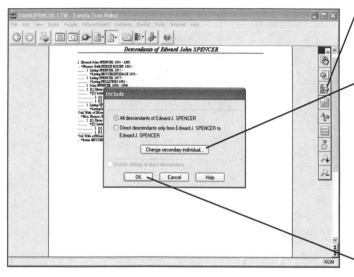

1. Click the **Individuals to Include** button from the vertical toolbar. The Include dialog box will open.

2. Click which individuals you want to include in your Outline Descendant Tree. If you want to include only the direct descendants from the primary person to a specific descendant, click the **Change secondary individual** button to change the selection. (To change the primary individual, go to that individual's Outline Descendant Tree.)

3. Click **OK** to save your changes and close the dialog box.

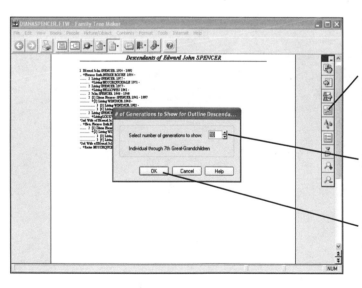

Choosing the Number of Generations to Display

1. Click the **Number of Generations** button from the vertical toolbar. The # of Generations to Show for Outline Descendant Tree dialog box will open.

2. Click the up and down arrows to choose how many generations you would like to show.

3. Click **OK** to save your changes and close the dialog box.

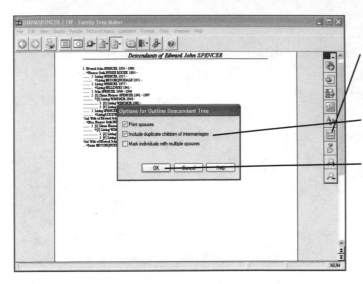

Choosing Options

1. Click the **Options** button from the vertical toolbar. The Options for Outline Descendant Tree dialog box will open.

2. Click a check box for each option you would like to include.

3. Click **OK** to save your changes and close the dialog box.

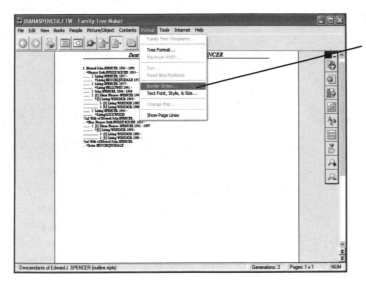

Choosing Borders

1. Click **Border Styles** from the **Format** menu. The Border Styles for Outline Descendant Tree dialog box will open.

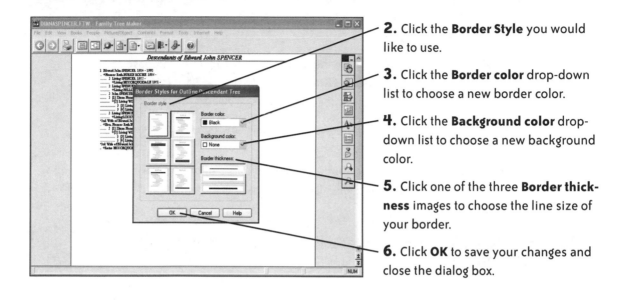

2. Click the **Border Style** you would like to use.

3. Click the **Border color** drop-down list to choose a new border color.

4. Click the **Background color** drop-down list to choose a new background color.

5. Click one of the three **Border thickness** images to choose the line size of your border.

6. Click **OK** to save your changes and close the dialog box.

Adding Titles and Footnotes

You can add titles and footnotes for Outline Descendant Trees in the same manner as Family Group Sheets, by clicking **Title & Footnote** from the **Contents** menu and making the changes in the dialog box that appears.

Choosing Text Font, Style, and Size for an Outline Descendant Tree

You can make font, style, and size changes to Outline Descendant Trees in the same manner as Family Group Sheets, by clicking **Text Font, Style, & Size** from the **Format** menu and making the changes in the dialog box that opens.

Kinship Reports

The Kinship report helps you determine how individuals in your database are related to a specific person. When you select a Kinship report from the Reports button, you will be taken to the Kinship report of the individual you last viewed.

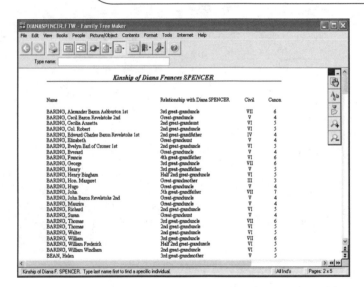

In the Kinship report, you can perform several of the same functions you learned about in Outline Descendant Trees. You can add a **Title & Footnote** (under the **Contents** menu), change the **# of Generations to show** (under the **Contents** menu), choose a **Border Style** (under the **Format** menu), and choose a **Text Font, Style, & Size** (under the **Format** menu).

Alternate Facts Reports

With the Alternate Facts report, you can view all conflicting facts in your Family File at once. You can double-click on a conflicting fact in the list to open the Edit Individual dialog box and begin making changes.

The Alternate Facts report has several of the options found in Outline Descendant Tree. You can select which **Individuals to Include** (under the **Contents** menu), add a **Title & Footnote** (under the **Contents** menu), choose a **Border Style** (under the **Format** menu), and choose a **Text Font, Style, & Size** (under the **Format** menu). In addition, you can sort the Alternate Facts report.

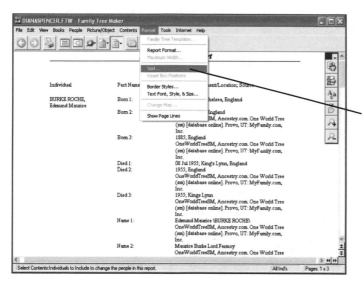

Sorting Names and Dates

You can change the order in which names and dates are sorted in many of the reports:

1. Click **Sort** from the **Format** menu. The Sort Report dialog box will open.

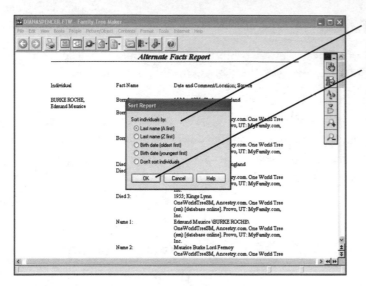

2. Click the radio button next to the sort method you would like to use.

3. Click **OK** to save your changes and close the dialog box.

Address Reports

The Address report may be useful for correspondence to living relatives or to keep track of an ancestor's main residence. When you select the Address report from the Reports button drop-down menu, it will list all names, addresses, and phone numbers you have entered in your Family File.

The Address report lets you use several functions already covered in this chapter: select which **Individuals to Include** (under the **Contents** menu), add a **Title & Footnote** (under the **Contents** menu), **Sort** your report (under the **Format** menu), choose a **Border Style** (under the **Format** menu), and choose a **Text Font, Style, & Size** (under the **Format** menu). In addition, you can adjust the column widths.

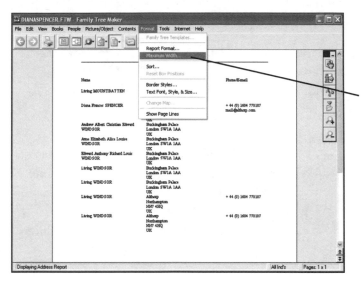

Adjusting Column Widths

You may want to increase the width of your columns to fit longer names:

1. Click **Maximum Width** from the **Format** menu. The Maximum Width for Each Column dialog box will open.

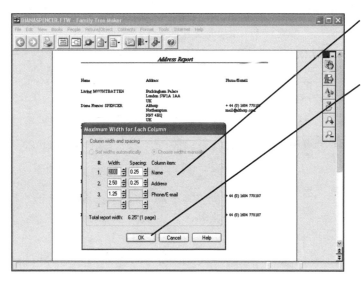

2. Click the up and down arrows, or simply type in the fields, to select the width and spacing for each column item.

3. Click **OK** to save your changes and close the dialog box.

Medical Information Reports

The Medical Information report lists the name, birth date, cause of death, and any other medical information you have entered about individuals in the Medical tab of the Edit Individual dialog box for each individual. This is especially useful for seeing trends in your family's health history.

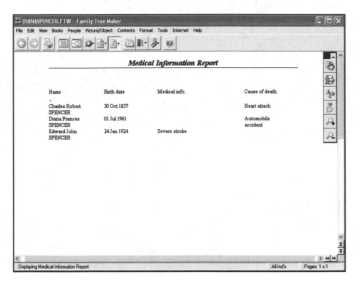

The Medical Information report lets you use several functions already covered in this chapter: select which **Individuals to Include** (under the **Contents** menu), add a **Title & Footnote** (under the **Contents** menu), choose the **Maximum Width** for each column (under the **Format** menu), **Sort** your report (under the **Format** menu), choose a **Border Style** (under the **Format** menu), and choose a **Text Font, Style, & Size** (under the **Format** menu).

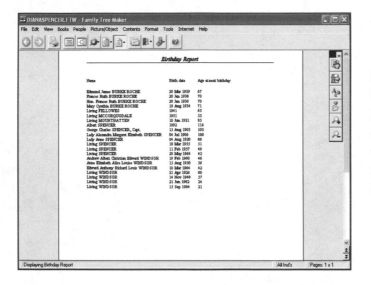

Birthdays of Living Individuals Reports

Family Tree Maker gathers all known birthdays of living individuals into the Birthday report. If the individual does not have a death date recorded and would still be under 120 years old, the program assumes the individual is still living.

The Birthdays of Living Individuals report lets you use several functions already covered in this chapter: select which **Individuals to Include** (under the **Contents** menu), add a **Title & Footnote** (under the **Contents** menu), select the **Maximum Width** for each column (under the **Format** menu), **Sort** your report (under the **Format** menu), choose a **Border Style** (under the **Format** menu), and choose a **Text Font, Style, & Size** (under the **Format** menu).

Marriage Reports

The Marriage report lists the names of the husbands, wives, the marriage date, and the relationship status for all marriages entered in your Family File.

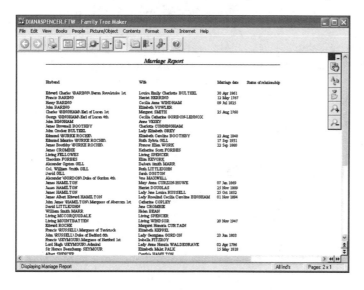

The Marriage report lets you use several functions already covered in this chapter: add a **Title & Footnote** (under the **Contents** menu), select the **Maximum Width** for each column (under the **Format** menu), **Sort** your report (under the **Format** menu), choose a **Border Style** (under the **Format** menu), and choose a **Text Font, Style, & Size** (under the **Format** menu).

Parentage Reports

The Parentage report lists each individual, the individual's parents, and the relationship between the individual and parents (e.g., natural, adopted, foster).

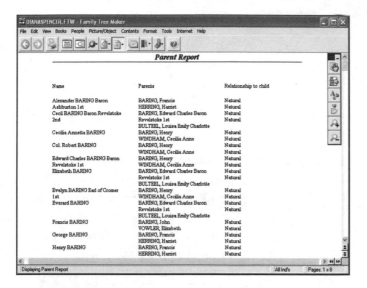

The Parentage report lets you use several functions already covered in this chapter: choose which **Individuals to Include** (under the **Contents** menu), add a **Title & Footnote** (under the **Contents** menu), choose the **Maximum Width** for each column (under the **Format** menu), **Sort** your report (under the **Format** menu), choose a **Border Style** (under the **Format** menu), and choose a **Text Font, Style, & Size** (under the **Format** menu).

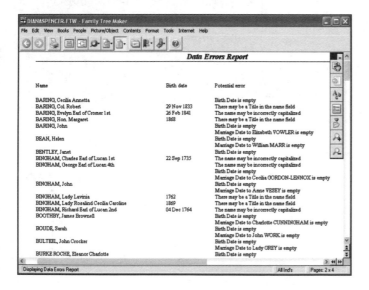

Data Errors Reports

The Data Errors report lists all instances where there is missing data or where Family Tree Maker believes there may be a mistake. This includes nonsensical dates (e.g., an individual being born before their parents were born), empty fields, duplicate individuals, typos, and more.

The Data Errors report lets you use several functions already covered in this chapter: choose which **Individuals to Include** (under the **Contents** menu), add a **Title & Footnote** (under the **Contents** menu), choose **Options** (under the **Contents** menu), **Sort** your report (under the **Format** menu), choose a **Border Style** (under the **Format** menu), and choose a **Text Font, Style, & Size** (under the **Format** menu).

> **NOTE**
>
> Family Tree Maker offers a few more specialized reports that can help you visualize particular aspects of your family history. These can be found under the View menu.

Timeline

To open the Timeline, click **Timeline** from the **View** menu. The Timeline displays a horizontal bar for each individual depicting his/her lifespan in a chronological chart. The Timeline also includes many significant historical events. You can choose to display these historical milestones to put the lives of your ancestors in historical context.

The Timeline also lets you use several functions already covered in this chapter: choose which **Individuals to Include** and **Items to Include** (under the **Contents** menu), add a **Title & Footnote** (under the **Contents** menu), **Sort** your timeline (under the **Format** menu), choose a **Box, Line and Border Style** (under the **Format** menu), and choose a **Text Font, Style, & Size** (under the **Format** menu).

> **TIP**
>
> You can add the Timeline button to the toolbar if you use it often. You can customize your toolbar in the Preferences dialog box, which will be covered in Chapter 16.

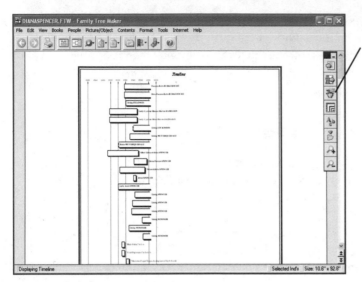

Formatting the Timeline

1. Click the **Format** button on the vertical toolbar. The Format for Timeline dialog box will open.

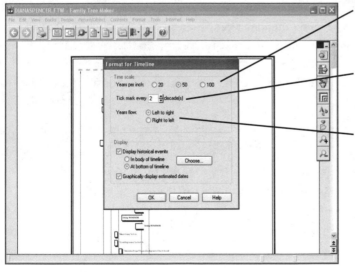

2. Click the **Years per inch** radio button that best suits how much detail you want squeezed into an area.

3. Click the **Tick mark every decade(s)** up and down arrows to indicate where you would like to show tick marks.

4. Click a **Years flow** radio button to indicate in which direction you would like the years to show.

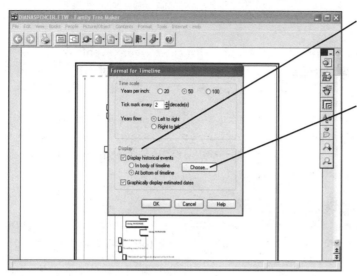

5. Click the check boxes and radio buttons to indicate if you want to display historical events in the **Display** box, and how you would like to display them.

6. Click **Choose** to open the Choose Historical Events dialog box.

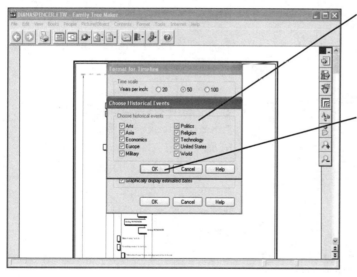

7. Click the check boxes to indicate which historical events you would like to display, ranging from arts to religion. You can choose as many historical events as you desire.

8. Click **OK** to save your changes and close the dialog box; then click **OK** to close the previous dialog box.

Maps

Family Tree Maker displays maps with labeled dots marking cities where events you have entered in your Family File took place, e.g., dates and locations where ancestors were born. You can change the map's format, size, and area.

The Map also lets you use several functions already covered in this chapter: choose which **Individuals to Include** and **Items to Include** (under the **Contents** menu), add a **Title & Footnote** (under the **Contents** menu), choose **Options** (under the **Contents** menu), and choose a **Text Font, Style, & Size** (under the **Format** menu).

> **TIP**
>
> You can add the Maps button to the toolbar if you use it often. You can customize your toolbar in the Preferences dialog box, which will be covered in Chapter 16.

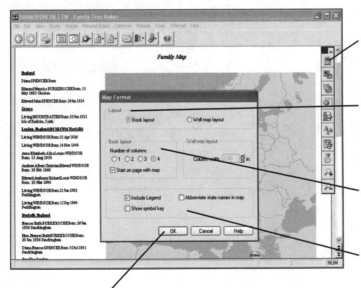

Changing the Map Format

1. Click the **Map Format** button from the vertical toolbar. The Map Format dialog box will open.

2. Click the radio button for a layout. The Book layout will format the map to fit on a single page, and the Wall map layout will create a larger map.

3. Click other options as necessary, depending on which layout you choose, the Book layout or Wall map layout.

4. Click the check boxes if you want to add a legend, symbol key, or if you want to abbreviate state names in a map.

5. Click **OK** to save your changes and close the dialog box.

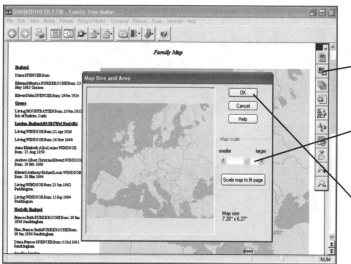

Changing the Map Size and Area

1. Click the **Map Size and Area** button from the vertical toolbar. The Map Size and Area dialog box will open.

2. Drag the scroll bar on the Map Scale indicator to make the map larger or smaller, or click **Scale map to fit page**.

3. Click **OK** to save your changes and close the dialog box.

TIP

You can change the map to cover another areas besides the United States. Click **Change Map** from the **Format** menu, then select the map you want to use from the Change Map dialog box.

Calendars

The calendar displays all birthdays and/or anniversaries added to your Family File. Use the scroll bar to move the page down and see each month. You can make some changes to your calendar's appearance by selecting which items to include and what basic style you want to give your calendar.

The calendar also lets you use several other functions covered in this chapter: choose which **Individuals to Include** (under the **Contents** menu), add a **Title & Footnote** (under the **Contents** menu), and choose a **Text Font, Style, & Size** (under the **Format** menu).

TIP

You can add the Calendar button to the toolbar if you use it often. You can customize your toolbar in the Preferences dialog box, which will be covered in Chapter 16.

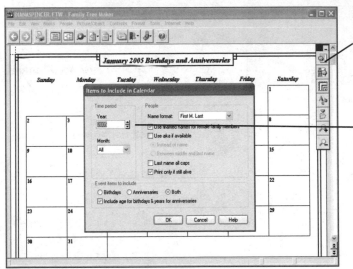

Choosing Items to Include

1. Click the **Items to Include** button from the vertical toolbar. The Items to Include in Calendar dialog box will open.

2. Click the drop-down arrows to select the calendar year and month you want to cover.

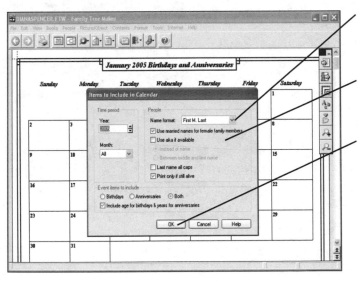

3. Click the **Name format** drop-down list to choose the way you would like names to appear in the calendar.

4. Click the check boxes that indicate what items you want to include in your calendar.

5. Click **OK** to save your changes and close the dialog box.

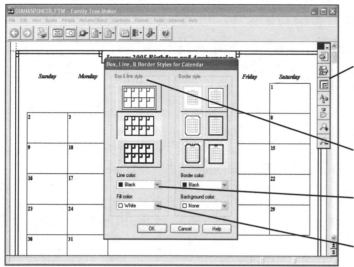

Choosing Box, Line, and Border Styles

1. Click the **Box, Line, and Border Styles** button from the vertical toolbar. The Box, Line, & Border Styles for Calendar dialog box will open.

2. Click the **Box & line style** you would like to use.

3. Click the **Line color** drop-down list to choose a line color.

4. Click the **Fill color** drop-down list to choose a fill color.

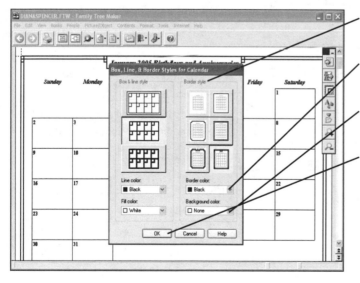

5. Click the **Border style** you would like to use.

6. Click the **Border color** drop-down list to choose a border color.

7. Click the **Background color** drop-down list to choose a background color.

8. Click **OK** to save your changes and close the dialog box.

Mailing Labels and Cards

Family Tree Maker can print labels or cards in a variety of sizes and shapes, depending on the type of label. By default, the labels or cards include some basic information about your family. You can change this information.

The Mailing Labels and Cards feature includes the following functions covered in other areas of this chapter: **Items to Include**, **Individuals to Include**, **Options** (all under the **Contents** menu); **Maximum Width for Each Picture/Object**, **Sort Labels/Cards**, **Text**, **Font**, **Style and Size**, and **Box and Line Styles** (all under the **Format** menu).

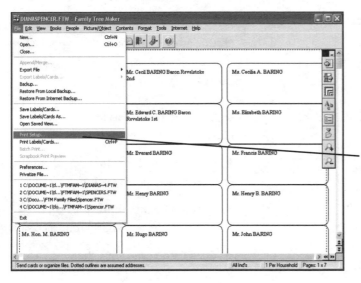

Setting Up Printing for Labels and Cards

It is important to use the right setup for Labels and Cards because they do not print to standard 8 ½" by 11" paper like most reports.

1. Click **Print Setup** from the **File** menu. The Print Setup for Labels/Cards dialog box will open. Mostly likely, you will want to keep the default settings for the default printer and print orientation.

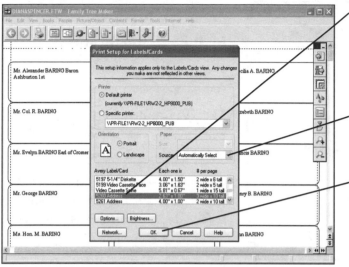

2. Click the description in **Avery Label/Card** that best matches the type of labels or cards you are using. The label number is typically on the box packaging.

3. If necessary, click **Manual** from the **Source** drop-down list so you can manually feed the labels into your printer.

4. Click **OK** to save your changes before printing the labels.

TIP

To sort your labels and cards, click **Sort Labels/Cards** from the **Format** menu. Then make your selection in the Sort Labels/Cards dialog box.

Custom Reports

Custom reports let you create reports with your own criteria. For example, just as Family Tree Maker can create a custom report for Birthdays of Living Individuals, you can create a custom report for Favorite Ice Cream if you have recorded that information for several individuals in your Family File. The Custom report defaults to a list of all individuals, birth dates, and death dates, so you can begin to customize it with all information intact.

In addition to specifying individuals and items to include in your custom report, you can also add a **Title & Footnote** (under the **Contents** menu), choose the **Maximum Width** for each column (under the **Format** menu), **Sort** your report (under the **Format** menu), choose a **Border Style** (under the **Format** menu), and choose a **Text Font, Style, & Size** (under the **Format** menu). These features were all covered earlier in the chapter with different reports, and will function in a similar way for custom reports.

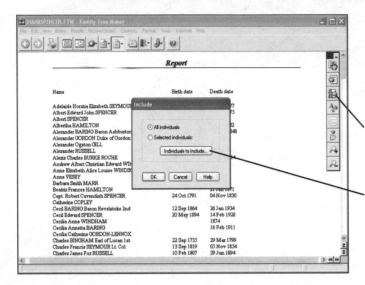

Choosing Individuals to Include in the Report

Begin by selecting which individuals you want to include in your report.

1. Click the **Individuals to Include** button on the vertical toolbar. The Include dialog box will open.

2. If you do not want to include all individuals in your file, click **Individuals to Include**. The Individuals to Include dialog box will open.

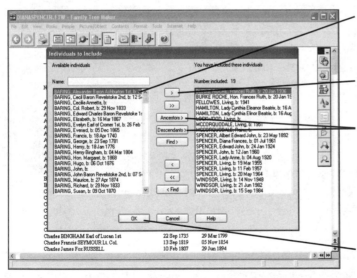

3. Click the individual you want to include in the **Available individuals** list.

4. Click the **right angle bracket (>)** button to move one individual.

5. Click the **Ancestors>** button to include an individual and all of the individual's ancestors, or click the **Descendants>** button to include an individual and all of the individual's descendants.

6. Click **OK** to save your changes and close the dialog box.

NOTE

If you click the inclusion button with two arrows instead of one, you will move all the items in the list at once instead of a single item you have selected. The Ancestors button will include the ancestors of the highlighted individual, while the Descendant button will include the descendants of the highlighted individual.

Choosing Items to Include in the Report

When customizing your report, you can also choose which items to include in your report.

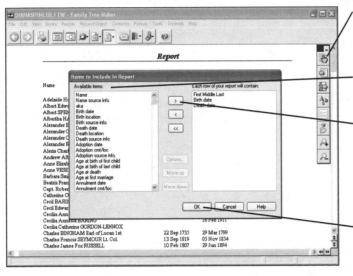

1. Click the **Items to Include** button from the vertical toolbar. The Items to Include in Report dialog box will open.

2. Click the item that you want to include in the **Available items** list.

3. Click the **right angle bracket** (>) button to move the item. An Options dialog box might open, depending on the item you've chosen to include. If it does, choose the options you would like.

4. Click **OK** to save your changes and close the dialog box. The items you selected will be included in your report.

Defining Specific Criteria

You may want to create a report with more specific criteria. For example, you may want to generate a report showing all individuals who were born in a particular city.

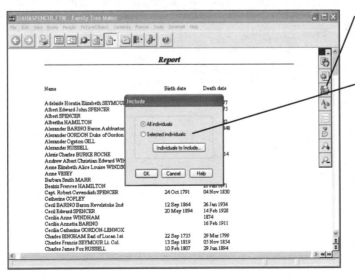

1. Click the **Individuals to Include** button from the vertical toolbar. The Include dialog box will open.

2. Click the **Selected individuals** radio button, then click the **Individuals to Include** button. The Individuals to Include dialog box will open.

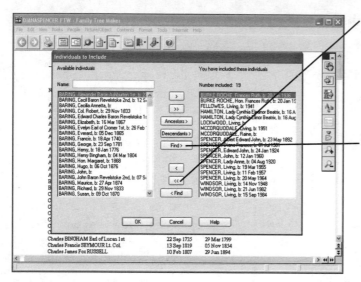

3. Click the **left double angle bracket** (**<<**) button to clear all individuals from the list on the right. If you do not clear the list, the individuals in the right box will be included whether or not they meet the criteria you are about to set.

4. Click the **Find>** button (make sure the arrow is pointing to the right). The Add Individuals dialog box will open.

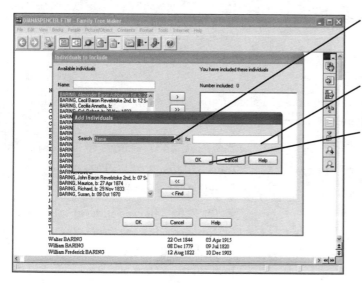

5. Click the **Search** drop-down list to choose the field for which you want to set the criteria, such as birth location.

6. In the **for** field, enter the date, name, etc. you seek, such as the name of a city.

7. Click **OK**. The list on the right will now include individuals who meet the criteria you have set.

Removing Individuals from the Report

Similar to how you performed a Find to generate a report showing all individuals who matched a certain criteria, you can remove individuals you have added with the Find remove button.

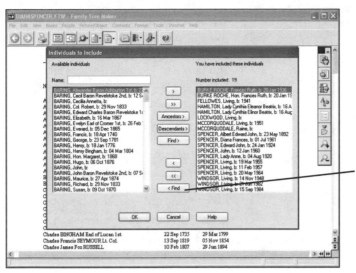

1. Click the **<Find** button. The Remove Individuals dialog box will open.

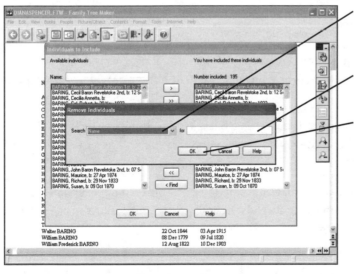

2. Click the **Search** drop-down list to choose the item you would like to remove.

3. In the **for** field, enter the name, date, etc., you want to remove.

4. Click **OK**. The names in the right list that match that criteria will be moved back to the left list.

TIP

You can use operators such as less than (<) and greater than (>) when you set your criteria. For a full list of options, click the Help button in the Add Individuals or Remove Individuals dialog box.

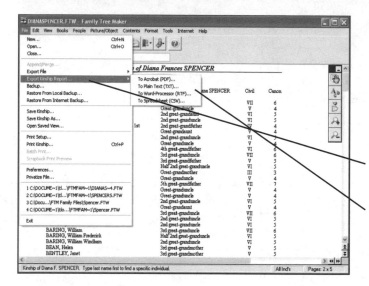

Exporting Reports to Other File Formats

You may want to export your reports to other file formats to share with others or to aid in your research. Make sure your report is open.

1. Click **Export Report** from the **File** menu. A sub-menu will appear.

2. From the sub-menu, choose how you would like to export your report. Choose one of these options:

Acrobat (PDF)—This format retains printer formatting and graphical elements so it resembles how the printed document will appear. You cannot make changes to the PDF from within Family Tree Maker, and you need the free Adobe Reader in order to read it. The Reader can be downloaded from the Adobe website.

Plain Text (TXT)—This format does not retain any of the formatting. This is a version that can be typically opened by any word processing or document-editing program and can be edited and resaved.

Word-Processor (RTF)—This format is based on a basic text file, but it can include information such as text style, size, and color. Also, this is a universal format, so it can be read by nearly all word processors.

Spreadsheet (CSV)—This format organizes information into fields (comma-separated values) and is meant to be imported into spreadsheet programs. Only reports in columnar format can be exported to this format.

NOTE

Not all reports can be exported to all formats. For example, reports with graphical elements, such as the Family Group Sheet and the Outline Descendant Tree, can be only exported to PDF format.

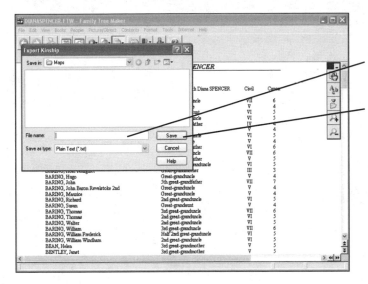

Once you have made your selection, the Export dialog box will open.

3. Enter a name for the file in the **File name** field.

4. Click **Save** to save the file in the directory shown, or open a different directory to save the file to a different location. The file will be saved, and the Export dialog box will close.

PART IV

Searching With Family Tree Maker

11

Using Family Tree Maker to Help Research Your Tree

Many of the views, charts, and reports in Family Tree Maker help you to see gaps in your research. Family Tree Maker helps you fill in these gaps by searching Ancestry.com for more information on the people in your Family File. In this chapter, you'll learn how to:

- Use the Web Search feature
- View Web Search results
- Merge Web Search results into your Family File
- View facts about your family name
- View research tips
- Contact other researchers

If you are connected to the Internet, you can use Family Tree Maker to search Ancestry.com for information about individuals in your Family File. You can find family members in Ancestry.com collections, learn facts about your family name, view personalized research tips, and contact others who are researching the same individuals you are.

Using the Web Search Feature

Family Tree Maker's Web Search performs behind-the-scene searches on the vast collection of genealogy records on Ancestry.com and looks for more information on the people in your Family File—without interrupting your work. Web Search can search thousands of databases including: census records; birth, marriage, and death records; court and land records; immigration records; military records; and more. With Web Search, you have a convenient starting point for researching and expanding your family history.

If you are connected to the Internet, the Web Search Resources button will change in appearance when Family Tree Maker has found a result that matches the ranking criteria you have set. Normally, the Web Search Resources button is a world with a magnifying glass. When Family Tree Maker finds a match, a star appears on the button. However, you do not have to wait for matches to appear. You can use the Web Search feature at any time.

> **NOTE**
>
> Web Search features in Pedigree View are also discussed in Chapter 5, "Navigating and Editing in Pedigree View."

Ranking Web Search Results

Family Tree Maker uses a five-star ranking system to indicate the probability of a data match to an individual in your Family File. The greater the number of stars, the more relevant the search result. Five-star matches are almost certain to contain information about a family member.

> **NOTE**
>
> One-star matches have the lowest probability of containing information about an individual in your file. However, the record may be still be worth researching.

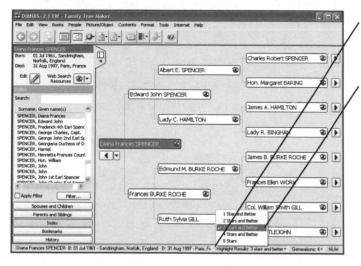

1. Click the **Highlight Results** drop-down list in the status bar at the bottom right section of the screen.

2. Click the number of stars you would like before Family Tree Maker indicates that search results meeting that quality level exist.

NOTE

You can also set your default search criteria from the Preferences dialog box, which will be covered in Chapter 17, or from the Web Search report, which will be covered later in this chapter when you learn about filtering Web Search results.

Viewing Web Search Results

You can view the Web Search results at any time, even if Web Search does not match the criteria you set. The report lets you compare side-by-side the information found online with the information already in your file.

Once the Web Search report opens, you may need to change the search criteria in order to see some potential matches. For example, the Web Search report may open and indicate there are no results for a quality level of five stars and above, so you may want to change it to three stars and above to widen the possibilities.

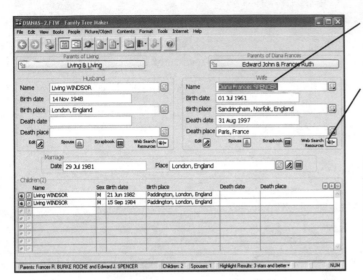

1. Click an individual. You can do this in Family View, Pedigree View, tree charts, and most reports.

2. Click a **Web Search Resources** button. The Web Search report will open.

TIP

You can also click **Web Search Results** from the **View** menu if you do not want to use the Web Search Resources button.

NOTE

You can view a Web Search report from Family View any time. Simply click the Web Search button below an individual's name to open that individual's Web Search report. In Pedigree View, click the **Web Search** button in the node if a Web Search result met the criteria you set or click the **Web Search Results** button in the details area of the Side Panel to view the Web Search report of the individual you clicked on in the tree. The Web Search report will open for the individual you have selected.

Understanding the Web Search Report

The Web Search report is divided into three sections.

1. The top half of the report lists the records found on Ancestry.com, with details about each possible match.

2. The bottom left box displays details about the information available in the Ancestry.com record you have highlighted in the top half of the report, is used for the Family Tree Maker Web Merge feature, and lets you compare information in your Family File with the Web Search results.

3. The bottom right box displays the details you have entered about the individual in your Family File. This makes it easier for you to compare your information with the potential matches Web Search has found.

> ### NOTE
>
> To see all of the details available in a record, you must either have a subscription to or be participating in a trial version of the associated data collection. You can subscribe using options in the Internet menu.

Columns in the top half of the report include:

1. Quality—Indicates the likelihood of a good match with stars. The more stars listed, the stronger the likelihood of a positive match.

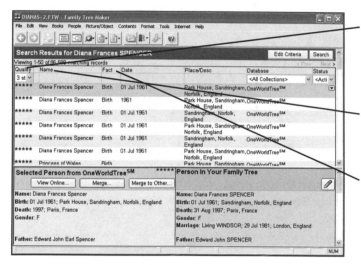

2. Name—Lists exactly how the name appears in the source in which it was found.

3. Fact—Lists the fact relevant to the source information found, e.g., Birth, Residence, Death.

4. Date—Lists the date found on the record.

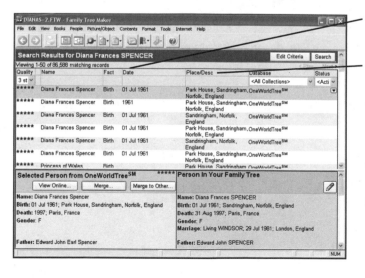

5. Place/Desc—You can often compare the place the record was found with possible locations the ancestor may have been. For example, if the birth record appears in Kentucky, USA, and you know your relative grew up in Kentucky, there is a possibility this is a good lead.

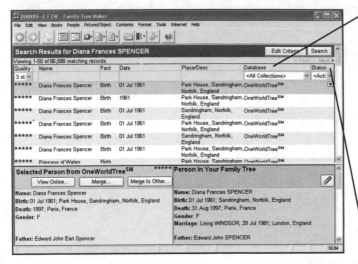

6. Database—The database in the Ancestry.com collection where the record was found by Family Tree Maker. The databases are all hyperlinked, so you can click on them to view the exact context for where the record was found—if you have a subscription to the collection at Ancestry.com. You can also use the Source feature to narrow down your search.

7. Status—Lets you set individual statuses for each search result: None, Ignore, Follow Up, Merged, or Done.

NOTE

If the name appears in angle brackets < >, the data collection may not have the exact name indexed. This is frequently the case with newspaper or other collections that primarily contain images.

Filtering Your Web Search Results

You can filter the Web Search results to view only the results that are most relevant. You can filter by Quality (likelihood of a positive match), Database (where the information was found, e.g., Census Records, Military Records), or Status (e.g., Follow up, Merged).

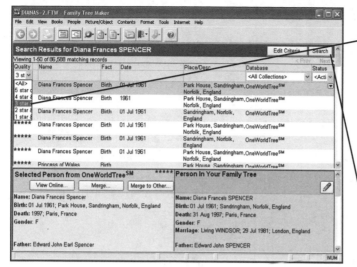

Sorting by Quality

1. Click the **Quality** drop-down list and choose the number of stars you want a source to have before Family Tree Maker will show the result. A filter will be applied, and matches with fewer stars than what you have selected will not appear.

2. Click **Search**.

TIP

While the ranking of the stars is an attempt to help you decide which search results to look at first, due to errors by census transcribers, etc., you may still find matches in the results with fewer stars. You may want to start with only five-star matches, then move down to four-star matches, and so forth.

If you see zero matches, you have narrowed the search too much. For example, you may have indicated you want to see only five-star matches, but if Family Tree Maker has found only four-star matches at best, you will not have any positive search results.

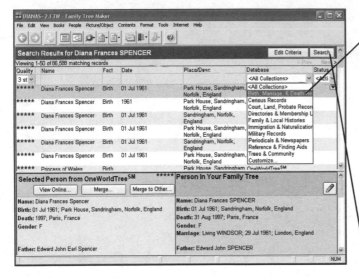

Sorting by Database

1. Click the **Database** drop-down list and choose a specific database. You can click **<ALL COLLECTIONS>** (the default setting) if you want to see results from all sources. The items in the search results will change to show only matches found for the database you have selected. For example, if you want to see only vital records, click **Birth, Marriage, & Death Records**.

2. Click **Search**.

Sorting by Status

To sort the Web Search Results by status, you first have to assign a status to an individual search result.

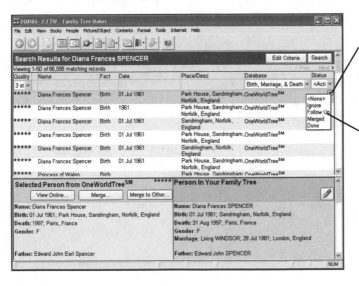

To assign a status to a search result:

1. Click an individual's search result row. The row will be highlighted, and a small down arrow will appear in the Status column.

2. Click the drop-down arrow in the **Status** column to choose a status. Unless you click "None," the column will indicate the status you have chosen.

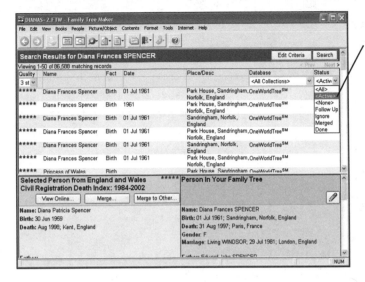

To sort by status:

1. Click the **Status** drop-down list and choose the status by which you want to sort your column.

a. All—Displays all search results.

b. Active—Displays all search results marked as either "Follow Up" or "None."

c. None—Displays all search results that have not been assigned a status.

d. Follow Up—Displays all search results marked "Follow Up."

e. Ignore—Displays all search results marked "Ignore."

f. Merged—Displays all search results you have merged through the Web Merge Wizard; this status will automatically be set after you merge a result.

g. Done—Displays all search results marked "Done."

2. Click **Search**.

NOTE

In Web Search results, any status for a result will apply only to that result for that individual, not other individuals in your Family File. In addition, you can always opt to remove the Ignore label.

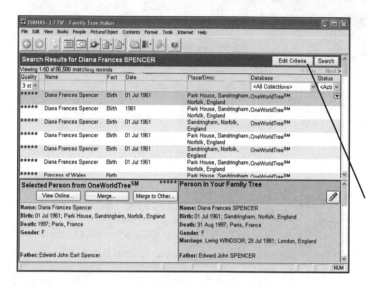

Changing Your Web Search Criteria

When you access Web Search results, you can change any search criteria that you want without having to select a new individual. This can be useful for checking for alternate spellings of names or married names.

1. Click **Edit Criteria**. The columns at the top of the window become editable.

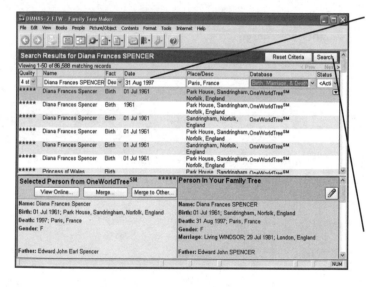

2. Change the search criteria as necessary.

a. Name—Enter a new name to search on. This can be useful when searching for alternate or married names.

b. Fact—Choose a new fact from the drop-down list.

c. Date—Enter a new date.

d. Place/Desc—Enter a new location.

3. Click **Search**. Web Search shows the new results.

NOTE

You can also change the Quality, Database, and Status criteria as explained earlier in this chapter.

Merging Web Search Results into Your Family File

If you find results in the Web Search report that you would like to add to your Family File, you can merge them into your file with the Family Tree Maker Web Merge Wizard. You can merge specific individuals and the individual's parents, spouses, and children, as long as those family members are associated with the record that Web Search found.

> **NOTE**
>
> Unlike a regular file merge, the Web Merge process will never overwrite any of your data. However, it is always a good idea to save a backup of your file.

Source information will automatically be included for each fact you add to your file, unless you opt to ignore the fact or individual completely. If you do not want source information to be included automatically, you can turn this feature off in Preferences.

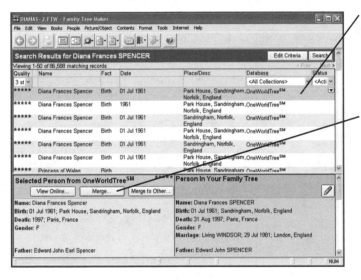

1. Click on the individual Web Search result you would like to merge into your Family File. The information available in the online record will appear in the Selected Person box.

2. Click **Merge**. The Web Merge Wizard will launch.

> **NOTE**
>
> If you want to merge the record with a person in your Family File that is different than the currently selected individual, click **Merge to Other**. Choose an individual and click **OK**.

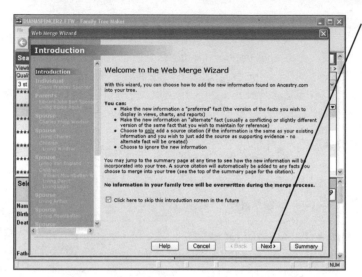

3. Read the welcome text for the Web Merge Wizard and click **Next >**. The Merge Primary Individual window will open.

> **NOTE**
>
> Click the **Skip introduction** check box if you do not want to see the introduction each time you use the Web Merge Wizard.

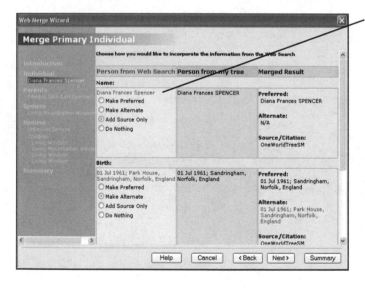

4. Click the radio buttons in the first column according to what you want to do with the information found on Ancestry.com.

a. Make Preferred—Make this the preferred fact/individual in your Family File.

b. **Make Alternate**—Make the information the alternate fact in your Family File.

c. Add Source Only—Add only the source information to the fact in your Family File, e.g., you may already have the same fact listed in your file, but you want to add this as another source to further validate the existing fact.

d. **Do Nothing**—Do not merge the information into your Family File, e.g., you may choose to ignore some facts from the Ancestry.com record, although it is usually a good idea to include all facts from a particular record in case they turn out to be relevant. This option will also ignore source information.

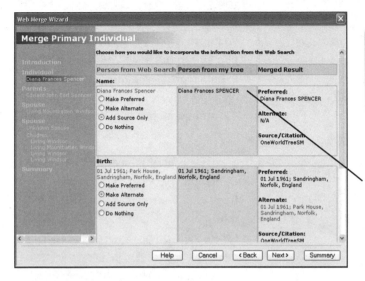

NOTE

The source information will automatically be included for the first three options (Make Preferred, Make Alternate, Add Source Only) unless you have the automatic sourcing feature turned off in Preferences.

5. View the information in the middle column to compare the information you already have in your Family File with what you are about to merge into your Family File.

6. View the information in the right-hand column to see how your selections in the first column will affect your Family File.

7. Click **Next >**. If the individual you want to merge has parents, spouse(s), or children that Web Search has found, the Web Merge Wizard will ask you if you want to add the information found for the first additional family member. If the individual does not have siblings or parents associated with this source, click **Next >** to go to the Summary window and skip to step 10. If the individual does have additional family members, continue to step 8.

NOTE

All names related to a Web Merge are listed in the blue navigation panel on the left side of the Web Merge Wizard. You can click on a name to skip to a specific individual, or let Family Tree Maker methodically go down the list, starting at the top.

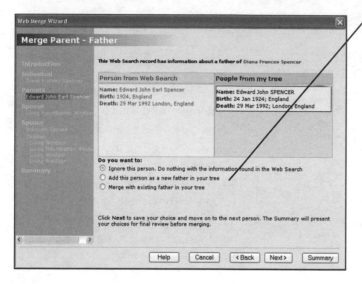

8. Click a radio button to choose what you want to do with each family member. **Ignore** the first additional family member; **add** the additional family member as a new Individual; or **merge** the additional family member with an existing individual.

The details about the additional family members appear in the **Person from Web Search** column, while the information you already have in your Family File appears in the **People from my tree** column. You can compare the information you have with what Family Tree Maker has found. If more than one individual appears in the **People from my tree** column, you will need to select the one with whom you want to merge the new information.

NOTE

If you do not want to go through each name the Web Merge Wizard wants to merge, click **Summary,** then click the **Merge Now** button. The additional family members will automatically be added if no equivalent family members exist in your file. However, if an immediate family member exists, Family Tree Maker will not default to adding the individuals as new people, since you may want to merge the information into the existing family member(s). In this case, you will default to ignoring the person.

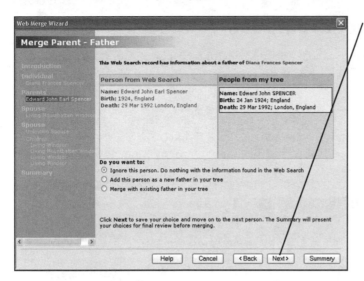

9. Click **Next >**. Complete step 8 for every name in the wizard until all additional family members have been looked through.

10. Verify your selections in the Summary page. You cannot undo a merge once it has been performed. However, none of your existing information will be overwritten, so if you decide you made a mistake, you can simply delete the fact or source that you added during the merge.

11. Click **Merge Now**. A Family Tree Maker dialog box will open to tell you when your Web Search result has been successfully merged into your tree. Click **OK** to close the dialog box.

NOTE

The Web Search report must be refreshed to see the new data you just added, but you can also view the information by opening Family View, Pedigree View, or the Edit Individual dialog box.

Viewing Facts About Your Family Name

You can use Family Tree Maker to search Ancestry.com for facts about your family name. You can discover interesting facts such as the meaning of your family name or your family's country of origin.

> **NOTE**
>
> You must register Family Tree Maker and have an Internet connection to use this feature.

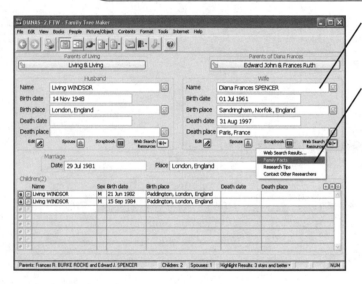

1. Click an individual. You can do this in Family View, Pedigree View, tree charts, and most reports.

2. Click the **Web Search Resources** button drop-down list and choose **Family Facts**. The Family Facts page will open.

> **NOTE**
>
> You can also view Family Facts by clicking **Family Facts** from the **View** menu.

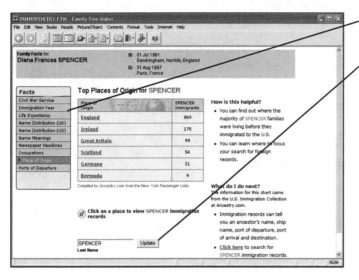

3. Click a fact in the **Facts** list. The new fact is displayed.

4. If you want to view Family Facts for a different individual or family name, enter a name in the **Name** fields and click **Update**. The fact for the new individual will open.

Viewing Research Tips

You can use Family Tree Maker to access personalized research tips for individuals in your Family File.

> **NOTE**
>
> You must register Family Tree Maker and have an Internet connection to use this feature.

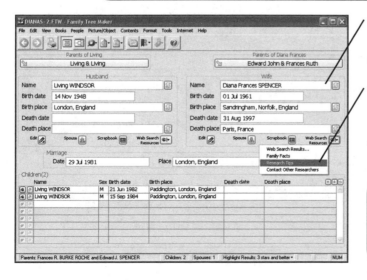

1. Click an individual. You can do this in Family View, Pedigree View, tree charts, and most reports.

2. Click the **Web Search Resources** button drop-down list and choose **Research Tips**. The Research Tips page will open.

> **NOTE**
>
> You can also access Research Tips by clicking **Research Tips** from the **View** menu.

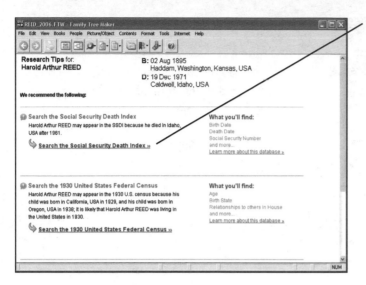

3. If you want to use the suggested research tip, click on a **Search** link. Family Tree Maker displays the relevant search results in the Web Search page.

Contacting Other Researchers

You can use Family Tree Maker to anonymously contact people who have submitted a family tree containing information about an individual in your Family File. Before you can do this, you must first use Web Search to find a OneWorldTree record for an individual and merge the record into your Family File.

NOTE

You must register Family Tree Maker and have an Internet connection to use this feature.

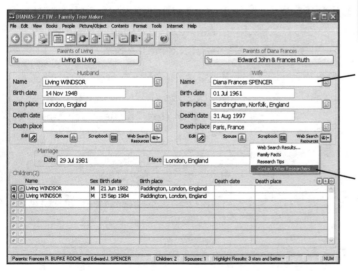

1. Click an individual. You can do this in Family View, Pedigree View, tree charts, and most reports. Make sure you have merged a OneWorldTree record for this individual.

2. Click the **Web Search Resources** button drop-down list and choose **Contact Other Researchers**. The Contact people page will open.

> **NOTE**
>
> You can also contact others by clicking **Contact Other Researchers** from the **View** menu.

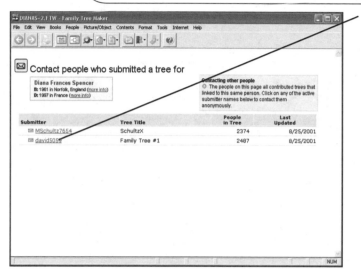

3. Click a submitter's e-mail link. An e-mail message will open. The e-mail is pre-populated with information about the individual in your Family File.

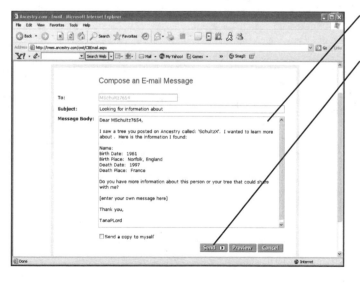

4. If you want, you can change or add information to the message.

5. Click **Send**.

12

Searching Data CDs

In addition to the Web Search feature for searching data on Ancestry.com, you can also use Family Tree Maker to view hundreds of data CDs containing information from marriage indexes, passenger and immigration lists, genealogy indexes, and more. In this chapter, you'll learn how to:

- View a data CD

- Navigate in a data CD

- Read data pages

- Search for names with the Search Expert

- Work with matches

- Exit a data CD

Family Tree Maker can search an extensive data CD-ROM collection sold through Genealogy. com with its built-in CD-ROM viewer. The data CD-ROMs contain information covering records such as: census; birth, marriage, and death; military; genealogies; bibliographies; and more.

You can purchase the data CDs individually as they meet your needs or even obtain the FamilyFinder Index, which is the index of the entire data collection from Genealogy.com. To see what data is available on the more than 300 discs, or to search for which CDs contain possible matches before buying, visit <www.genealogy.com/cdhomelist.html >.

The data on these CDs comes in four varieties:

- **Image**—Microfilmed images of records, such as census or military records

- **Data**—Information from marriage records, death records, and much more

- **Text**—Text from books, such as local histories or genealogies

- **World Family Tree**—Family trees that were submitted by other family historians

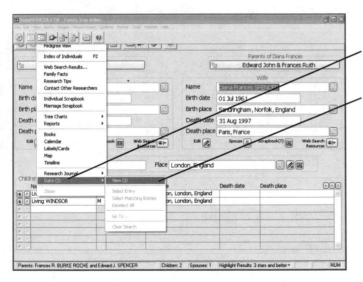

Viewing a Data CD

1. Click **Data CD** from the **View** menu. A sub-menu will open.

2. Click **View CD**. The About this Family Archive dialog box will open.

> **NOTE**
>
> The information that appears in the following dialog boxes will vary depending on the CD data collection you are viewing.

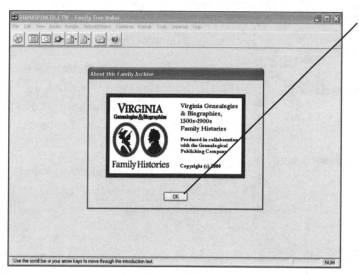

3. Click **OK**. The License Agreement dialog box will open. Read the license agreement, then click **OK**. Family Tree Maker will open to the introduction window of the CD.

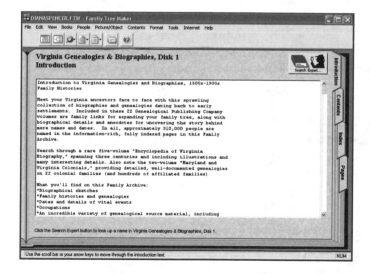

Navigating in a Data CD

Although Family Tree Maker automatically opens to the Introduction tab in the data CD, there may be other tabs as well, depending on the type of data CD. For example, many data CDs contain a Contents tab, which is a Table of Contents, and a Records tab, which lists all the records in the CD first in alphabetical order, then by locality. Other CDs may contain an Index tab and a Pages tab that show images of the original records.

TIP

You can click and drag the scroll bar to move the text up and down on the page as you read or scan the text, or you can click in the text and use the up and down arrows on your keyboard.

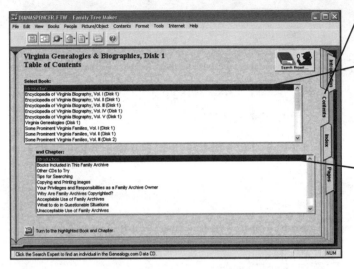

1. Click the **Contents** tab to view the data CD's table of contents.

2. Click an item in the **Selection** section to choose an area of the CD that you want to view. The Chapter section will open with a list of each chapter or record section.

3. Double-click the chapter you want to read. The text or image for that section will open.

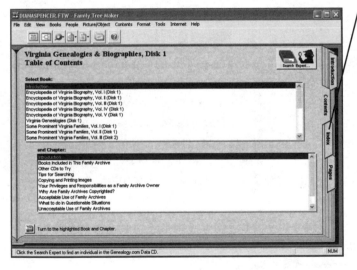

4. Click another tab to view other details, for example, the **Records** tab or **Index** tab, if one exists in the data CD you are viewing. A list will appear.

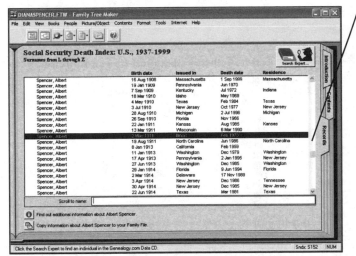

5. Click and drag the scroll bar up and down to browse the information on the tab you have open, if there is more information than what fits on the screen.

> **NOTE**
>
> When viewing names, you can double-click to open the More About dialog box, where you can read additional details about the individual.

> **NOTE**
>
> You can also click the blue Information button (where available) for additional information about an individual. The blue button will always appear in the same area of the window if that feature is available for the current data CD.

Reading Data Pages

Some data CDs (such as those containing family histories), will have pages within, which you can read much like a book. You will know this feature is available if the Pages tab appears when you open the data CD.

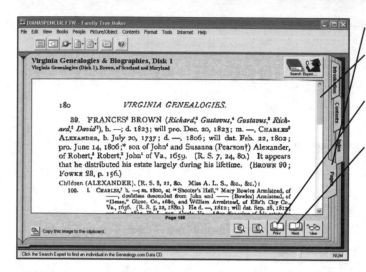

1. Click the **Pages** tab.

2. Click and drag the scroll bar to read further down on the page.

3. Click the **Prev** button to go to the previous page.

4. Click the **Next** button to go to the next page.

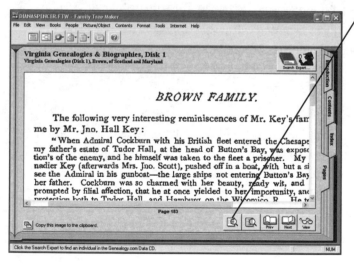

5. Click the **Magnify** button to increase the size of the text on the page. When you go to a Next or Previous page, Family Tree Maker will revert the new page to the default image size.

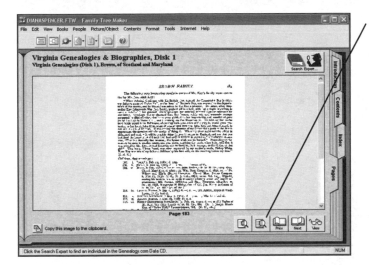

6. Click the **De-magnify** button to decrease the size of the text on the page.

Searching for Names with the Search Expert

The Search Expert is the recommended way to search for a name in CDs, either in the FamilyFinder Index or on the actual data CD. When the Search Expert finds a matching name in the FamilyFinder index, it tells you which data CD contains more information about the name. Reading the information in the data CD will help you determine if you have actually found your ancestor or just someone with a similar name. When you do find one of your ancestors, you can add information from the data CD directly to the Family File. With many of the data CDs, you can use the Search Expert to select and search on a name from the Family File you have open.

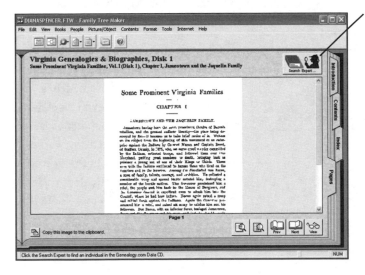

1. Click the **Search Expert** button. The Search Expert dialog box will open.

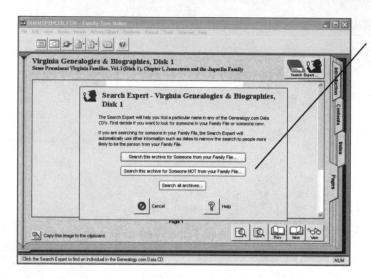

In this example, the Search Expert has three search options, which function in three different ways.

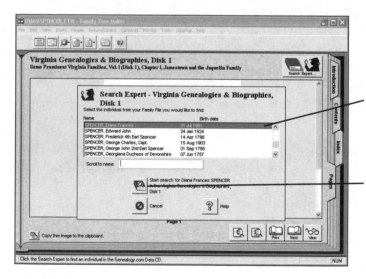

a. Click **Search this archive for Someone from your Family File**. A dialog box will open that lists the names of all individuals in your Family File.

1. Click a name when you find one that you want Family Tree Maker to search. (You can use the scroll bar to look through the names.)

2. Click the **Start search for** button to have Family Tree Maker search the data CD for that individual. If no match is found, Family Tree Maker will display a dialog box stating that no matches were found. If a match is found, Family Tree Maker will take you back to the Records page with the name highlighted. You can then double-click to view more details about the individual.

NOTE

If your search returns zero results, your ancestor may still be in the record. The individual could be in a record that was not indexed, or the name could have been recorded incorrectly. The FamilyFinder Index is made up of many different sources, including hand-written census records more than a century old, so there can be spelling errors, misinterpretations of names, transpositions of first and last names, first initials being used instead of last names, abbreviated names, and other complications. In addition, if you are searching for a woman in the Social Security Death Index, you will likely need to search under her married name, not her maiden name. You may want to review the introduction tab at the beginning of the CD to search for other hints on finding an individual in that particular data CD.

NOTE

If the data CD contains images, there will be a magnifying glass next to each page number below the image. If the information in the data CD is in records, there will be a magnifying glass to the left of the matches. When a field in a record contains too much information to fit in the allotted space, Family Tree Maker places an ellipsis (…) button to the right. Click the ellipsis button to view the additional information.

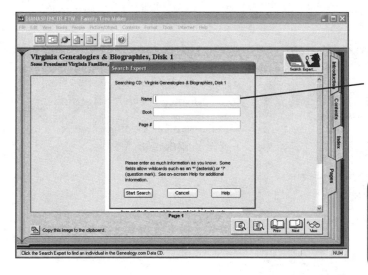

b. Click **Search this archive for Someone NOT from your Family File**. The Search Expert dialog box will open.

1. Enter information about the individual in the corresponding fields. You may want to include less information for a higher chance of a successful match.

NOTE

On some data CDs, you can search for name only, while in others you can search for other information such as dates and location.

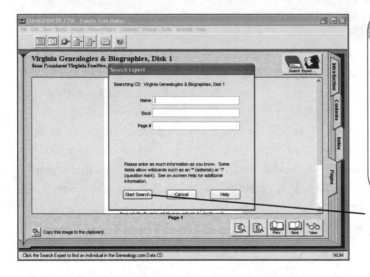

2. Click **Start Search** when you are done entering information in the fields.

c. Click **Search all archives**. You will need to insert the FamilyFinder Index to search all the FamilyFinder archives for a match. The FamilyFinder Index is a set of CDs containing an index to all of the Family Tree Maker data CDs. This CD set can tell you which CD-ROM(s) contain the records for which you are searching, but they do not contain records.

Working with Matches

When you find a match, you can click Next to move forward and click Previous to move backwards through the matches.

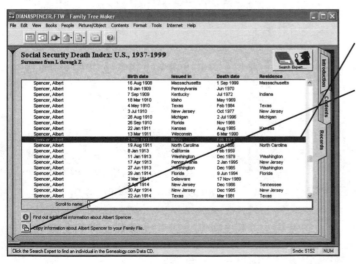

To save a match into your Family File:

1. Click on the name you want to save to your Family File in the **Records** tab.

2. Click the **Copy** button. The Copy Information to Family File dialog box will open.

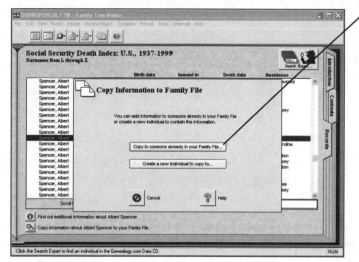

3. Click **Copy to someone already in your Family File** if you want to add the information found to an existing name in your Family File.

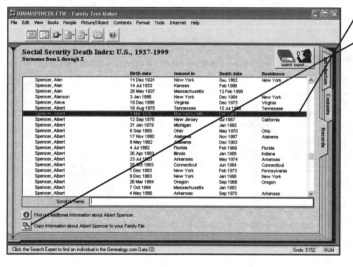

4. Click a name from the list.

5. Click the **Copy** button. The Facts to Import dialog box will open.

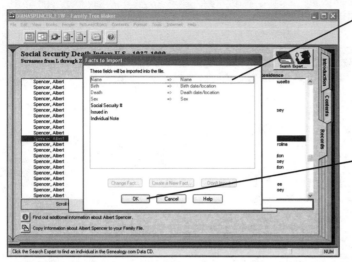

6. View the information in the dialog box to select what information you want to add to the Family File. The list in the left column shows what information will be added to your Family File, and the list in the right column shows what information is already in your Family File.

7. Click **OK** if you are happy with the information you are going to add to your Family File. The Merge Individuals dialog box will open.

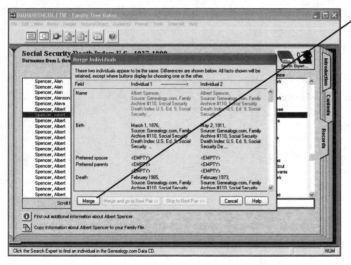

8. Click **Merge**. The information will be merged to your Family File.

Exiting a Data CD

When you are done with your data CD, simply open your CD-ROM drive and take the CD out. Family Tree Maker will not be able to read the CD if the CD is not in the drive. You can insert a new data CD, as long as you are still in **View CD** in Family Tree Maker. Family Tree Maker will automatically view the new data, or you can click a button in the toolbar to leave the CD data page and go another window, e.g., Family View or Pedigree View.

PART V

Sharing Your Research with Others

13

Creating a Family History Book

For many researchers, the ultimate goal is to publish a record of their ancestry. Family Tree Maker has long offered one of the easiest ways to put a variety of reports together to share with family, friends, or colleagues. Because the process is so easy, you can even create preliminary versions of your book at different stages in the research process. In this chapter, you'll learn how to:

- Create a book
- Select reports and trees to include
- Organize selected items
- Add additional text
- Work with images
- Add page breaks
- Create an index
- Edit a book
- Finalize and share your book

You can create a book complete with charts, reports, photos, stories, and an automatically generated table of contents and index. The book will be saved to a PDF format, allowing others to view or print the book without having to use the Family Tree Maker software program.

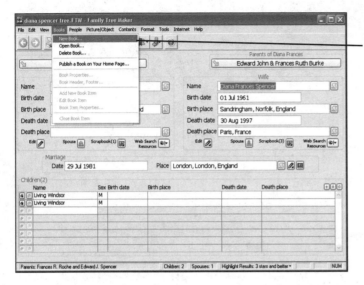

Creating a Book

1. Click **New Book** from the **Books** menu. The New Book dialog box will open.

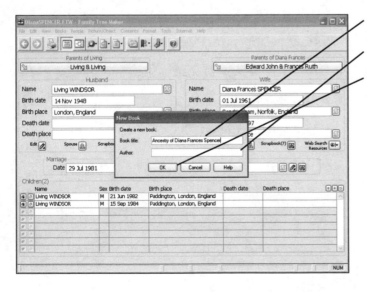

2. Enter a title in the **Book title** field.

3. Enter a name in the **Author** field.

4. Click **OK**. The New Book dialog box will close and the Book page will open.

Selecting Specific Reports and Trees to Include

You will create your book by selecting items from the Available items list and moving them to the Outline list for your book. You can first create your front matter, such as Foreword, Dedication, Copyright, etc. Then, you'll select trees and reports to add to your book.

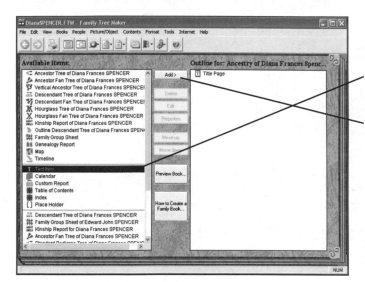

Selecting and Editing Front Matter

1. Click **Text Item** in the **Available items** list. The item will be selected.

2. Click **Add>**. The Add text item dialog box will open.

TIP

You can also double-click **Text Item** instead of using the Add> button.

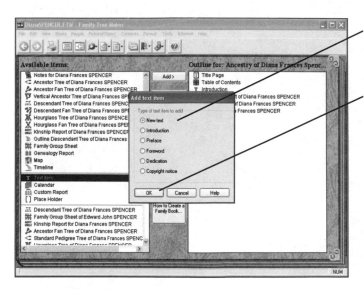

3. Click the radio button for the desired type of text item. The item will be selected.

4. Click **OK**. The selected item will be added to the Outline list. The buttons located between the Available items list and the Outline list will be activated once you click on the new item you have added to your outline.

NOTE

Family Tree Maker automatically adds the Title Page, because this page is required to create the book. It has been placed in the Outline list to indicate it is part of the Book selection.

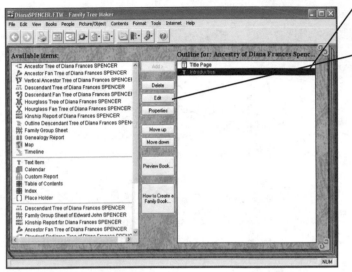

5. In the **Outline** list, click on the item you added in step 2.

6. Click **Edit**. A text-editing window will open.

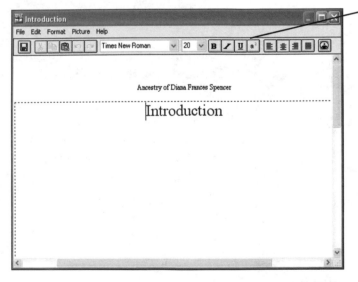

7. Click the toolbar buttons in the text-editing window to make changes to the item.

TIP

The toolbar buttons are similar to those found in word-processing programs. If you click on one of the toolbar buttons, such as italic, before you type, then the text you enter will be in italics. You can also drag your mouse over a word to highlight it, then click a button, such as italics, to change the appearance of the word. The most commonly used toolbar buttons are the B for bold, I for Italicize, and U for Underline.

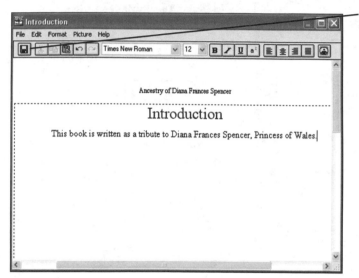

8. Click the **Save** button in the text-editing window to save your changes.

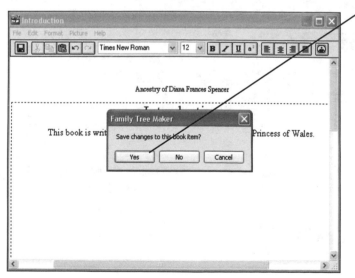

9. Click the **X** button to close the editing window. If you forget to save your changes, a Family Tree Maker dialog box will open, asking if you want to save changes. Click **Yes**. The dialog box will close.

Adding Trees and Reports

You can include several different trees and reports in your book. Make your selections based on the audience who will receive the book. For example, you may want to share more personal and informal trees and reports with family, but you will likely want to remove information about living relatives when sharing your family tree with other genealogists.

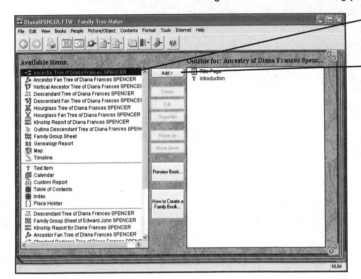

1. Click the tree or report you want to add in the **Available items** list.

2. Click **Add>**. The tree or report will be added to the Outline list.

TIP

Select as many trees or reports as you would like. You can also double-click on a report instead of clicking the Add> button. You will learn how to organize your selections later in this chapter.

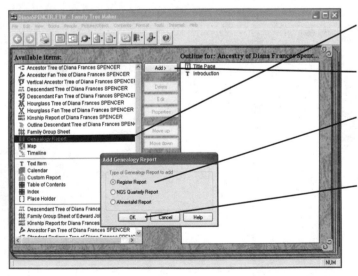

3. Click **Genealogy Report** in the **Available items** list.

4. Click **Add>**. The Add Genealogy Report dialog box will open.

5. Click the radio button for the type of Genealogy Report you would like to add.

6. Click **OK**. The Add Genealogy Report dialog box will close, and the Genealogy Report will appear in the Outline list.

Organizing Selected Items

The items in the Outline list are displayed in the order you added them and will also be printed in that order. However, you can change that order and decide where you would like new chapters in your book to begin.

> **NOTE**
>
> The Title Page must be the first item on the list, and the Index page must be the last item on the list.

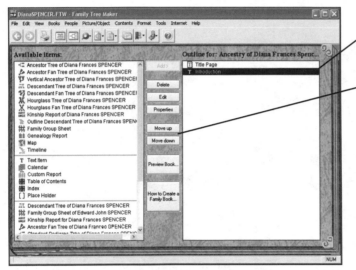

Rearranging the Outline

1. Click on the item you want to move in the **Outline** list.

2. Click **Move up** or **Move down** to move the highlighted item up or down in the Outline.

> **NOTE**
>
> You can also move items in the Outline list by clicking on the item with the left mouse button, and dragging the highlighted item to where you would like it to be on the outline. When you let go of the button, the item will be placed in the new location.

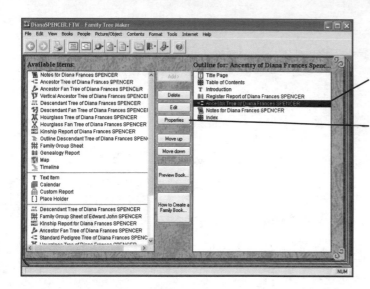

Using the Item Properties Dialog Box

1. Click a report or tree in the **Outline** list.

2. Click **Properties**. The Item Properties dialog box will open.

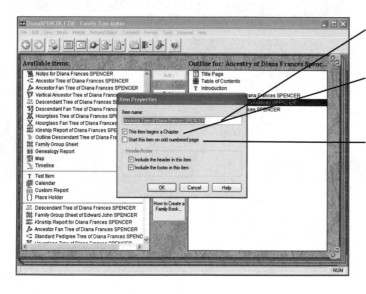

3. Enter or rename the chart or tree in the **Item Name** field.

4. Click the **This item begins a Chapter** check box if you want this item to begin a new chapter in the book.

5. Click the **Start this item on odd numbered page** check box if you want to control the page on which this item will begin.

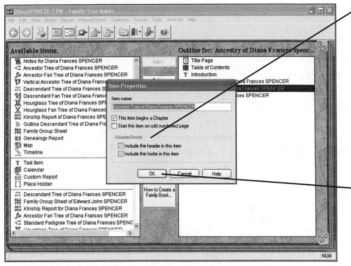

6. Click the **Header/Footer** options if you want headers and footers to appear on the book's pages.

> ### TIP
>
> The header is usually the title of the book. The footer is usually the page number.

7. Click **OK** to save your changes and close the dialog box.

Renaming Outline Items

You can rename the items in your book outline if you want.

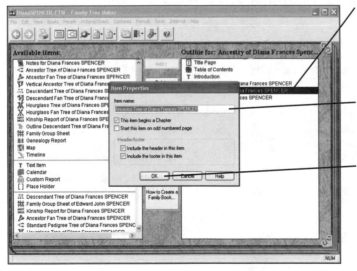

1. Click on the appropriate item in the **Outline** list.

2. Click **Properties**. The Item Properties dialog box will open.

3. Highlight the name in the **Item name** field and enter a new name. This will replace the old item name.

4. Click **OK**. The Item Properties dialog box will close, and the item name will change in the Outline list.

Adding Place Holders

You can use a place holder to reserve a set number of pages anywhere in your book. Place holders are especially helpful if you plan to incorporate a story, chart, photo, etc. from somewhere outside of Family Tree Maker.

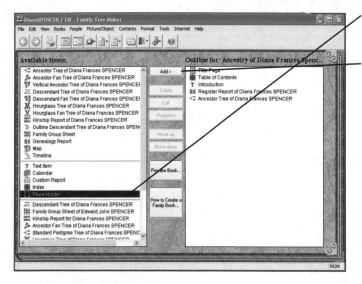

1. Click **Place Holder** in the **Available items** list.

2. Click **Add>**. The Place Holder Properties dialog box will open.

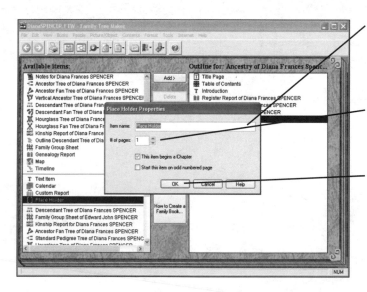

3. Enter the name of the item in the **Item name** field. The words "Place Holder" will be replaced with the name you have entered.

4. Click the **# of pages** arrows to choose the number of pages to use as a place holder.

5. Click **OK**. The Place Holder Properties dialog box will close.

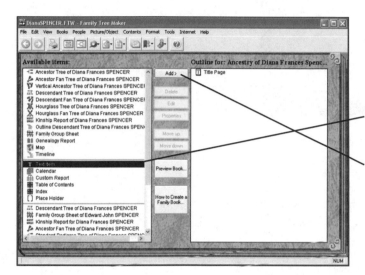

Adding Additional Text

You can add additional text to your book that you have not entered anywhere else in your Family File.

1. Click **Text Item** in the **Available items** list.

2. Click **Add>**. The Add text item dialog box will open.

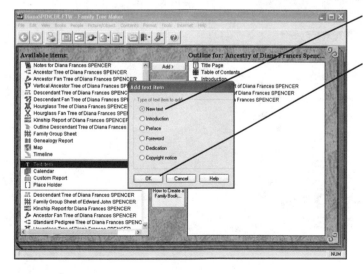

3. Click the **New Text** radio button if it is not already selected.

4. Click **OK**. The item will be added to the Outline list.

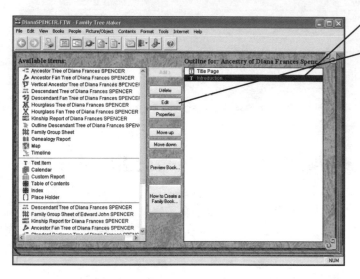

5. Click **Text Item** in the **Outline** list.

6. Click **Edit**. A text editing window will open.

7. Enter or paste your text into the text editor. Click the **Save** button when you are done, then click the **X** button to close the text editor.

Working with Images

Although you have already learned that you can add images to trees and reports before you even select them for your book, you can also add images to a text item and then incorporate the text item into your book.

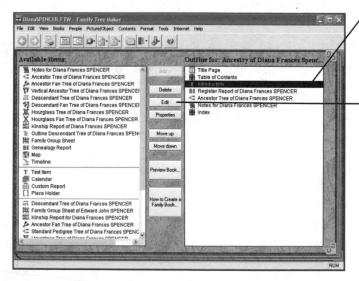

1. Click on the item you want to add an image to in the **Outline** list. The buttons located between the Available items list and the Outline list will be activated.

2. Click **Edit**. The Text Item edit window will open.

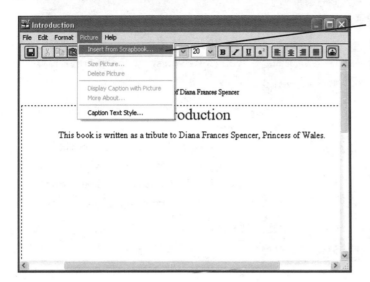

3. Click **Insert from Scrapbook** from the **Picture** menu. The Individuals with Scrapbook Pictures dialog box will open.

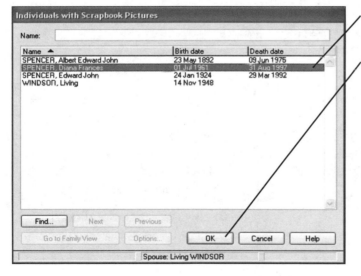

4. Click the individual whose scrapbook you want to access.

5. Click **OK**. The Insert Scrapbook Picture dialog box will open.

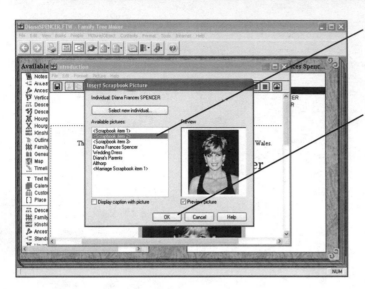

6. Click the image you would like from the **Available pictures** list. The picture you chose will show in the Preview window.

7. Click **OK** if the picture in the Preview window is the one you want. The dialog box will close and the picture will be displayed in the text edit window. You can also click **Select new individual** if you want to choose a different picture than the one in the Preview window.

8. Enter the text you want to associate with the image in the Text Edit dialog box.

> **TIP**
>
> You can move the image by clicking on the image and dragging it to a new location.

9. Click the **Save** button. The changes to the item will be saved.

10. Click the **X** button or click **Close** from the **File** menu. The Text Item window will close.

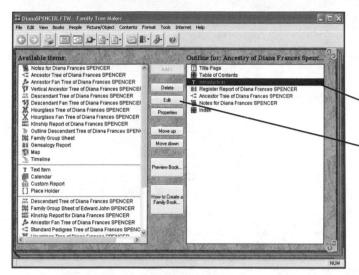

Adding Page Breaks

You can separate your text onto individual pages.

1. Click the text item you want to edit from the **Outline** list.

2. Click **Edit**. The Text Item window will open.

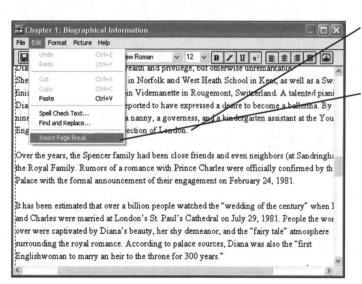

3. Click where you want to place your page break. The cursor indicator will show where you have clicked.

4. Click **Insert Page Break** from the **Edit** menu. A new page will be added in the Text Item window.

NOTE

You may want to maximize your editing window by pressing the maximize button in the upper right corner of the text window and/or using the scroll button to move down, to view where you have inserted a page break.

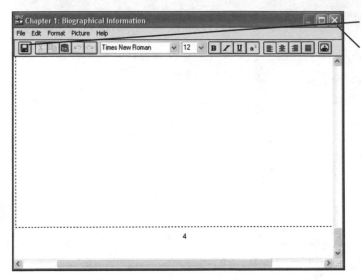

5. Click the **Save** button.

6. Click the **X** button or click **Close** from the **File** menu. Family Tree Maker will prompt you to save your changes, and the Text Item window will close.

> **TIP**
>
> You can undo the page break by clicking at the front of the text of the new page you have created and pressing the Backspace key on your keyboard.

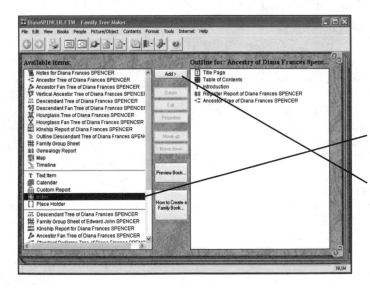

Creating an Index

Family Tree Maker automatically creates an index for you as long as you select it for your outline. In addition, you can customize how the index will appear.

1. Click **Index** in the Available items section.

2. Click **Add>**. The Index will be moved to the **Outline** list.

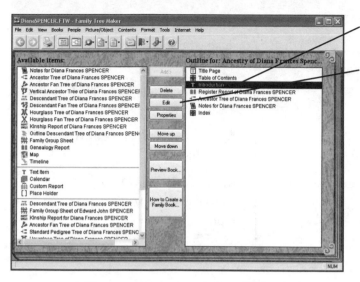

3. In the **Outline** list, click on **Index**. The Index will be highlighted.

4. Click **Edit**. The Index of Individuals Report will appear.

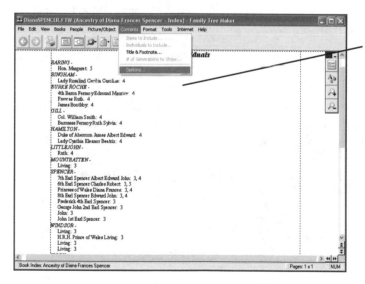

5. Click **Options** from the **Contents** menu. The Options for Book Index dialog box will open.

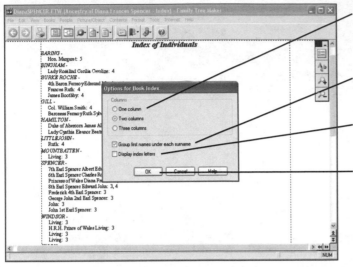

6. Click the radio button next to the number of columns you would like your index to have.

7. Click the **Group first names under each surname** check box.

8. Click the **Display index letters** check box.

9. Click **OK**. Family Tree Maker will make the requested changes to the report.

TIP

If you do not like the changes you have made, follow steps 3–10 again, selecting and deselecting check boxes and radio buttons.

Editing a Book

After you have created a book and saved it, you can add additional reports or make changes at a later time. Once you have created a book, the book is saved to your Family File.

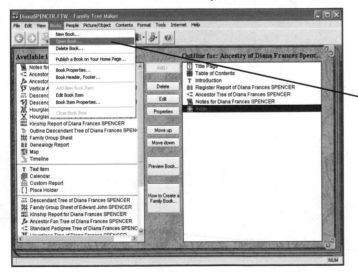

Adding Saved Reports to Books

1. Click **Open Book** from the **Books** menu. The Open Book dialog box will open.

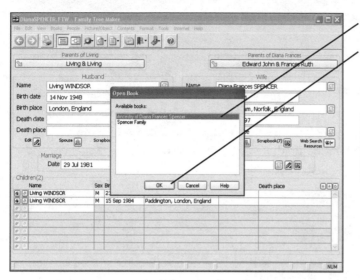

2. Click the appropriate book.

3. Click **OK**. The Open Book dialog box will close, and the Book view will open.

> **NOTE**
>
> The previously saved reports will always appear at the bottom of the Available items list.

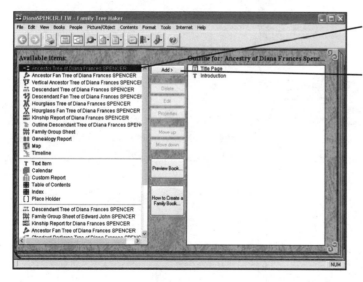

4. Click the appropriate saved report from the **Available items** list.

5. Click **Add>**. The report will be added to the Outline list.

TIP

Although Family Tree Maker uses the name of the main individual in the title of many charts and reports, some of the charts and reports have generic names, e.g., Family Group Sheet. You may want to rename the chart or report to better represent who is included in your report. To do this, open the report, click **Title & Footnote** from the **Contents** menu. In the Title & Footnote dialog box, click the **Custom title** radio button and then type the new title in the field. Refer to Chapter 10, Creating Specialty and Custom Reports, for additional help.

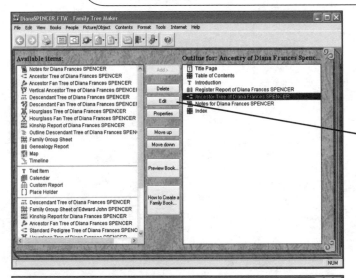

NOTE

At this point, the saved report can be repositioned or edited like the other items in the Outline list.

6. Click **Edit**. The report will open for editing.

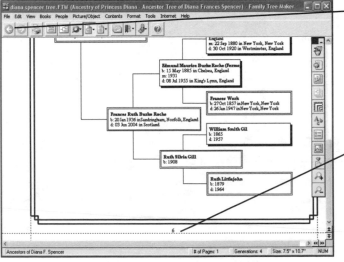

7. Click the **Back** button to return to the Books window. Your work will automatically be saved.

NOTE

You can see the page number that has been assigned based on where the report is presently located in the book. This number will change if the report is moved up or down in the Outline list in the Books view.

Adding Reports About Other Individuals

When a book is first created, it relies on the reports of the selected individuals. Once a book has been saved, though, you can add additional reports about other people, giving you a lot of flexibility in your book and its layout.

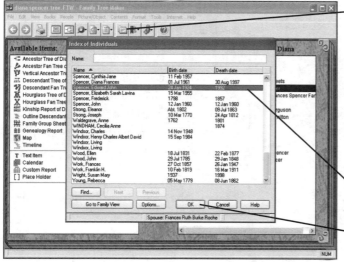

1. Click the **Index of Individuals** button. The Index of Individuals dialog box will open.

> **TIP**
>
> You can also press the F2 key to open the Index of Individuals dialog box.

2. Click the name of the desired individual.

3. Click **OK**. The Index of Individuals dialog box will close, and the **Available items** section in the Books view will reflect the change in individual.

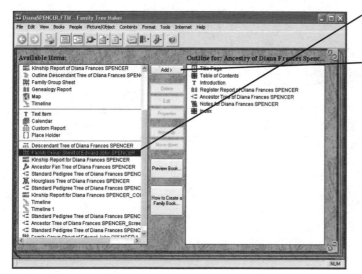

4. Click the appropriate item in the **Available items** list.

5. Click **Add>**. The selected item will be added to the bottom of the Outline list, just above the Index item.

> **TIP**
>
> If you click on the selected item in the **Outline** list, you can use the various buttons to reposition the item, edit it, or change its properties. It is now part of the book unless you decide to delete the item.

> **NOTE**
>
> Notice that while you changed the focus of the individual in the Available items list, your saved reports are still available.

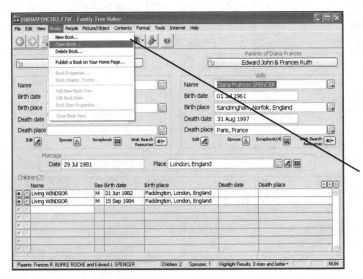

Adding Notes to Books

If you have spent time adding notes about the individuals in your Family File, there will be times when you will want to include the notes in your book, especially when sharing with family members.

1. Click **Open Book** from the **Books** menu. The Open Book dialog box will open.

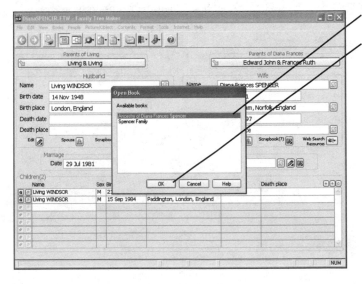

2. Click the appropriate book.

3. Click **OK**. The Open Book dialog box will close, and the Book window will open.

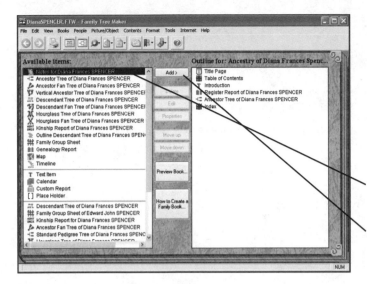

The Notes item will only appear in the Available items list if the individual selected has notes. If this is not the individual you want, you can access the Index of Individuals using the F2 key.

4. Click **Notes for** in the **Available items** list.

5. Click **Add>**. A message box will open.

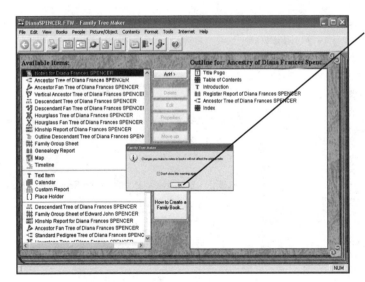

6. Click **OK**. The message box will close, and the Notes item will be added to the Outline list to be included in the book.

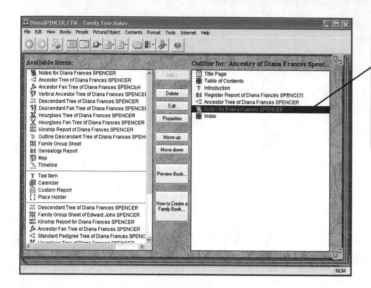

NOTE

Once in the Outline list, the notes can be edited as appropriate for the book. Remember, any changes made at this stage will not affect your notes in your Edit Individual dialog box or Edit Marriage dialog box.

Finalizing and Sharing Your Book

There are several ways to share your book with others. You can print copies to distribute, share the book on a CD-ROM, or even send it via e-mail.

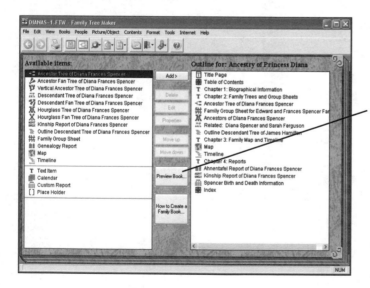

Previewing Your Book

You can preview the final version of your book before printing or sending the book to others.

1. Click **Preview Book**. A Saving dialog box will open, and a blue bar indicates that Family Tree Maker is saving your book for preview. Next, a Family Tree Maker dialog box will open, that says "Processing" across the top. Other Family Tree Maker dialog boxes will open and close as Family Tree Maker prepares the document for previewing. The Family Tree Maker book will open in Adobe Reader as a PDF file.

NOTE

You will need to install Adobe® Reader® to see the preview of the book. Go to <www.adobe.com> for a free download.

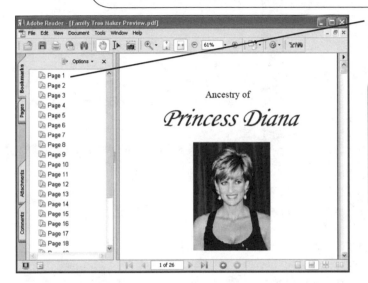

2. Click on each link in the Bookmarks pane to move from page to page.

NOTE

The PDF may open on your computer but remain minimized. If you see a new label at the bottom of your screen, typically which reads "Adobe Reader" click on it to bring up the PDF file.

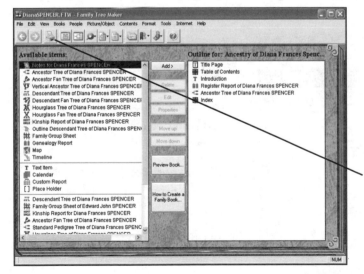

Printing Your Book

You can print your book from the Book page of Family Tree Maker or by pressing the print button in the PDF file you are previewing.

To print from the Book page of Family Tree Maker:

1. Click the **Print** button. The Print Book dialog box will open.

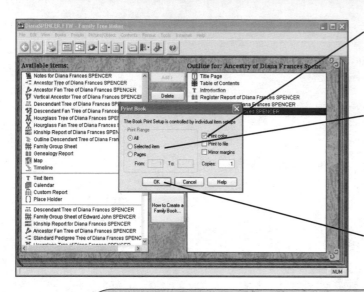

2. Click the **Print color** check box if you want to print in color. If you are printing in black and white, you can deselect the box.

3. Click the **All** radio button if you want to print the entire book; click **Selected Item** to print only the item you have clicked on; or click **Pages** and enter the page numbers of the book that you want to print.

4. Click **OK**. The book will print.

NOTE

You can print more than one copy of a book at a time. Change copies from "1" to the number of copies of the book you would like to print. You may prefer to print just one copy of the book and then photocopy the rest to save time and wear on your printer.

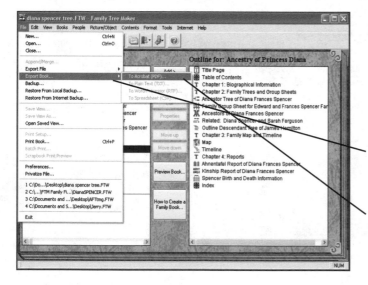

Exporting to PDF

After previewing your book you can save it to your computer for future reference or to send via e-mail. You can also export your book as a PDF directly without previewing it:

1. Click **Export Book** from the **File** menu. The Export book sub-menu will appear.

2. Click **To Acrobat (PDF)**. The Export Books dialog box will open.

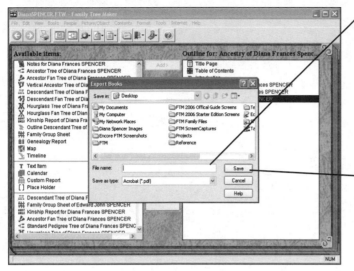

3. Enter the name that you would like to use for this saved file.

NOTE

Make sure you note where you have chosen to save your PDF so you can find it later on.

4. Click **Save**. The book will be saved.

14

Creating Your Personal Family Tree Maker Home Page

While publishing a family history is still traditionally done by putting your research on paper, the Internet provides a new way for people to publish their family histories. When publishing to paper, people tend to delay publishing until everything is "perfect." The Internet saves people from this need to delay, as they can always upload a revised version of their pages. In this chapter, you'll learn how to:

- Create your first home page

- Enhance your home page

- Add charts, reports, and books to your home page

- Add photographs to your home page

- Remove items from your home page

Creating Your First Home Page

Family Tree Maker makes it easy for you to create your own home page on the Internet. Your Family Home page will include your own personal touches, a list of all surnames and photos, an index of everyone you choose to include, up to five reports or charts, and an interactive pedigree tree. You will be able to view and share your Family Home Page on Genealogy.com. To create, edit, and view your Family Home Page use the Internet menu tools in Family Tree Maker.

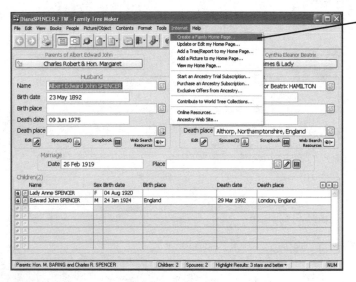

1. Click **Create a Family Home Page** from the **Internet** menu. The Family Home Page dialog box will open.

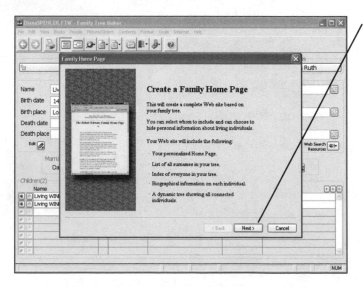

2. Read the summary about Family Home Pages, then click **Next**. The Individuals to Include page will appear.

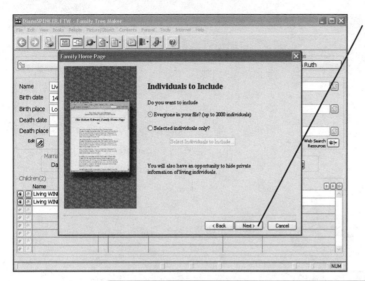

3. Click **Next** to include everyone in a specific Family File in your Family Home Page. The Pictures page will appear.

NOTE

If you want to select specific individuals to include in your Family Home Page, choose **Selected individuals only?** The **Select Individuals to Include** button will be activated, and you can click the button to open the Individuals to Include dialog box, which you learned about in earlier chapters, including Chapter 10. If you are concerned about publishing names of living individuals, you do not have to hand select individuals. Family Tree Maker gives the option to hide living individuals' information before publishing.

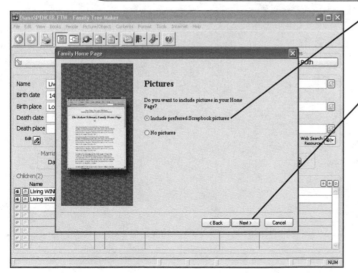

4. Click the **Include preferred Scrapbook pictures** radio button if you have images you want to share on your Family Home Page.

5. Click **Next**. The Hide Info on Living Individuals page will appear.

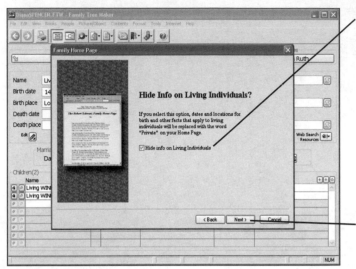

6. Click the **Hide info on Living Individuals** check box.

7. Click **Next**. The Make a Connection page will appear.

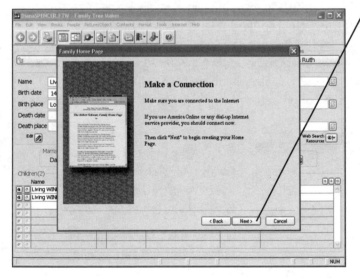

8. Log onto the Internet if you are not already connected, then click **Next**. The Terms of Service dialog box will open.

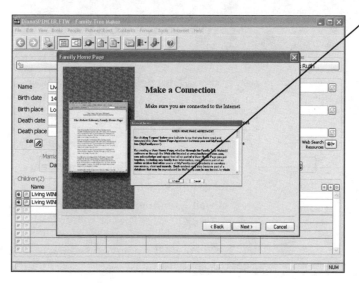

9. Read the Terms of Service and click **I Agree**. The dialog box will open and tell you that your home page is building. When the Family Home Page is done building, a dialog box informs you that your information has been uploaded.

10. Click **OK** to close the message.

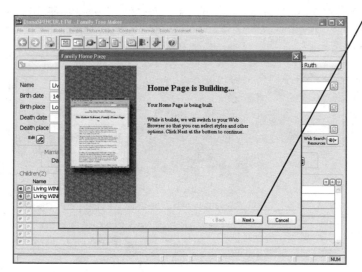

11. Click **Next**. Your Web browser will open to your new home page location, which reads "Create Your Own Home Page."

NOTE

If you have never visited Genealogy.com, or if you have deleted your cookies, you will see a registration page before you see your new home page. You will be prompted through the registration process.

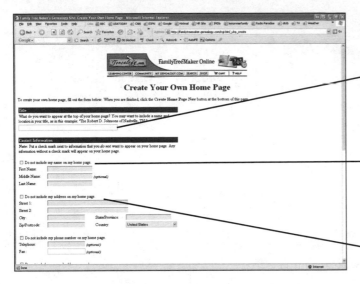

Enhancing Your Home Page

1. In the **Title** field of the Create Your Own Home Page Web page, enter the name you want to appear at the top of your home page.

2. Click the **Do not include my name on my home page** check box if you do not want your name included on the Web page.

3. Complete the name and contact information as necessary.

> **NOTE**
>
> This Web page will be longer than your computer screen. You may want to use the scroll bar to the right to move up and down the page. The screen shots depicted here do not show the full length of the Web page.

4. Describe your website in the text box.

> **TIP**
>
> You are more likely to have visitors that you can learn from and who will learn from you if you provide a clear description of your research, what your purpose is, and introduce visitors to your site.

5. Click a **Style** radio button to choose a style for your Web page.

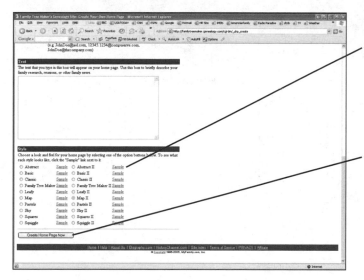

TIP

Click on the Sample link next to each style for an example of how it will look. Then, use the Back button on your browser to return to making your selection.

6. Click **Create Home Page Now**. The page will be created and shown in your browser.

Adding Charts, Reports, and Books to Your Home Page

After you upload your family tree, you can continually enhance it by adding additional reports or even a book. You can update your tree at any time.

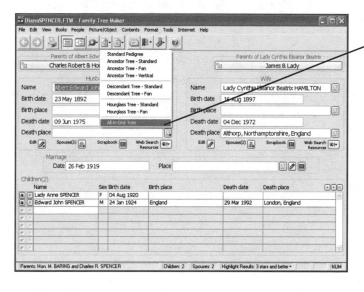

Adding Charts and Reports

1. Click the **Tree Charts** or **Reports** button, then click the tree or report that you want to appear on your home page. The tree or report will appear.

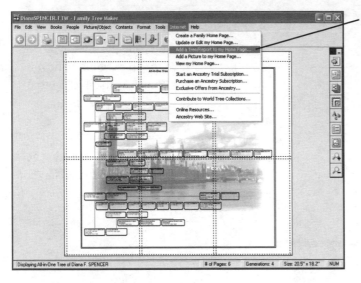

2. Click **Add a Tree/Report to my Home Page** from the **Internet** menu. The Add a Tree or Report to your Home Page dialog box will open.

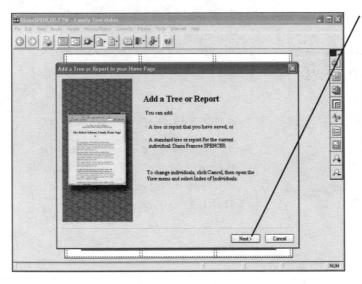

3. Click **Next**. The Add a Tree or Report page will open.

NOTE

Family Tree Maker should already select the tree that is open. If you still want to publish that tree, you only need to check to make sure that it is selected. Or use the scroll bar to move up and down the menu, then click on the new tree you would like to publish.

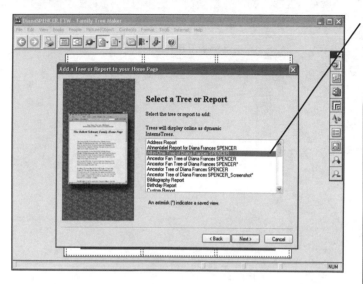

4. Click the tree or report you would like to publish and click **Next**. The Select type of Tree Upload page will open.

NOTE

Since you can post only one InterneTree to your home page, you may want to choose the All-in-One Tree because it is the most comprehensive selection. The interactive InterneTree lets visitors move through the generations in a tree by using an index of names. Visitors can view name, birth date, and death date information.

TIP

The InterneTree can hold up to 2,000 individuals. This is important to remember if you have chosen to upload a report that includes all the individuals in your database.

You may need to click the Refresh button in your Internet browser to see the InterneTree in the list of reports on your home page.

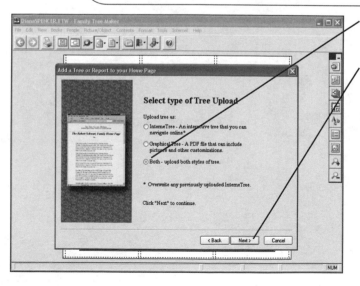

5. Click the type of tree you want to upload.

6. Click **Next**. The Info on Living Individuals page will open. If you want to hide information about living individuals, make sure you have privatized your file.

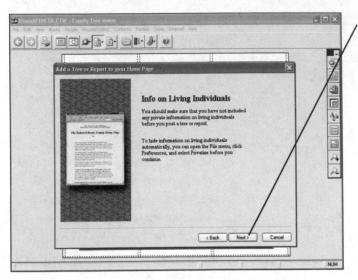

7. Click **Next**. The Make a Connection page will open.

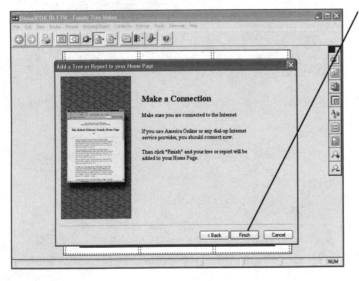

8. Make sure you are connected to the Internet, then click **Finish**. Family Tree Maker will open a dialog box to let you know your chart or report has successfully uploaded and will be linked to your home page and available within fifteen minutes.

TIP

As you learned earlier in this chapter, you can view changes to your home page. Click **View my Home Page** from the **Internet** menu.

Adding a Book

You can add your family book to your home page. If you update your book, you can simply upload a new version of the book to your home page.

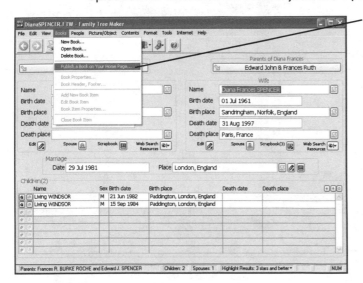

1. Click **Publish a Book on Your Home Page** from the **Books** menu. The Select Book to Upload dialog box will open.

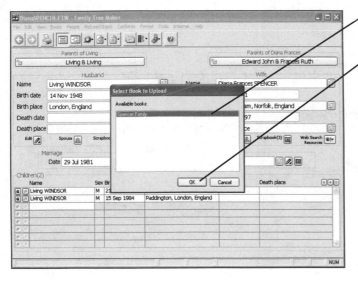

2. Click the book you want from the **Available books** list.

3. Click **OK**. The Select Book Format dialog box will open in front of the Book window.

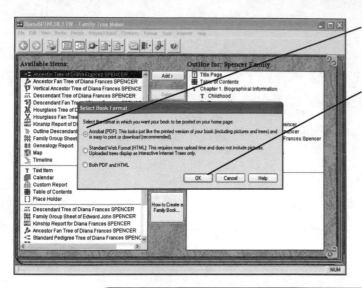

4. Click the radio button that corresponds to the type of book format you want.

5. Click **OK**. A Book Upload dialog box will open.

NOTE

You may see a few different dialog boxes with short instructions or questions. If you have left required items out of your book, Family Tree Maker will ask you if it is okay to add the mandatory items. Click **Yes** or **OK**. In addition, you may be asked if you want to contribute to the World Tree Collections project. This is a set of user-submitted family tree collections compiled by MyFamily.com, Inc., for researchers interested in sharing their information.

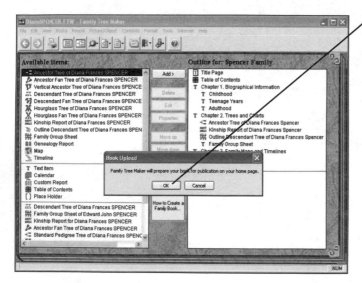

6. Click **OK**. The Saving to disk dialog box will open as Family Tree Maker prepares to save the book to the Internet. Then, a dialog box will open to tell you when you have successfully posted to the Web.

NOTE

You can have only one book uploaded to your home page at a time. If you upload a new book, it will replace the existing book.

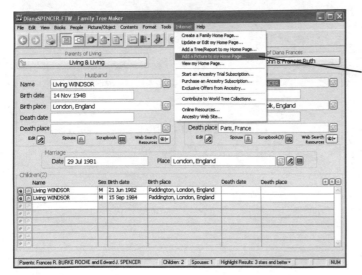

Adding Photographs to Your Home Page

1. Click **Add a Picture to my Home Page** from the **Internet** menu. The Individuals with Scrapbook Pictures dialog box will open.

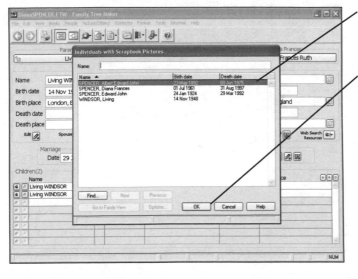

2. Click an individual from the Individuals with Scrapbook Pictures dialog box.

3. Click **OK**. The dialog box will close, and the Insert Scrapbook Picture dialog box will open.

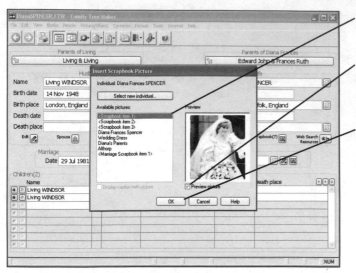

4. Click a picture from the **Available pictures** list.

5. Click the **Preview Picture** check box if a preview picture is not showing. A picture will appear.

6. Click **OK**. The Title and Description dialog box will open.

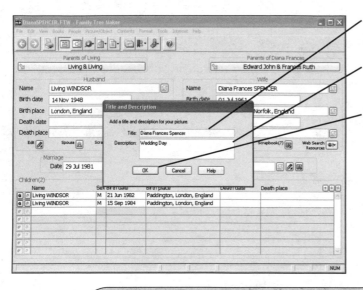

7. Enter a title for the picture in the **Title** field.

8. Enter a description in the **Description** field.

9. Click **OK**. A message indicates whether you have successfully posted to your home page. Click **OK** again.

NOTE

You can upload any photos on your computer to your home page, even if the photo is not in your scrapbook, by uploading directly from the Web page.

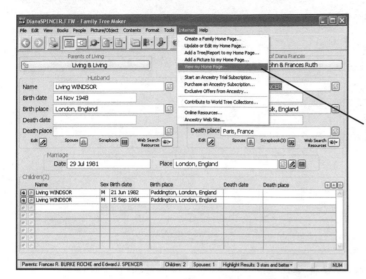

Removing Items from Your Home Page

You can remove items from your home page if you no longer want them online.

1. Click **View my Home Page** from the **Internet** menu. Your Internet home page will open.

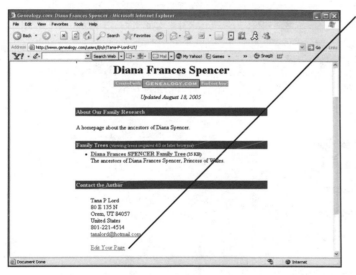

2. Click the **Edit Your Page** link. The Author Options page will open in your browser.

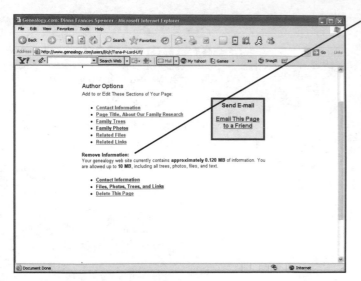

3. Scroll to the **Remove Information** section at the bottom of the edit page and click the link for the information you want to remove. The Removing Files, Photos, Trees & Links page will appear.

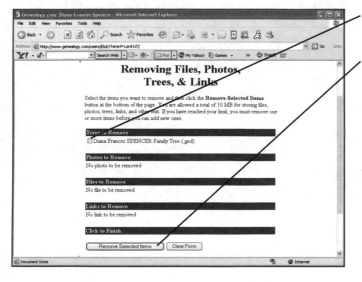

4. Click the check box next to the item you want to remove.

5. Click **Removed Selected Items**. The item(s) will be removed.

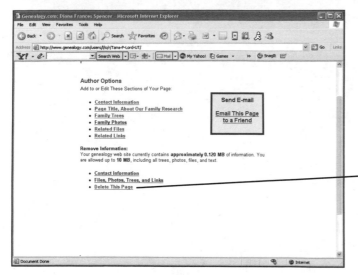

Deleting Your Home Page

If you would prefer to delete your entire home page, you may do so. You can always re-create your home page at a later date.

1. Follow steps 1–3 in "Removing Items from Your Home Page."

2. Scroll to the **Remove Information** section at the bottom of the page and click the **Delete This Page** link. A message asks you to confirm the deletion.

3. Click the **Yes, Delete My Home Page** link. Your home page will be deleted. All reports and trees you have created will no longer be online.

15

Working with Other Family Files

At some point, you may receive a file from another researcher, or you may want to share your research with others. Sharing is usually done through the GEDCOM (GEnealogical Data COMmunications) computer file format. There will also be times when you will want to keep some of your research in a separate Family File or compare two files. In this chapter, you'll learn how to:

- Export all or part of your Family File

- Work with older versions

- Import a GEDCOM file to an existing Family File

- Import a file from Ancestry Family Tree

- Open two Family Files to compare

- Merge Two Family Files

- Back up your Family Files

You may want to share a Family File with another researcher, or import or merge another individual's Family File with your own file. Family Tree Makr allows for many file merging and sharing scenarios.

Exporting All or Part of Your Family File

GEDCOM is the standard file format used to transfer data between different genealogy software packages. When you share your file with others, you will likely use the GEDCOM format. To save a copy of your file as a GEDCOM, first make sure Family View is displayed.

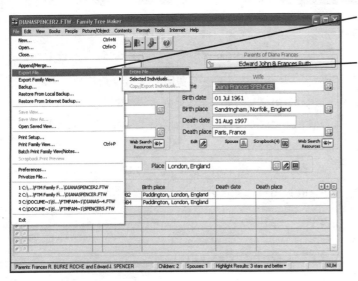

1. Click **Export File** from the **File** menu. A sub-menu will appear.

2. Click **Entire File**. The New Family File dialog box will open.

NOTE

While Family Tree Maker lets you add digitized images, sounds, and objects, these items will not be included in the GEDCOM file.

NOTE

If you want to select specific individuals to include in the file, click **Selected Individuals** from the **Export File** sub-menu. The Individuals to Include dialog box will open. As in previous chapters, select individuals to include by using the **right angle bracket (>)** button to move them into the "Included individuals" list. Then click **OK**.

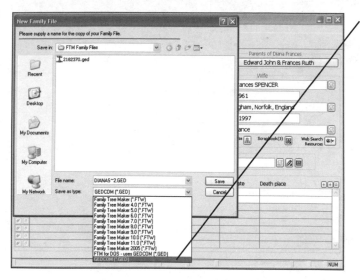

3. Click the **Save as type** drop-down list and click **GEDCOM (*.GED).**

NOTE

Family Tree Maker automatically names the GEDCOM file with the same name as the Family File. If you want to use a different name, you can change it in the **File name** field. Make sure the file extension ends in GED, for example, "SmithFamily. GED".

TIP

Make note of where the file is saved, so you can find it later.

4. Click **Save**. The Export to GEDCOM dialog box will open.

NOTE

The default settings for exporting your GEDCOM file are usually correct. However, if you are a Latter-day Saint creating a file for TempleReady, you will want to use the Destination drop-down list to choose TempleReady.

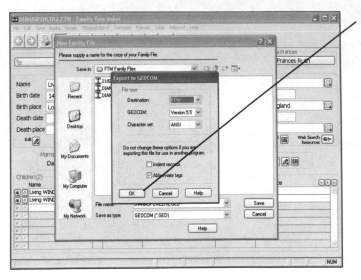

5. Click **OK** to save the file and close the dialog box.

Working with Older Versions of Family Tree Maker Family Files

You cannot open Family Tree Maker 2006 files in older versions of Family Tree Maker. However, you can save a copy of your Family Tree Maker 2006 file that is compatible with an older version of Family Tree Maker if you want to share your file with someone who does not have the latest version.

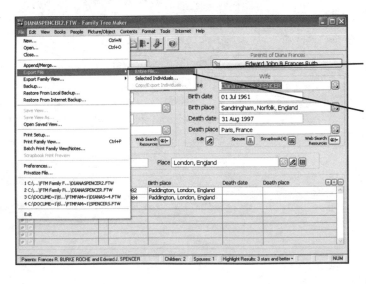

1. Open the Family File you want to share.

2. Click **Export File** from the **File** menu. A sub-menu will appear.

3. Click **Entire File**. The New Family File dialog box will open.

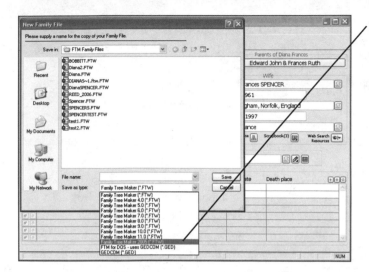

4. Click the **Save as type** drop-down list and click the desired version of Family Tree Maker.

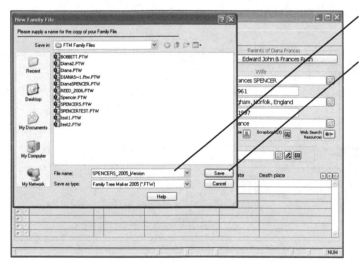

5. Enter a name for the file in the **File name** field.

6. Click **Save**. The new version will be saved to the designated file. You can then save this version to a disk or e-mail it can be opened in an older version of Family Tree Maker.

NOTE

Once you save a file as an older version of FTM, do not open the new file in FTM 2006, or it will be re-saved as an FTM 2006 file.

Importing a GEDCOM File to an Existing Family File

You can import a GEDCOM file directly into your Family File.

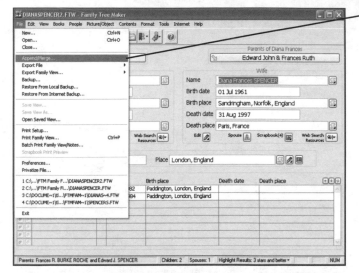

1. Click **Append/Merge** from the **File** menu. A message asks if you want to create a backup. It is a good idea to back up your file on a regular basis, and especially before any major alteration. Click **Yes** to back up, or click **No** to skip to the next step. The dialog box will close, and the Select File to Merge or Append dialog box will open.

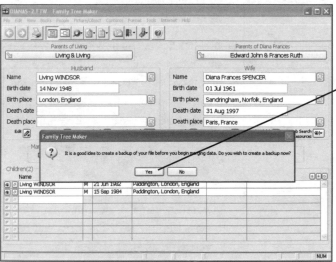

NOTE

To create a backup, click **Yes**. Choose where you would like to save your Family File, then click **Backup**. Family Tree Maker will back up your file and alert you that the backup was successful. Click **OK** when the dialog box opens. Then, click **Yes** to return to the merge process.

TIP

Save a new GEDCOM as a separate Family File first. This lets you evaluate the data before it is included in your own Family File. Once you have determined its accuracy, you can then follow the steps described here to add this file to your personal Family File.

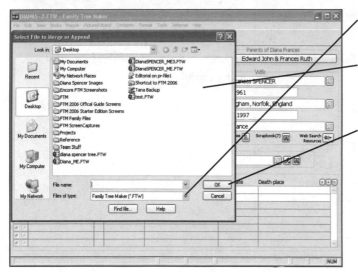

2. Click the **Files of type** drop-down list and click **GEDCOM (*.GED)**.

3. Click the GEDCOM file you'd like to merge or append. The file name will appear in the File name field.

4. Click **OK**. The Import from GEDCOM dialog box will open.

> ### TIP
>
> If you cannot find the GEDCOM file in the list of names, you may be looking in the wrong location. Click the **Look in** drop-down list to find the location where you may have saved the item.

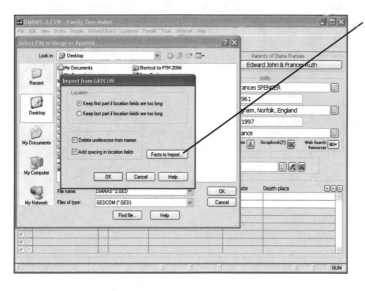

5. Click **Facts to Import**. The Facts to Import dialog box will open.

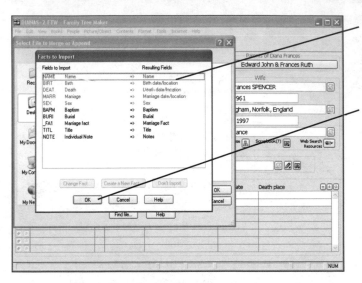

6. Scan through the list and make sure you agree with where Family Tree Maker wants to put some of the facts that will be imported.

7. Click **OK**. The Facts to Import dialog box will close.

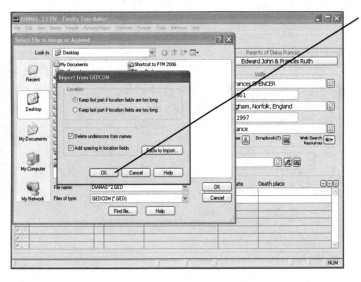

8. Click **OK**. The Import from GEDCOM dialog box will close, the GEDCOM file will be appended to the Family File, and a message box will open stating that your merge was successful.

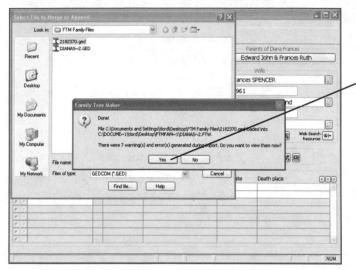

NOTE

If there were errors in the import process, a message asks if you want to view them. Click **Yes** to view the errors; click **No** to continue the import process and open the Individuals to Include dialog box.

9. Click **OK**. The message closes, and the Individuals to Include dialog box will open.

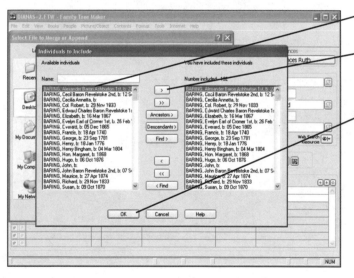

10. Click the individual that you want to add from the **Available individuals** list, then click the **right angle bracket** (>) button to move the individual to the Included Individuals list.

11. Click **OK**. The Append File dialog box will open.

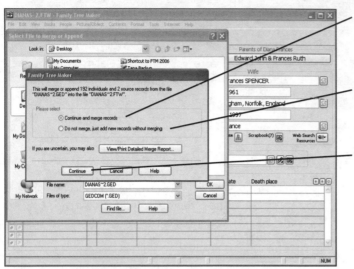

12a. Click the **Continue and merge records** radio button.

Or

12b. Click the **Do not merge, just add new records without merging** radio button.

13. Click **Continue**. The Likely Matches dialog box or Force Merge dialog box will open depending on which option you chose.

TIP

If you need a refresher on how to check the Family File for duplicate individuals, see Chapter 4, "Editing Your Family File."

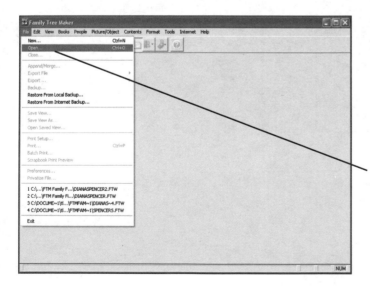

Opening a GEDCOM File as a New Family File

You can use a GEDCOM file to create a new Family File.

1. Click **Close** from the **File** menu to close the currently opened Family File.

2. Click **Open** from the **File** menu. The Open Family File dialog box will open.

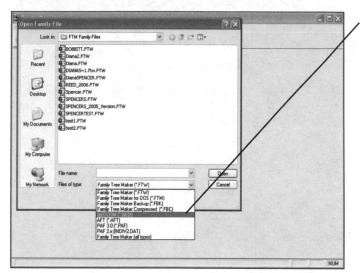

3. Click the **Files of type** drop-down list and click **GEDCOM (*.GED)**.

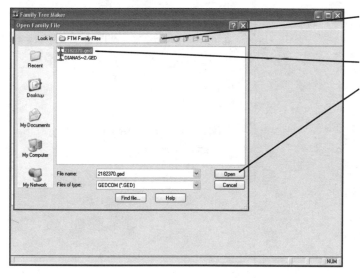

4. Click the **Look in** drop-down list and open the folder where the GEDCOM is located.

5. Click the appropriate GEDCOM file.

6. Click **Open**. The Import File dialog box will open.

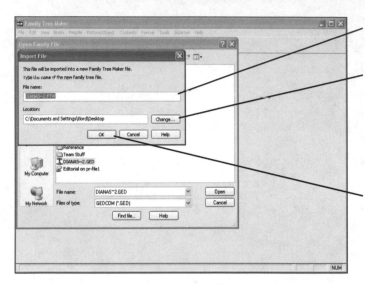

7. Enter a new name for the GEDCOM file in the **File name** field.

8. If you want Family Tree Maker to save the file to the default location (in a folder called FTM which is in your My Documents folder), continue with step 9. If you want to change the location, click **Change** and choose a new location.

9. Click **OK**. The Import from GEDCOM dialog box will open.

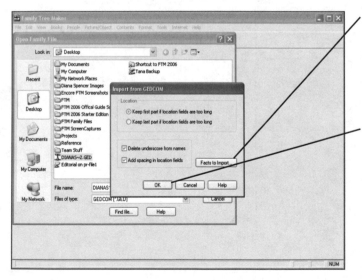

10a. Click **Facts to Import**. The Facts to Import dialog box will open. Make any necessary changes and click **OK** to return to the new Family File.

Or

10b. Click **OK**. A message tells you the import is complete.

Importing a File from Ancestry Family Tree

If you created a Family File in Ancestry Family Tree, you can import the file into Family Tree Maker. Make sure you know where your AFT file is saved on your computer before proceeding with these steps in Family Tree Maker.

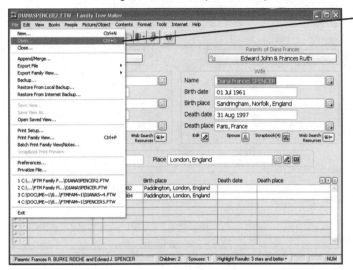

1. Click **Open** from the **File** menu. The Open Family File dialog box will open.

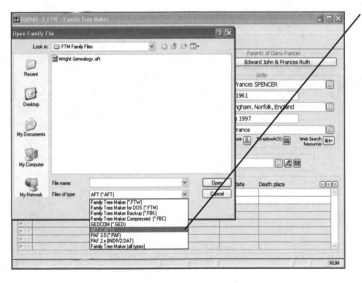

2. Click the **Files of type** drop-down list and click **AFT (*.AFT)**. All files you have saved as an Ancestry Family Tree in that folder will appear.

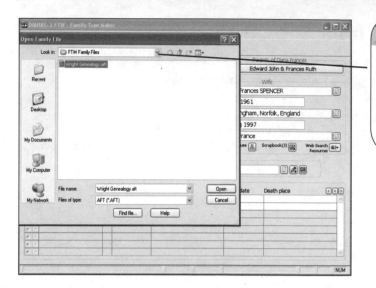

NOTE

If the AFT file you want is not in the folder, you will need to select the correct folder by clicking the **Look in** drop-down list, then clicking the appropriate folder.

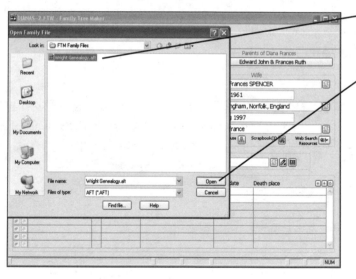

3. Click the AFT file you want to open. The name will appear in the File name field.

4. Click **Open**. The Import File dialog box will open, with the same file in the File name field, except the extension has changed from .AFT to .FTW.

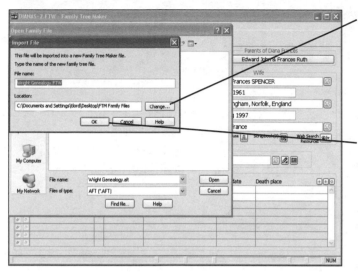

5. If you want Family Tree Maker to save the file to the default location (which is in your My Documents folder, in a folder called FTM), skip to step 6. If you want to change the location, click **Change** and choose a new location.

6. Click **OK**. A message tells you if you have successfully saved your Ancestry Family Tree file as a Family Tree Maker file.

7. Click **OK**. The dialog boxes will close, and your new Family File will open in Family Tree Maker.

NOTE

If there were errors in the import process, a message asks if you want to view them. Click **Yes** to view the error report; click **No** open the new Family File.

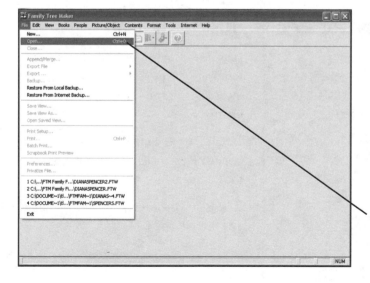

Opening Two Family Files to Compare

You may have more than one Family File. Perhaps your second file is for individuals with the same surname only or for individuals with whom you do not yet understand the connection. You can have these files open at the same time for easy comparison.

1. Click **Open** from the **File** menu. The Open Family File dialog box will open.

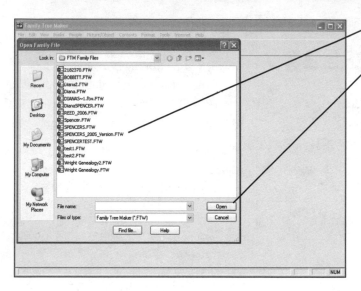

2. Click the **Family File** you want to open.

3. Click **Open**. The Family File will open.

4. Follow steps 1–3 again, but with a different Family File that you want to open. A second Family Tree Maker window will open with the new Family File.

TIP

When you have two Family Files open, you can copy and paste between the two of them. For more information on how to copy and paste, see Chapter 3.

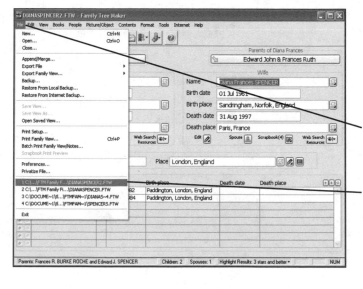

Using File History

Family Tree Maker remembers the last four Family Files you have opened, including the one you currently have open.

1. Click the **File** menu. The recently opened files are listed at the bottom of the File menu.

2. Click on the Family File you want. The file will open.

Merging Two Family Files

Rather than simply comparing two Family Files, you can always merge the Family Files. Make sure you have one of the two Family Files open and that you are in the Family View.

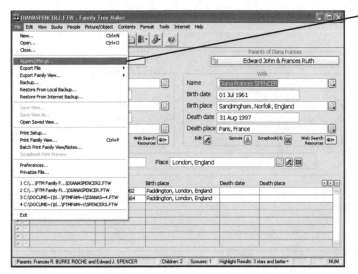

1. Click **Append/Merge** from the **File** menu. A message asks if you want to create a backup. It is a good idea to back up your file on a regular basis, especially before any major alteration. Click **Yes** to back up or click **No** to skip to the next step. The dialog box will close, and the Select File to Merge or Append dialog box will open.

NOTE

To create a backup, click **Yes**. Choose where you would like to save your Family File, then click **Backup**. Family Tree Maker will back up your file and alert you that the backup was successful. Click **OK** when the dialog box opens. Then, click **Yes** to return to the merge process.

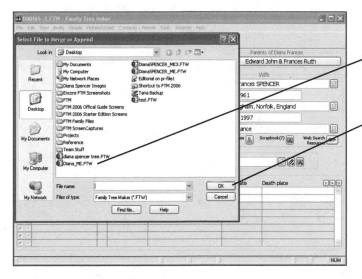

2. Click the file you'd like to merge. The file name will appear in the File name field.

3. Click **OK**. The Individuals to Include dialog box will open.

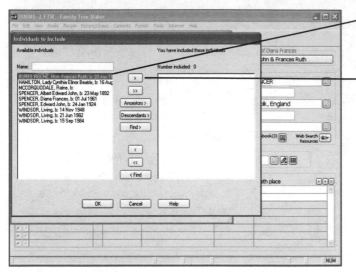

4. From the **Available individuals** list, click the individual that you want to move to the open Family File , then click the **right angle bracket** (>) button to move the individual to the Included Individuals list.

> **NOTE**
>
> You can find more detailed information on how to use this dialog box in Chapter 5.

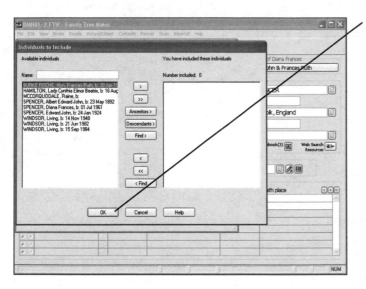

5. Click **OK** when you have finished choosing which individuals to merge into your Family File.

6. Click **OK** again if you see a dialog box noting that no additional source information was found. This occurs when Family Tree Maker has found no matching individuals or source information. Family Tree Maker will simply add the individuals, instead of merging them, if this occurs.

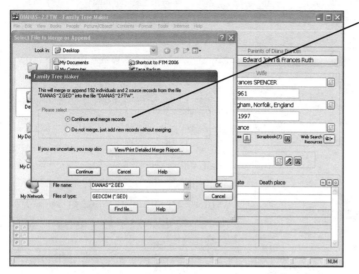

7. Click a radio button to select if you want to merge records or add new records without merging additional information. Depending on the data, Family Tree Maker may not allow you to perform one of the options.

NOTE

You can click **View/Print Detailed Merge Report** to view the information Family Tree Maker found regarding the merge and what actions Family Tree Maker will take.

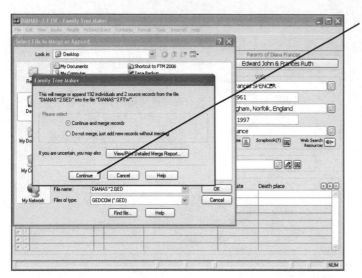

8. Click **Continue**. The Likely Matches dialog box will open and show you a list of likely matches between the two files.

NOTE

If Family Tree Maker finds sources in both files that appear to be the same, the Merge Sources dialog box will open. If the fields have different information, it will ask you to choose which to keep. Sources that are identical will automatically be merged and new sources will automatically be added.

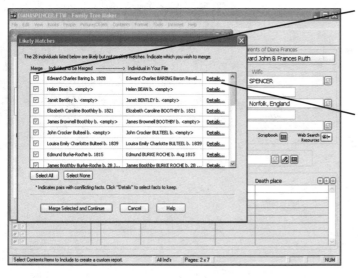

9. Click to check or uncheck the boxes. If you remove a check mark from a check box in the left column, you will prevent the merge of the two individuals.

10. Click the details column to see more information about the individuals to help you make your decision, or skip to step 12.

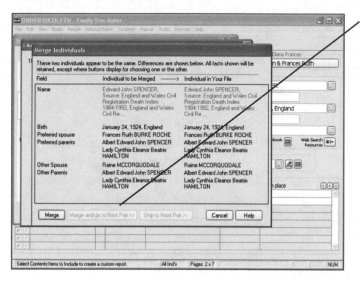

11. Click one of the following buttons according to what action you want to perform for the first pair of individuals:

a. Merge—This will merge the two individuals and close the dialog box.

b. Merge and go to the Next Pair— This will merge the individuals but keep the details database open to see the details for the next set of individuals.

C. Skip to the Next Pair—This will prevent the merge of these two and move on to the details of the next pair.

d. Cancel—This will close the dialog box and return the information to the list with the check boxes.

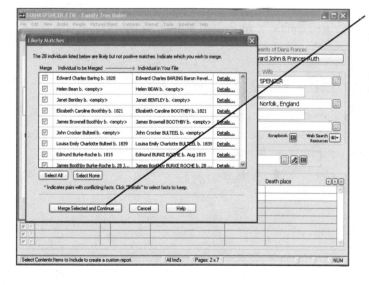

12. Click **Merge Selected and Continue** when you have finished making your selections. Your merge will be completed and the dialog box will close.

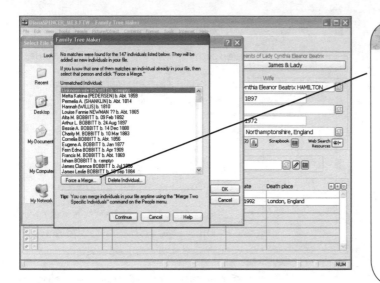

NOTE

You can undo the file merge immediately after the merge if you think you made a mistake. If you make any other changes to your file, you cannot undo the merge. To undo the merge immediately, click **Undo** from the **Edit** menu.

Backing Up Your Family Files

Your Family File is important: not only does it contain your family's history, it also represents hours of your labor. Family Tree Maker automatically saves your information while you are working. Unfortunately, all computer files are vulnerable and can become corrupted or accidentally destroyed. Family Tree Maker can better preserve your family history if you regularly make backups of your files.

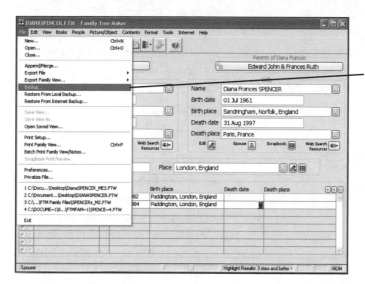

1. Open the Family File for which you want to create a backup.

2. Click **Backup** from the **File** menu. The Backup Family File dialog box will open.

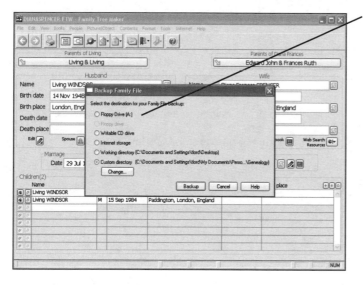

3. Click one of the following backup methods:

a. Floppy Drive—Saves your file to a floppy diskette.

If you are backing up a large file, Family Tree Maker will ask you to insert new diskettes as needed. When the backup requires multiple diskettes, be sure to label them in the order in which they are used.

b. Writable CD drive—Saves your file to a CD-ROM.

The first time you back up your file to a CD-ROM, you may get a message asking you to install a driver—this message will appear only once.

CAUTION

If you name the backup file the same name as a file that is already on the CD, the backup will write over the original file.

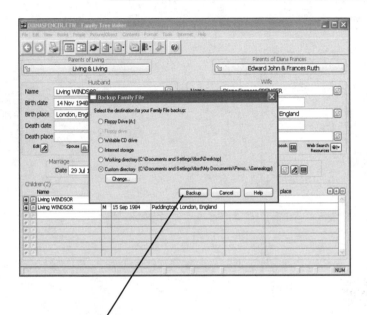

c. Internet storage—Saves your file to a MyFamily.com, Inc., website.

To use this feature, you must be a registered user of Family Tree Maker and have an Internet connection. Family Tree Maker includes three months of free Internet backups. Beyond this period, a subscription to this service is available for a small fee.

d. Working directory—Saves your file to the directory where your current Family File is saved on your hard drive.

e. Custom directory—Saves your file to a directory that you choose. Click **Change** to choose a new location.

4. Click **Backup**. A message tells you when the file has been backed up successfully.

PART
VI

Working with Preferences and Tools

16

Setting Family Tree Maker Preferences

Family Tree Maker is a powerful program that offers many features and options. To help you get the most out of the software, Family Tree Maker lets you define your preferences for many of the windows and more common activities. In this chapter, you'll learn how to change:

- General preferences
- Editing preferences
- Date preferences
- Label, titles, and LDS preferences
- Image preferences
- Reference number preferences

Family Tree Maker has many standard settings that let you change the way dates are displayed, automatically save your Family File for you as you work, and check for name errors when you enter data. You can change these default settings and many others in the Preferences dialog box.

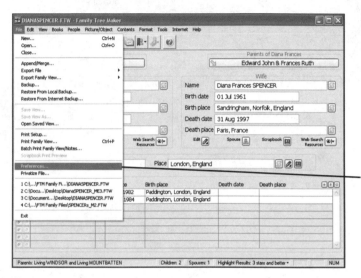

Opening the Preferences Dialog Box

The Preferences dialog box features six tabs that let you change the preference settings by category: General; Editing; Dates; Labels,Titles,LDS; Images; and Reference Numbers.

1. Click **Preferences** from the **File** menu. The Preferences dialog box will open.

2. Click a tab to view the associated preferences.

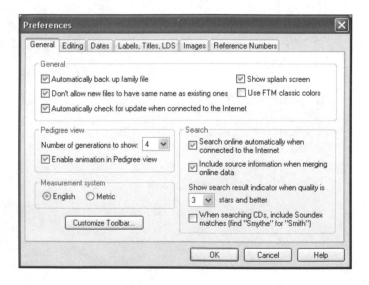

General Tab

When you open the Preferences dialog box, the dialog box opens the General tab by default (if it does not, click the **General** tab). Click the check boxes to select or deselect any of the desired options. Family Tree Maker will ignore items that are not selected. Click OK at the bottom of the Preferences dialog box to save your changes. The features of the General tab will be covered by section (General, Pedigree View, Measurement System, and Search).

General Section

• **Automatically back up Family File**—Click this check box if you want Family Tree Maker to automatically back up your Family Files. Family Tree Maker automatically saves a copy of your Family File when you exit the program. The backup file has the same name as the original file, but with the extension ".FBK". You can use this backup file if your original file is ever lost or damaged. However, since the backup file takes up space on your computer's hard drive, you may want to deselect this option if your computer's hard drive space is limited.

• **Don't allow new files to have same name as existing ones**—Click this check box if you don't want to have multiple files with the same name. This prevents you from accidentally working in the wrong file.

TIP

It is a good idea to leave both of these options turned on (by leaving the check mark in the check box). This not only creates a backup of your file when exiting the program, but prevents you from overwriting an existing Family File when creating a new Family File.

• **Automatically check for update when connected to the Internet**—Click this check box if you want Family Tree Maker to look automatically for updates to Family Tree Maker 2006 and alert you if an update exists.

• **Show splash screen**—Click this check box if you want the splash screen to appear each time you open Family Tree Maker.

• **Use FTM classic colors**—Click this check box if you want to use the classic yellow background used in previous versions of Family Tree Maker. Family Tree Maker 2006 colors are now based on the program colors of your Windows operating system. Selecting this option will also cause the program background color to change to green if you privatize the file or if you make the file a read-only.

Pedigree View Section

• **Number of generations to show**—Click the drop-down list to select the default number of generations that appear in Pedigree View. You can also change the number of generations when you're in the Pedigree View.

• **Enable animation in Pedigree View**—Click this check box to use animation in the Pedigree View. The Pedigree View animation shows names shifting up or down a tree when you select a new primary individual or visit an ancestor or descendant not on the current display. The purpose of this animation is to help you visualize where ancestors are shifted along the tree as you work.

Measurement System Section

• **English**—Click this radio button if you want to use feet, inches, pounds, and ounces.

• **Metric**—Click this radio button if you want to use meters, centimeters, grams, and kilograms.

> **NOTE**
>
> The measurement system setting applies only to the Family File you have open and will not carry over into other files. This setting is used for height and weight on the Medical tab of the Edit Individual dialog box.

Search Section

• **Search online automatically when connected to the Internet**—Click this check box if you want Family Tree Maker to automatically search Ancestry.com for more information on the individuals in your file (when your Internet connection is enabled). The program will conduct a search on each person—as they come into view through Family View, Pedigree View, or the Web Search report—and alert you when matches meet your criteria (see Show search result indicator below). If you deselect this feature, you can still view Web Search results by navigating to an individual's Web Search report, as long as you have Internet connectivity. (You must have an Ancestry.com subscription to view this information.)

• **Include source information when merging online data**—Click this check box to include source information when you use Web Merge.

• **Show search result indicator**—Click the drop-down list to choose when Family Tree Maker will indicate that a Web Search result meets your criteria. Family Tree Maker categorizes the search results with a "star" ranking system. Five-Star Matches are virtually certain to contain information about someone in your Family File. The higher the number of stars, the more likely the match will be relevant, but setting too high of a threshold may also cause you to miss relevant information. If a Web Search result matches the quality level you set, the Web Search icon will change to include a gold star in both the Family and Pedigree Views.

• **When searching CDs, include Soundex matches**—Click this check box so that Family Tree Maker searches for Soundex results, which help you find matches where the name could be the same but the spelling is different. Spelling differences could arise from translation errors, for example, spelling "Smith" as "Smythe."

NOTE

These settings apply only to the Family File you have open and will not carry over into other files.

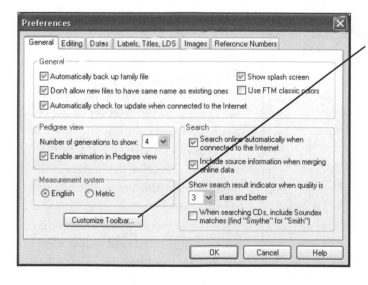

Customizing the Toolbar

1. On the **General** tab, click **Customize Toolbar.** The Customize Toolbar dialog box will open.

The default toolbar buttons are listed under "Current toolbar buttons." You can add additional buttons to the toolbar (from "Available toolbar buttons"), change the order of the buttons, and add separators to show spaces between buttons.

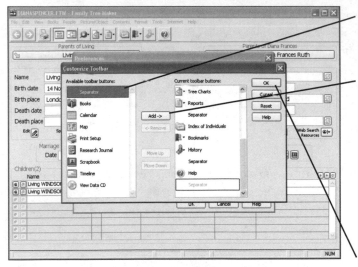

2. Click the item you would like to add to the toolbar from the **Available toolbar buttons** list.

3. Click **Add->**. The item will be moved to the Current toolbar buttons list.

4. Click the item you want to remove from the toolbar from the **Current toolbar buttons** list.

5. Click **<-Remove**. The item will be moved to the Available toolbar buttons list.

6. Click **OK** to save your changes.

NOTE

You can click the **Reset** button if you want to return the toolbar to its default setting.

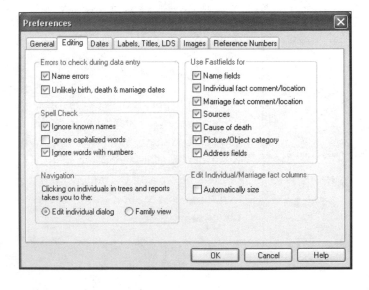

Editing Tab

You can click the Editing tab in the Preferences dialog box to view and change your editing preferences. Click the check boxes to select or deselect any of the desired options. Family Tree Maker will ignore items that are not selected. Click OK at the bottom of the Preferences dialog box to save your changes. The features of the Editing tab will be covered by section (Errors to check during data entry, Spell Check, Navigation, Use Fastfields for, and Edit Individual/Marriage fact columns).

> **NOTE**
>
> If you change the preference for any item in the Editing tab, except the Spell Check features and the Edit Individual/Marriage fact column, the preference selection will apply only to the current Family File and will not carry over into other files. You will need to make this selection again for other Family Files.

Errors to Check During Data Entry Section

• **Name errors**—Click this check box if you want Family Tree Maker to warn you when you enter names that do not look right (for example, names that include numbers).

• **Unlikely birth, death & marriage dates**—Click this check box if Family Tree Maker should warn you when you enter unlikely dates (for example a death date that occurs earlier than the individual's birth date).

Spell Check Section

Specify how Family Tree Maker's spell check should work, specifically what words it should ignore. The default setting is to "Ignore known names" and "Ignore words with numbers." Some people prefer to enter surnames in capital letters to distinguish them from first and middle names. If this is your preference, you will likely want spell check to ignore capitalized words.

Navigation Section

By default, the Edit Individual dialog box opens when you double-click a name in trees and in reports or when you double-click a name in Pedigree View. You can change the default to open Family View. However, if you do, keep in mind that this guidebook assumes that when you double-click on a name, you will open the Edit Individual dialog box, not Family View.

Fastfields Section

Fastfields speed up data entry by automatically filling in repetitive data as you type in the Family View fields and elsewhere. For example, if you type "San Jose, California" into a location field, then go to another location field and begin to type "San," Family Tree Maker will recognize the similarity and suggest "San Jose, California." By default, all Fastfield options are selected, but you may deselect any that you want to turn off. Fastfields are discussed in Chapter 1.

Edit Individual/Marriage Fact Columns Section

Family Tree Maker will automatically adjust the width of the columns in the Edit Individual and Edit Marriage dialog boxes for you. Leave this check box deselected if you would rather adjust the columns yourself by placing your mouse on a column and dragging it to the desired size.

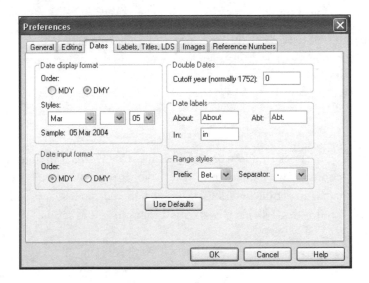

Dates Tab

You can click the Dates tab in the Preferences dialog box to view and change your date formatting preferences. Click OK at the bottom of the Preferences dialog box to save your changes. The features of the Dates tab will be covered by section (Date display format, Date input format, Double Dates, Date labels, and Range styles). If you do not like the selections you make, you can always reset your preferences to Family Tree Maker's default settings by clicking the Use Defaults button.

Date Display Format Section

• **Order**—Click the **MDY** radio button if you want the month to appear before the day (e.g., January 07, 2006). Click the **DMY** radio button if you want the day to appear before the month (e.g., 07 January 2006). By default, Family Tree Maker displays dates in the accepted genealogical date standard, DMY.

•**Styles**—Click the drop-down lists and make selections for the month, day, and year formats, e.g., 5 Mar 2006 vs. 05 March 2006.

Date Input Format Section

• **MDY** or **DMY**—Click a radio button to select how you want Family Tree Maker to interpret the information you input for dates, in Month Day Year order or Day Month Year order.

Double Dates Section

• **Cutoff year**—Change the year in this field to change the default double date cutoff year. If you do not want double dates to print, set the double date cutoff year to zero.

NOTE

Calendars changed systems in 1752, moving from Julian to Gregorian. In the Julian system, the first day of the year was March 25. In today's Gregorian system, January 1 is the first day of the year. A date that falls between January and March before 1752 can be interpreted in two ways, and some genealogists prefer to show both dates. For example, February 22 could fall in the year 1750 according to the Gregorian calendar, so the date would be noted as 22 February 1750/51. You can set the year at which you want to display both date interpretations.

NOTE

This setting applies only to the Family File you have open and will not carry over into other files. The default setting is 0, but if you open a file that already has a cut-off year selected, Family Tree Maker will retain that setting in that particular file.

Date Labels Section

• **About**—If you want Family Tree Maker to display different text for the term "About" (meaning "Circa") in reports, trees, and other views, enter your preferred label in the field.

• **Abt**—If you want Family Tree Maker to display a different abbreviation for the term "Abt" in reports, trees, and other views, enter your preferred label in the field.

NOTE

When entering dates/location information, if you change the preference for this item, it will only apply to the window from which you opened the Preferences dialog box and any window in which you enter dates from this point. Dates which have already been entered using a different date label, e.g., using Abt instead of Ca, will remain unchanged.

NOTE

This setting applies only to the Family File you have open and will not carry over into other files.

Range Styles Section

• **Prefix**—Click the drop-down list and make a selection for the date range prefix (Bet., Btn., or blank).

• **Separator**—Click the drop-down list and make a selection for the date range separator (-, to, and, or &).

NOTE

If you change the preference for Prefix or Separator, the change will apply only to the current Family File. You will need to make this selection again for other Family Files you create or have created.

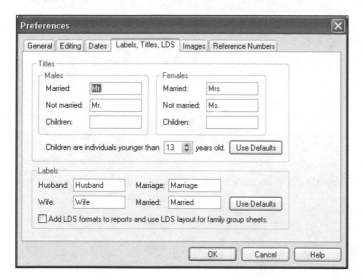

Labels, Titles, LDS Tab

You can click the Labels, Titles, LDS tab in the Preferences dialog box to change how fields in the program are labeled. These are fairly standard labels that you will not likely need to change. Click OK at the bottom of the Preferences dialog box to save your changes. The features of the Labels, Titles, LDS tab will be covered by section (Titles and Labels). If you do not like the selections you make, you can always reset your preferences to Family Tree Maker's default settings by clicking the Use Defaults buttons.

NOTE

If you change the preference for any item in the Labels, Titles, LDS tab, it will apply only to the Family File you have open and will not carry over into other files. You will need to make this selection again for other Family Files you create or have created.

Titles Section

Enter titles to use for married and unmarried males, females, and children if you do not like the default titles.

Children are individuals younger than—Click this drop-down list and choose the age at which an individual should be assigned an "adult" title, such as "Mr."

Labels Section

Enter labels that will be used to refer to basic family relationships. For example, you can change Husband and Wife to Father and Mother or Spouse 1 and Spouse 2.

Add LDS formats to reports and use LDS layout for family group sheets—Click this check box to add the following report formats of particular interest to members of The Church of Jesus Christ of Latter-day Saints (LDS church). These appear in the Report Format dialog box in most Reports views:

– LDS: Incomplete Individual Ordinances

– LDS: Incomplete Marriage Sealings

Also note that if you select the LDS check box, the labels for Husband, Wife, Marriage, and Married revert to defaults. The Family Group Sheet will also change. In addition, you can use special LDS Ordinance codes even if you do not select this preference.

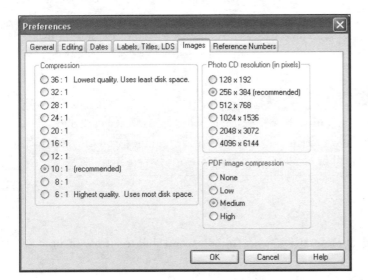

Images Tab

You can click the Images tab of the Preferences dialog box to view the preferences for image compression and resolution. Click OK at the bottom of the Preferences dialog box to save your changes. The features of the Images tab will be covered by section (Compressions, Photo CD Resolution, and PDF Image Compression).

> **NOTE**
>
> Family Tree Maker has established default quality settings for images imported into your scrapbook. While the defaults are usually suitable, there are times when you may want to see what changing the settings does to the quality of the output. You can make changes only while importing the original file, so you will need to access the original image and import it again.

Compression Section

Click the radio button corresponding to the degree of compression that you want for your picture. Higher ratios give you a greater loss in picture quality, but the pictures will take up less space on your hard disk. Lower ratios give you pictures with less quality loss, but the images will take up more disk space.

Photo CD Resolution Section

Click the radio button next to the size you would like your photo CD pictures to be when you add them to the scrapbook. In general, a higher resolution will present a clearer picture. However, the higher the resolution, the larger the file size, and the more of your hard disk space the picture will use.

> **NOTE**
>
> These settings apply only to the Family File you have open and will not carry over into other files.

PDF Image Compression Section

Click the radio button next to the compression quality you would like. The radio buttons allow users to improve print quality, which can suffer when images have been resized and then converted to PDF format. (This problem may affect certain Family Tree Templates, such as USA Flag and New World.) When selected, this option improves picture quality, but it also results in very large PDF output files. You may want to experiment with the compression to see how it changes the picture. Remember that the less compression used, the larger the picture file will be on your hard drive.

> **NOTE**
>
> This setting applies only to the Family File you have open and will not carry over into other files.

Reference Numbers Tab

You can click the Reference Numbers tab of the Preferences dialog box to set up reference numbers for individuals and marriages. Some researchers prefer to use reference numbers for each individual to coincide with their pedigree chart numbers or filing system. At one time, genealogy programs relied on these numbers to find someone in the database. Today's software uses names; Family Tree Maker searches for individuals using the Index of Individuals dialog box or the bookmark or history features. The features of the Reference Numbers tab will be covered by section (Individuals and Marriages).

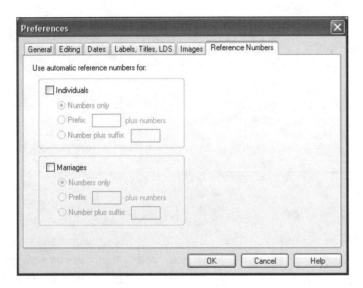

NOTE

This preference setting will cause Family Tree Maker to automatically assign reference numbers, but you can also type in your own reference number for each individual in the Edit Individual dialog box, under the Options tab.

Individuals Section

Individuals—Click this check box to activate reference numbers for individuals. Also, click the radio button that corresponds to the way you want to format your reference numbers.

NOTE

After you have turned on this preference option, you can view the reference number for each individual on the General tab in the individual's Edit Individual dialog box or Edit Marriage dialog box.

Marriages Section

Marriages—Click this check box to activate reference numbers for marriages. Also, click the radio button that corresponds to the way you want to format your reference numbers.

> ### NOTE
>
> Once the reference number options have been selected, you will need to remember to turn on the display options in the appropriate reports to view the numbers.

17

Using Family Tree Maker Tools

While researching and entering information about your family, you may need to figure out how individuals are related or to calculate the approximate birth year of an individual. Also, you may want to check how many individuals or generations you have entered in your Family File. Family Tree Maker offers calculators and other tools to assist you with these functions and more. In this chapter, you'll learn how to:

- Use relationship, Soundex, and date calculators

- View general statistics about a Family File

- Enter user information

- Compress a Family File

Family Tree Maker has special tools to help you calculate dates and figure out how people are related. You might know your great-grandfather's estimated age when he died and the year he died. Use the date calculator to figure out an approximate year of birth so you can look for him in census records. You can also view statistics about the number of names added to your Family File, who compiled the Family File, and more.

> **NOTE**
>
> In addition to the tools explained in this chapter, Family Tree Maker has two other main tools you can use—the spell checker and the Find Error feature. Both of these tools are covered in Chapter 4, "Editing Information in Family View."

Using Relationship, Soundex, and Date Calculators

Family Tree Maker has three calculators to assist you with relationships between individuals, names, and estimated dates and ages.

Relationship Calculator

The Relationship Calculator automatically calculates the relationship for any two individuals in your Family File. It also gives you their canon and civil numbers and, in some cases, will identify their nearest common relative.

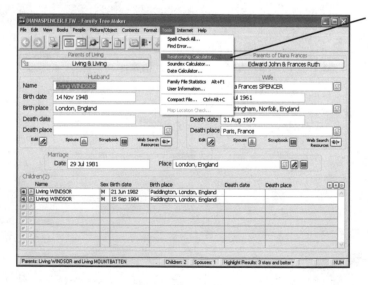

1. Click **Relationship Calculator** from the **Tools** menu. The Relationship Calculator will open, and two names will be selected based on the names you are currently viewing in your Family File.

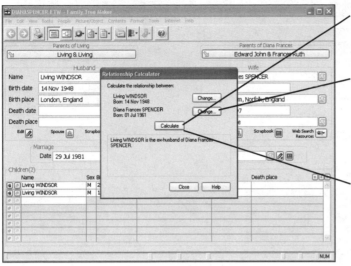

2. Click **Calculate**. The box below the Calculate button shows you the relationship between two individuals.

3. Click the **Change** buttons to change the individuals whose relationship you would like to compare. The Index of Individuals dialog box will open. Choose a name and click **OK**.

4. Click **Calculate**. The box below the Calculate button shows you the relationship between the two new individuals you have selected.

Soundex Calculator

Soundex is a familiar term to genealogists. The Soundex method is a coding system that was used by the government to create indices of the U.S. census records based on how the surname sounds rather than how the surname is spelled. This was done in order to accommodate potential spelling errors. For example, "Smith" may be spelled "Smythe," "Smithe," and "Smyth." The Soundex index was created by coding surnames on their consonant sounds rather than their spelling. By Soundex, the Smith examples given all sound the same, so they would be identified by the same Soundex code (S530). Family Tree Maker can automatically determine the Soundex code for any name, the code can then be used to find microfilms of certain census returns.

1. Click **Soundex Calculator** from the **Tools** menu. The Soundex Calculator will open.

2. Enter a surname into the **Name** field or click **Choose** to select a name from the Index of Individual dialog box.

The Soundex value automatically changes as you enter the information into the field.

Date Calculator

You can use the Date Calculator to calculate an individual's birth date, an individual's age at the time of an event, or the date of an event. You need to know two of these items to calculate the third. Try this sample date calculation:

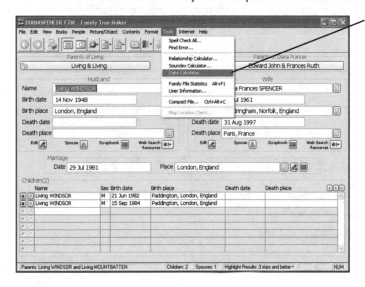

1. Click **Date Calculator** from the **Tools** menu. The Date Calculator will open.

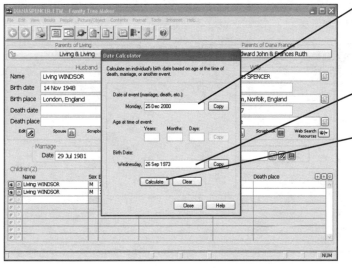

2. Enter "December 25, 2000" in the **Date of event** field. The date will automatically change to standard genealogy format.

3. Enter your birth date in the **Birth Date** field.

4. Click **Calculate**. The remaining field, Age at time of event, will be filled in. You now know your age on December 25, 2000.

Try another calculation. If you know the date an ancestor was married and their approximate age, you can fill that in, then click **Calculate**. Since the Birth Date field may still be populated from your last entry, Family Tree Maker will ask you to clarify which detail you want calculated. Click **Birth Date**. The birth date will be calculated.

> **TIP**
>
> You can use the Date Calculator to figure out the passage of time. For example, enter the date your parents were married in the **Birth Date** field. Then, enter today's date in the **Date of event** field. Click **Calculate**. The resulting field, Age at time of event, will display the number of years, months, and days that your parents have been married.

Viewing General Statistics About a Family File

You can learn some general statistics about the size of your Family File, and the number of generations and surnames included in the file.

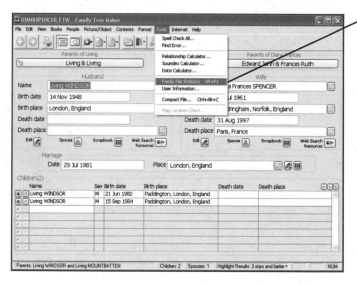

1. Click **Family File Statistics** from the **Tools** menu. The statistics will appear automatically in the Family File Statistics dialog box, except for the total number of generations and total number of different surnames.

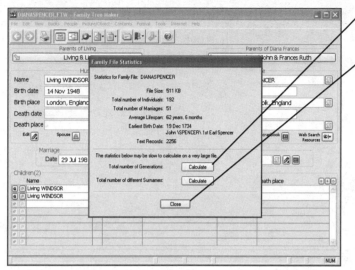

2. Click **Calculate** next to **Generations** and **Surnames** to calculate those figures.

3. Click **Close** when you are finished viewing the statistics.

Entering User Information

Family Tree Maker provides a form in which you enter information that identifies you as the person who created the Family File. This information is then automatically added to your file if you contribute your tree to a world tree collection.

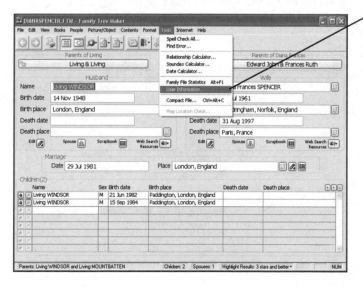

1. Click **User Information** from the **Tools** menu. The User Information dialog box will open. If you are viewing someone else's Family File, the details of this page may be filled in.

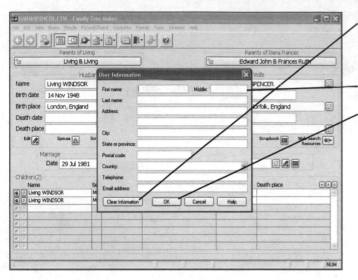

2. If you want to change the information that already appears, click **Clear Information**.

3. Enter your information in each field.

4. Click **OK**. The dialog box will close, and the information will be saved to your Family File.

Compressing a Family File

Family Tree Maker contains a database in which you may add and delete quite a bit of data. However, even when the data has been removed from the file, the file may still remain at a larger size. You should compress your file periodically to optimize the Family File, remove unnecessary items, and re-index the file to make it more efficient. This process may also find and correct problems with your file.

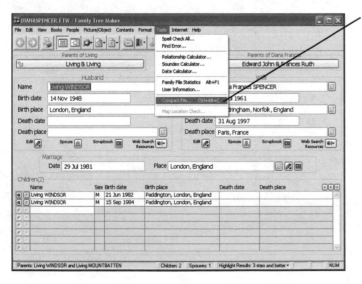

1. Click **Compact File** from the **Tools** menu. The Compact File dialog box will open.

> **NOTE**
>
> You should back up your file before compressing. Make sure you click the **Backup file before compacting file** check box.

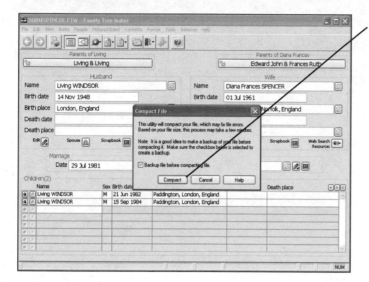

2. Click **Compact**. The file will be compressed.

PART VII

Appendixes

Installing Family Tree Maker 2006

Family Tree Maker has been designed to be easy to install. In this first appendix, you will learn how to:

- Install Family Tree Maker
- Uninstall Family Tree Maker

Installing Family Tree Maker

Most computers use an auto-run feature when you put a new program CD into your CD-ROM drive—the CD begins to run without your having to do anything.

NOTE

Close any programs you have running before you begin to install Family Tree Maker.

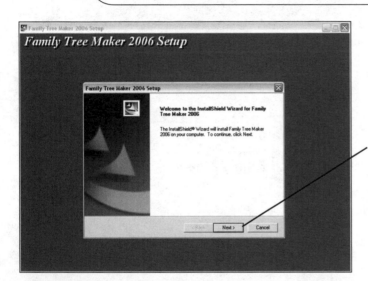

1. Insert the Family Tree Maker 2006 CD into your computer's CD-ROM drive. An animated tour will launch. Click **Install** to start the automatic installer. The Family Tree Maker 2006 Setup dialog box and InstallShield Wizard will open.

2. Click **Next**. The Access Your Online Data dialog box will open.

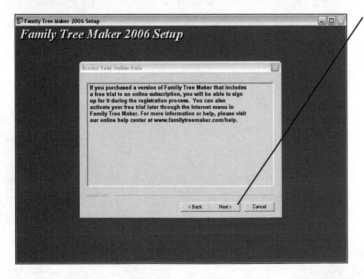

3. Read the message and click **Next**. The License Agreement will open.

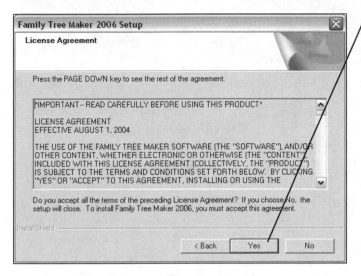

4. Read the license agreement. You can use the scroll bar on the right to view the entire agreement. Click **Yes** to accept the agreement. The Choose Destination Location dialog box will open.

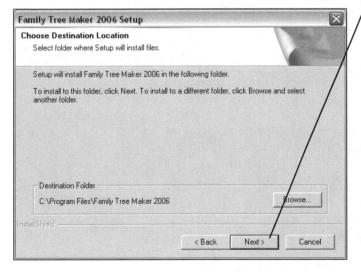

5. Click **Next** if you want to install Family Tree Maker in the default location (recommended) or click **Browse** to choose your own location. The Components dialog box will open.

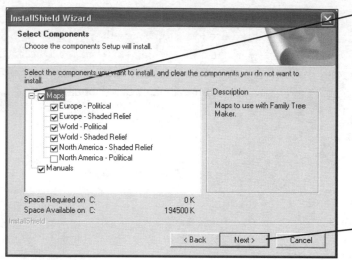

6. Click the check box next to each component you want to install.

7. Click **Next**. The Select Components dialog box will close, and Family Tree Maker will begin to install. After the initial installation is completed, you will be asked to select your Internet Connectivity Options.

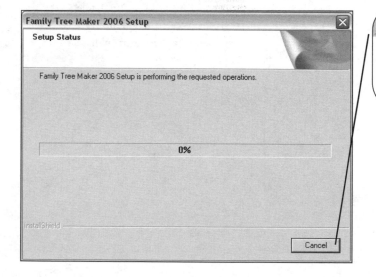

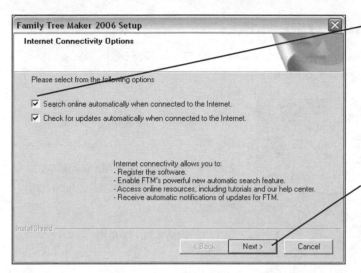

8. If necessary, you can change the recommended Internet connection settings. If you do not want to automatically search online and automatically search for updates when connected to the Internet, click the check boxes to remove the check marks. You can change these settings later.

9. Click **Next** to save your selections. You will be taken to the InstallShield Wizard Complete dialog box.

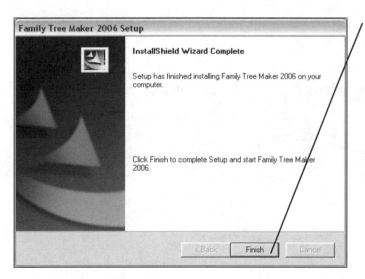

10. Click **Finish**. The installation window closes.

Uninstalling Family Tree Maker

There might come a time when you need to remove Family Tree Maker from your computer. Family Tree Maker has included an uninstall option.

1. Click the **Start** button and select **All Programs**. The Programs menu will appear.

2. Select **Family Tree Maker 2006**. The Family Tree Maker 2006 menu will appear.

3. Click **Uninstall Family Tree Maker 2006**. The InstallShield Wizard will open.

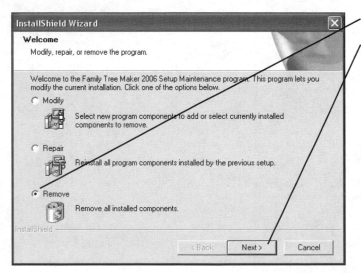

4. Click the **Remove** radio button.

5. Click **Next**. The InstallShield will verify that you want to remove the program. Click **Yes** to uninstall Family Tree Maker.

> **NOTE**
>
> On occasion you may find it necessary to reinstall the program if you are having problems. To do this make sure to select the Repair option. If you want to add maps that you did not install originally, select the Modify option.

B

Using Keyboard Shortcuts

Many people prefer not to have to reach for the mouse when they are entering information. Keyboard shortcuts let you perform many tasks on the keyboard instead of with the mouse. Throughout the book, your attention has been called to some of the keyboard shortcuts included in this appendix, but here you can see the information at a glance. In this appendix, you'll learn how to:

- Use the keyboard shortcuts in Family Tree Maker

- Use keyboard combinations in text windows

Learning Keyboard Shortcuts

As you spend more time with Family Tree Maker, you will find these shortcut keys especially useful.

Don't forget, you learned in Chapter 2 how to find shortcuts for most functions in Family Tree Maker. This appendix is simply a table of the most commonly used shortcuts.

Getting Help

Although you can always open the Help menu, you can use the keyboard shortcuts shown in the following table to get to the help you need more quickly.

To execute this command	Do this
View Help for the Current Window	Press F1

Working in Family Tree Maker

The following table puts the keyboard shortcuts related to Family Tree Maker commands together for an easy reference.

To execute this command	Do this
Create a new Family File	Press Ctrl+N
Open a different Family File	Press Ctrl+O
Print a report	Press Ctrl+P
Undo/Redo	Press Ctrl+Z
Create a new To-Do item	Press Ctrl+T
Access the Index of Individuals	Press F2
View a source	Press Ctrl+S
Open the Other Spouses dialog box	Press F3
Add bookmark	Press Ctrl+B

To execute this command	Do this
More about Picture/Object dialog box	Press Ctrl+M
Compact File	Press Ctrl+Alt+C
Get Family File status	Press Alt+F1
Get system information	Press Ctrl+F1
Exit Family Tree Maker	Press Alt+F4

Working with Text

While most of the entries in Family Tree Maker are made in fields, there are a number of text windows for entering notes. The following tables contain some shortcuts you might find useful when working in the text windows.

Selecting Text

The first step in manipulating your text is to select it. The following table offers some keyboard combinations for selecting a letter, a word, a line, or more.

To execute this command	Do this
Highlight the character to the right of the insertion point	Press Shift+Right Arrow
Highlight the character to the left of the insertion point	Press Shift+Left Arrow
Highlight an entire word to the right of the insertion point	Press Ctrl+Shift+Right Arrow
Highlight an entire word to the left of the insertion point	Press Ctrl+Shift+Left Arrow
Highlight an entire line	Press Shift+End
Highlight a paragraph one line at a time	Press Shift+Down Arrow for each line of the paragraph
Highlight all lines above the insertion point	Press Ctrl+Shift+Home

Copying and Pasting Text and Records of Individuals

After you select the text or individual(s) you want to work with, you might want to remove it or copy it for placement elsewhere. The following table contains the keyboard combinations you need to manipulate selected text or information about individuals.

To execute this command	Do this
Copy text	Press Ctrl+C
Cut text	Press Ctrl+X
Paste text	Press Ctrl+V
Delete text	Press Del
Copy Selected Individual	Press Ctrl+I
Copy All individuals in Family Page	Press Ctrl+A

Glossary

Ahnentafel. German for *ancestor table*. In addition to being a chart, it also refers to a genealogical numbering system.

Ancestor. A person from whom one descends.

Ancestor Tree. Also known as a *Pedigree Chart,* this chart begins with a specific individual and displays direct lineage of all of the individual's ancestors.

Annotation. Personal notes or comments that either explain or critique. Family Tree Maker employs annotations in the Bibliography Report.

Bibliography. A report that shows a list of sources used to compile the information included in the genealogy. The sources follow an accepted format, which Family Tree Maker has built into the program.

BMP. Bitmap. A file format for graphics.

Book. In Family Tree Maker, a compilation of reports generated for a family or an individual, including family trees, miscellaneous reports, stories, photos, a table of contents, and an index.

Brightness. An adjustment that can be made to scanned images to make the image lighter or darker.

Browser. See *Web browser.*

Case Sensitive. Differentiating between uppercase and lowercase characters.

Citation. The accepted notation of the source of information.

Cite. The act of making note of the proof that supports a conclusion or claimed fact in the genealogy.

Click. The action of pressing and releasing a mouse button. Usually, when a program instructs you to click an item, it is referring to the left side of the mouse. A program may specify "left-click" or "right-click." You can also double-click by pressing and releasing the mouse button twice in rapid succession.

Clipboard. A memory feature of the Windows environment that allows a person to copy or cut text or graphics from one document and paste them into another.

Contrast. An adjustment made to scanned images that causes the image to brighten or dim.

Compression. A setting that determines the quality of the images and the size of the image files you are working with in Family Tree Maker that will be put in your scrapbook and printed out on trees and reports.

CSV. Comma Separated Value(s). A file that separates data by commas which then allows importing into a spreadsheet program.

Cue Cards. The pop-up help windows that appear when you move from screen to screen in Family Tree Maker. They can be turned on or off in the system preferences.

Descendant. A person who descends lineally from another.

Descendant Tree. A chart that lists an individual and his or her descendants.

Dialog Box. Small windows that display on your screen and help you carry out different tasks for the program. Generally, dialog boxes contain command buttons and various options to help you carry out a command or task.

Endnotes. Source citations and explanatory notes that appear at the end of a document, specifically a tree or report.

Export. To transfer data from one computer to another or from one computer program to another.

Family File. Family Tree Maker's name for the database that contains the information about your lineage, e.g., you could create a Family File for Smith family and Jones family.

FamilyFinder Index. A genealogical list containing over 750 million names that is included in Family Tree Maker's CDs and online at Genealogy.com.

Family Group Sheet. A form that displays information on a single, complete family unit.

Family View. The main screen in Family Tree Maker, into which you enter information about a particular individual and family.

File Format. The file format in which you save a document indicates what program will open the file. Each file can only be opened by certain programs. The file formats are automatically attached to the end of a file name, but you can change the file format when you are saving it. Family Tree Makers uses the .FTW extension file format, or, for backup copies, it uses .FBK.

Fastfields. Family Tree Maker remembers the names of the last 50 locations you have typed in so that as you begin to type a place in a new location field, Family Tree Maker shows you possible matches based on the letters you have typed up to that point.

Format. One of Family Tree Maker's options for developing the style and look of reports and trees.

GEDCOM. GEnealogical Data COMmunication. A standard designed by the Family History Department of the Church of Jesus Christ of Latter-day Saints for transferring data between different genealogy software packages.

Genealogy Report. A narrative style report that details a family through one or more generations and includes basic facts about each member in addition to biographical information that was entered through Family Tree Maker.

Generation. The period of time between the birth of one group of individuals and the next—usually about 25 to 33 years.

GIF. Graphic Interchange Format. A graphic file format that is widely used in Web page documents.

Given Name. The first name (and middle name) given to a child at birth or at his or her baptism. Also known as a *Christian name*.

Home page. The main page of a website.

Hourglass Tree. A chart showing both the ancestors and the descendants of a selected individual. When printed, the tree resembles an hourglass because the ancestors spread out above the selected individual and the descendants spread out below.

HTML. Hypertext Markup Language. The standard language for creating and formatting Web pages.

Icon. A small graphic picture or symbol that represents a program, file, or folder on your computer. Clicking an icon with a mouse generally causes the program to run, the folder to open, or the file to be displayed. Sometimes, you have to double-click an item instead of just clicking once. (See Click in glossary.)

Import. To bring a file into a program that was created using another program.

Edit Individual Dialog Box. A multi-tabbed dialog box that lets you easily edit and view information for a specific individual you have recorded in Family Tree Maker.

Edit Marriage Dialog Box. A multi-tabbed dialog box that lets you easily view and edit personal information about a marriage or similar relationship between two individuals.

Inline Notes. The sources that appear within the text as opposed to at the bottom or end of a page in Family Tree Maker's genealogy reports.

Kinship. In genealogy, this refers to the relationship between one individual and any or all of his or her relatives. This can be displayed through the Kinship Report in Family Tree Maker.

JPEG. Joint Photographic Expert Group. Graphics that use the .jpg extension include a compression technique that reduces the size of the graphics file.

Maternal Ancestor. An ancestor on the mother's side of the family.

Merge. The ability in Family Tree Maker to take the information of two individuals who appear to be the same person and combine them into a single individual in the Family File.

NGSQ. *National Genealogical Society Quarterly.* A periodical published by that society. Also refers to the NGS Quarterly numbering system offered in descending genealogy reports.

OLE. Object Linking and Embedding. A technology that lets you create items in one program and place them in another, including video clips, still images, pictures, word-processing files, and spreadsheet files.

Outline Descendant Tree. A chart that shows in an indented outline format an individual's children, grandchildren, great-grandchildren, and so on through the generations.

Paternal Ancestor. An ancestor on the father's side of the family.

PDF. Portable Document Format. A file format that retains printer formatting so that when it is opened it looks as it would on the printed page. Requires Adobe Acrobat Reader to open and view a file that ends in the .PDF extension.

Pedigree Chart. A chart that shows the direct ancestors of an individual. Known in Family Tree Maker as an *Ancestor Tree.*

Pedigree View. The second main screen in Family Tree Maker, into which you view the linear relationship between individuals in an interactive pedigree chart.

Preferred. A term Family Tree Maker uses in reference to parents, spouses, or duplicate events, meaning that you want to see that selection first or have it displayed in trees and reports.

Primary or Root Individual. The main individual in any of the Family Tree Maker charts or reports.

Red-Eye Removal. The method of removing the red, or hollow, look of eyes from flash photographs that have been digitized.

Register. Refers to the descending genealogy format used by the New England Historic Genealogical Society. This also refers to their periodical by the same name.

Reports. Any of a number of standard and custom displays in various formats that Family Tree Maker can create.

Research Journal. A record used by genealogists to keep track of their research findings and tasks to be accomplished.

Resolution. In Family Tree Maker an option allowed when working with Kodak Photo CD files that lets you increase the size of a picture thus making it a clearer picture.

Re-Writable CD-ROM. A CD-ROM drive that lets you save files to a CD-RW disc, a disc designed to be used like a floppy disc and to which you can write to more than once (different from a Writable CD-ROM).

RTF. Rich Text Format. A cross-platform, cross-application text document format. It retains some of the formatting information that is supported by many word processors.

Root or Primary Individual. The main individual in any of the Family Tree Maker charts, reports, or views.

Saturation. The amount of color in each pixel of an image. When the saturation is high, the image shows bright, vivid colors. When the saturation is low, the picture may look black and white.

Scrapbooks. The term used by Family Tree Maker for the collections of photographs, images, video, sound, and OLE objects that can be stored for each individual and marriage in the Family File.

Siblings. Children of the same parents.

Source. The record, such as a book, an e-mail message, or an interview, from which specific information was obtained.

Spouse. The person to whom another person is married.

Surname. The family name or last name of an individual.

Threshold. As used in the Red-Eye Removal Dialog box, the minimum degree of redness for the pixels to be fixed.

Tree. The term Family Tree Maker uses to refer to its various charts. See *Ancestor Tree, Descendant Tree*, and *Outline Descendant Tree*.

URL. Uniform Resource Locator. The address used by a Web browser to locate a page on the Web.

User Home Page. The section of Genealogy.com where individual researcher's data is shared on the Web.

WAV. Windows Audio Visual. The sound files that work with Media Player and Sound Recorder.

Web browser. The software that lets you access pages on the Web. The browser reads the HTML code and converts it to the pictures, colors, menu options, and overall design that you view on your monitor.

Web Merge. A Family Tree Maker wizard that lets you merge Web results you have found on Ancestry.com to your Family File.

Web Search. A Family Tree Maker function that automatically searches Ancestry.com for records containing information about your ancestors.

Web page. A document on the Internet that is written using a scripting language such as HTML.

Website. A location on the Internet maintained by a single individual, company, or entity that provides information, graphics, and other items.

World Family Tree (WFT) Project. A multi-volume CD and online collection created by Genealogy.com from the genealogies submitted electronically by family history enthusiasts and indexed in the FamilyFinder Index.

World Wide Web. A graphical interface that is composed of Internet sites that provide researchers with access to documents and other files.

Writable CD-ROM. A CD-ROM drive that lets you save files to a CD-R disc, a disc designed to be used like a floppy disc.

Index

N

O

P

T

U

V

W

About the Author

Tana Pedersen Lord has been writing and editing in the technology industry for almost ten years. In that time, she has earned several awards for her writing including the Distinguished Technical Communication award from the Society for Technical Communication. She is currently Editorial Services manager for Ancestry.com and a contributing editor to *Ancestry* Magazine and *Genealogical Computing*.